London Trar

CONNE

1945–1985

..... wallis

The 98B was probably the most celebrated of post war independently operated bus routes within the London Transport Area. Independent operations commenced on 15 February 1966 consequent upon London Transport's withdrawal of their service on routes 98 and 98B between Ruislip and Rayners Lane Station from 30 January 1966. The first five years of independent operation of the 98B were turbulent, with gaps in coverage occurring as six successive operators struggled and failed in their attempts to run the service. Stability for the 98B finally arrived when Elmtree Transport took up operation from 24 May 1971. Six months into Elmtree's operation reg.no. PHN 859, a 1953-built Eastern Coach Works-bodied Bristol LS5G originally supplied new to United Automobile Services, is seen at Ruislip on 25 November 1971.
P R Wallis

Capital Transport

The prospective lady passenger, probably conditioned by previous experience of local travel to expect nothing other than the appearance of a large, red London Transport bus, seems uncertain at the prospect of boarding Thamesmead Motor Services diminutive 1965-built 12-seat Austin J2 Omnicoach fleet no. 6 (JHK 421C) at Slade Green Station. In the early 1970s Thamesmead started operating Sundays only bus services in the Bexleyheath area which replaced sections of routes not worked by London Transport (and London Country) on that day of the week. Thamesmead's ambitions to expand further into operation of daily bus services within the LT area were largely frustrated by the Executive's refusal to give its 'Agreement' to Thamesmead's route proposals. Short-lived Route 696, between Slade Green Station and Orpington, was introduced on 21 February 1971 as a daily operation. A G Bassom

First published 2003

ISBN 185414 257 7

Published by Capital Transport Publishing
38 Long Elmes, Harrow Weald, Middlesex

Designed by Tim Demuth

Printed by CS Graphics Singapore

© Philip Wallis 2003

CONTENTS

Acknowledgements   4

Preface   5

Conventions followed in the text   6

Chapter 1   A Restricted Monopoly   7

Chapter 2   Essex   20

Chapter 3   Hertfordshire and the Chiltern Hills   46

Chapter 4   The Thames Valley   73

Chapter 5   Surrey   87

Chapter 6   North Sussex and Kent   103

Chapter 7   Central Area Independents 1955–1969   121

Chapter 8   Orpington Area 1963–1985   143

Chapter 9   GLC Area Independents 1970–1985   159

Bibliography   174

Operators' Index   175

ACKNOWLEDGEMENTS

The late John King of The Omnibus Society was particularly active in developing the Society's route recording system. The publications which he produced on London and the South East form the kernel around which it has been possible to expand this book. Derek Persson, who collaborated with John King, has given me invaluable and unstinting support, generously making available to me his comprehensive records of independently operated London bus routes during the period reviewed. Members of the London Historical Research Group of The Omnibus Society have helped with answers to queries raised in that Group's Bulletins. Laurie Akehurst of that Group has kindly provided much information on relevant London Transport Country Area routes. The Omnibus Society's Libraries at both Coalbrookdale and Acton contained much useful research material.

Latterly the London Omnibus Traction Society has maintained records of London area operations and I am most grateful to them for permission to extract information from their publications. As usual The PSV Circle proved to be an invaluable and authoritative source of information on vehicle related matters. I am most grateful to them for permission to extract information from their comprehensive range of publications.

Both Chris Stewart and Michael Yelton filled gaps in my knowledge of City Coach Company, Westcliff-on-Sea and Eastern National operations. Richard Delahoy expounded his detailed knowledge of Southend Transport's incursions into the London area. Graham Smith provided me with much helpful information about operations on the Bedfordshire – Hertfordshire borders, in particular concerning Birch Bros. Peter Trevaskis expanded my knowledge of Aldershot & District operations abutting the London Transport area. Nicholas King of the M & D and East Kent Bus Club provided much detailed information about Maidstone & District's operations in North Kent. Andrew Bassom, Alan Lewington and John Wylde, men with 'hands on' knowledge gained from running independent bus services within the London Transport Area, have discussed their experiences with me. As well as loaning many of the tickets illustrated, David Seddon kindly provided me with detailed notes on ticket-related matters, much of which has been incorporated into captions. That doyen of bus enthusiasts, John Gillham, has given good advice as well as affording me access to his extensive photographic records. John Aldridge, John Burch, R J Edgington, Ted Gadsby, Barry LeJeune, Roy Marshall, David Stewart, Mike Stephens and Ian Taylor also gave me help and guidance.

Quality imaging brings a text to life. I am most appreciative of the time spent by the various photographers in searching out the best from their collections for possible use in the book, I am only sorry that space constraints have prevented use of some of this excellent material. Thanks are due too to Tony Wright for helping me with photographic services. I would like to thank my wife Rosalind for both her forbearance during my time devoted to writing this book as well as for her keyboard skills in transferring my manuscript onto a PC. Thanks are also due to the staff at Aries Business Centre, Basingstoke for additional help with manuscript presentation. The specially drawn maps are by Mike Harris.

The privatisation process of London Transport's bus operations could be considered to have begun on 13 July 1985 when certain routes from the first tranche previously put out to tender were taken up by independent or National Bus Company operators. It gained an unstoppable momentum with the decision to sell off London Transport's 'Red Bus' operating divisions which process was completed in 1996. Under the Transport *for* London regime effective from 3 July 2000, masterminded by London's new Mayor Ken Livingstone, even the name London Transport has been done away with. At the time of writing virtually all London bus routes are operated by private sector businesses awarded their routes under a tender system now controlled by London Bus Services Ltd. Today's *status quo* represents a stark contrast with the times when state controlled London Transport held near monopoly status for bus service provision in the London area – and yet back in those days exceptions existed.

In the 1950s I travelled between Reading and London on Thames Valley limited stop bus routes A and B whenever I could in preference to the railway. This introduced me to the virtual 'Iron Curtain' which surrounded London Transport's operational area – for at Slough Thames Valley stopped (except for Route B) and London Transport began. Visits to other 'border' towns such as Aylesbury and Guildford emphasised this rigid divide in operating territory – as well as revealing a host of small independently-operated services working in the wedges between London Transport's area and those of neighbouring territorial operators. In June 1961 I went to Wood Green to marvel at the sight of frequent green Eastern National buses on Route 251 to Southend operating amidst a host of red London Transport buses and soon to disappear trolleybuses. I remember waiting ten years later on a draughty tree lined avenue in London's north western suburbs not altogether sure if I was in the right spot to snatch a photograph of one of Elmtree Transport's second hand buses working celebrated Route 98B.

These memories and more besides sowed the seeds of the idea for this book. The period covered ranges from the end of the Second World War – hostilities in Europe ceased on 8 May 1945 – until 12 July 1985, the day before current London route tendering started. The varying transport policies of twelve Governments over that forty year period impacted the London bus scene. The most profound change saw the hiving off of London Transport's Country Bus Department to the National Bus Company on 1 January 1970. From that date the fortunes of other operators in the Country Area leave the scope of this book. Operations of London Country Bus Services Ltd and Green Line, are excluded from coverage too. Although subject to increasing changes from the late 1970s complex operations across the GLC boundary continued to patterns established by London Transport long before the divide. The book examines ordinary 'stage carriage' bus services available for public use. In general special entertainment, forces, school, sport or works services are excluded as are airport links, long distance express services as well as excursions and tours.

I very much hope that readers will enjoy recalling that host of operators who met up with London Transport to form LONDON TRANSPORT CONNECTIONS 1945–1985.

Philip Wallis, Bramley, Hampshire, April 2003

Conventions followed in the text

London Transport

London Transport is referred to by that name or the abbreviation LT. During the period reviewed the official title of the body was variously:

London Passenger Transport Board	(8 May 1945) – 31 December 1947
London Transport Executive	1 January 1948 – 31 December 1962
London Transport Board	1 January 1963 – 31 December 1969
London Transport Executive	1 January 1970 – 28 June 1984
London Regional Transport	29 June 1984 – (12 July 1985)

Route Profiles

These are intended to help the reader more easily assimilate changes to the structure of particular routes. They are very much summaries of salient developments. The route recording enthusiast seeking more exhaustive details is recommended to the publications of either The Omnibus Society or London Omnibus Traction Society. Similarly selective details of vehicles operated are given. Those readers seeking fuller and more comprehensive vehicle information are recommended to the publications of The PSV Circle.

Times and dates

Time period stated is frequency of service ie, x journeys, 30 minutes, 1 hour, etc.

Introduction dates of routes are the first day of operation.

Withdrawal dates of routes are the last day of operation.

Weekdays means Mondays – Saturdays inclusive.

Operators' Addresses

These usually refer to the Registered Office.

Other Abbreviations

BET	–	British Electric Traction
BOAC	–	British Overseas Airways Corporation
BTC	–	British Transport Commission
ECW	–	Eastern Coach Works
GLC	–	Greater London Council
LPTA	–	London Passenger Transport Area
NBC	–	National Bus Company
ORTA	–	Orpington Rural Transport Association
THC	–	Transport Holding Company
c	–	circa
no.	–	number
reg.no.	–	registration number
t/a	–	trading as

CHAPTER 1

A Restricted Monopoly

London Passenger Transport Area

The 1933 London Passenger Transport Act (1933 Act) was a complex piece of legislation uniting as it did the London General Omnibus Co Ltd with most other bus and all tramway and trolleybus interests in the London area along with the Metropolitan and Underground Railways into the London Passenger Transport Board.

The Board was charged with securing the provision of an adequate and properly co-ordinated system of passenger transport within an area defined as the London Passenger Transport Area with due regard to efficiency, improvement of facilities, and the avoidance of wasteful competition. It was lawful for London Transport to run stage carriage (ordinary bus) or express carriage services anywhere within the LPTA. Such services were allowed to extend to a distance of up to half a mile (one mile in Berkshire) beyond the LPTA's boundary for the purpose of reaching a convenient terminal point on which journeys local passengers could be carried. An exception was the borough of Luton where London Transport was not permitted to carry local traffic. London Transport was empowered to work services to up to a ten mile radius outside the Area's boundary (five miles in Kent) if agreement to

Map of the London Passenger Transport Area as established by the 1933 London Passenger Transport Act. The dotted lines show the London Special Area (see page 8).

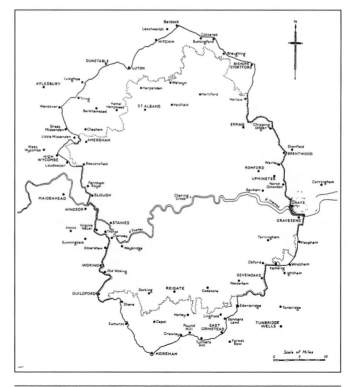

do so could be reached with an operator already authorised to run services in such area. There were certain specified roads outside the LPTA on which London Transport could work without restriction, as well as other roads upon which London Transport could work but subject to constraints on carrying local traffic. In a complimentary manner there were certain specific roads within the LPTA on which other operators could work without constraint.

Special Area

A 1600 square mile area within the London Passenger Transport Area was known as the 'Special Area'. Parts of the Special Area's boundary were conterminous with the boundary of the LPTA whilst the remaining parts of the Special Area boundary fell short of the LPTA's boundary. Within the Special Area London Transport held a veto over road passenger transport service provision, with the exception of long distance express services. London Transport was also freed from the necessity of obtaining road service licences from the Metropolitan Traffic Area Commissioner for services within the Special Area although they were obliged to obtain approval for the roads used. Other operators were allowed to work into the Special Area for a distance of up to half a mile from the boundary in order to reach a convenient terminal point over which distance local traffic could be carried. (The sole exception was the borough of Gravesend where the carriage of local traffic was not permitted).

Provisions in the 1933 Act allowed London Transport, at its discretion, to give written 'consent' to other operators to provide services in the Special Area. Such 'consents' were subject to review and renewal by London Transport on an annual basis. Applicants also had to obtain a road service licence.

Bus routes into Central London worked by operators other than London Transport were rare. On 27 March 1949 Birch Bros no. K 183, a Leyland Titan PD1 with bodywork built by the operator, swings out of Kings Cross Coach Station in Judd Street. Visible in the left distant background is the tower of the Midland General Hotel at St Pancras Station. Through workings on hourly Route 203 to Rushden were resumed following wartime disruption on 11 March 1946. With a journey time of around 3 hours Route 203 operated for 22 hours a day 7 days a week.
J D Bentley/courtesy J C Gillham

In practice bus service provision between the boundary of the Special Area and that of the LPTA fell to either London Transport or independent operators. Hants & Sussex Group company F H Kilner's Northern Coachbuilders bodied Leyland Titan PD1 no. LO 54 is seen at Horsham Carfax in April 1949. Major operators were wary of Hants & Sussex proprietor's Basil Williams expansionist plans. Even the unassailable London Transport became edgy, making a counter bid against Williams' attempt to purchase Tillingbourne Valley in 1949. J C Gillham

The continuation of Walton-on-Thames Motor Company's route from Walton Bridge to Walton Station in independent hands after the 1933 Act represented an anomaly in London Transport policy; although it lay outside the Metropolitan Police District (within the confines of which mandatory acquisition of all independent bus services was stipulated by the Act), it operated wholly within the London Special Area., within which London Transport's policy was to negotiate to acquire any such operations. In contrast, other local bus services in Walton-on-Thames provided by Ben Stanley has been acquired by London Transport in April 1934. The company's 1937-built Willmot-bodied Bedford WTB reg.no. DLD 407 is seen in Walton-on-Thames High Street in Summer 1952. C Carter

Outside the Special Area

Within the 400 square mile area where the boundaries of the Special Area fell short of the boundaries of the LPTA London Transport enjoyed the right to provide services but not with a monopoly status. London Transport had to apply to the Metropolitan Traffic Area Commissioner for road service licences for any services that it wished to work in that area. Other proprietors could also seek approval for services in that area. A further important constraint applied to certain specific operators within this area. When the 1933 Act was being drafted negotiations took place with a number of substantial territorial companies, referred to in the Act as the 'provincial operating companies', these comprised: Aldershot & District, Chatham & District, Eastern National, East Kent, Hants & Dorset, Maidstone & District, Redcar, Southdown, Thames Valley. The purpose of these discussions was twofold. One aim was to retain within the LPTA most bus routes operated by London General Country Services Ltd – formed in 1932 by an amalgamation of East Surrey Traction Co Ltd in the south with National Omnibus and Transport Co Ltd in the north. The second objective was to leave substantially intact the existing territorial boundaries of the 'provincial operating companies'. As a *quid pro quo* the 'provincial operating companies' agreement not to operate services in the LPTA (except for up to half a mile to reach a convenient terminal) without London Transport's written consent was incorporated into the 1933 Act. London Transport was also empowered to negotiate to acquire any remaining passenger transport operators within, or mainly within, the LPTA.

London Transport displayed antipathy towards the concept of establishing joint workings with other operators to provide through services crossing

The paucity of bus services working across the LPTA boundary was not an inevitable legal consequence of the 1933 Act. Rather, it reflected London Transport's determination to retain both direct control and direct operation of most services within the LPTA. From its inception in 1933 until well into the post-war years LT shunned provisions in the Act allowing joint working with other operators of services crossing the LPTA boundary. Thus in Essex former Eastern National Route 31 (Purfleet – Grays – Tilbury), which could have continued as a joint EN/LT operation, was split at the LPTA boundary in Grays from 17 April 1934 – to the considerable inconvenience of through passengers. Eastern National's no. 3880, a 1943-built Brush utility-bodied Guy Arab I, reverses at Tilbury Ferry in June 1949 prior to taking up a journey on Route 37A back to the 'boundary' at Grays.
V C Jones / courtesy Ian Allan Publishing Ltd

Another consequence of the 1933 Act was the creation of 'border' towns where London Transport territory abutted that of various territorial companies. Independent operators filled any gaps. At the end of World War II Bishop's Stortford was served by no less than six independents. One was H Monk who operated three rural routes into the town. Monk's 1938 Thurgood-bodied Bedford WTB reg.no. DUR 534 is seen, possibly in 1945, with wartime headlamp masks still fitted.
J F Parke / courtesy J C Gillham

the boundary of the London Passenger Transport Area. Co-operation, such as that initiated on 24 April 1935 between London Transport and independents A. T. Brady and Tillingbourne Valley Services Ltd to provide joint time-tabling and inter-availability of return tickets on bus routes in south west Surrey, was extremely rare. In general the boundary of the London Passenger Transport Area formed a barrier to the operation of the through bus services, setting the pattern for much bus service provision for at least the next half century.

The spectre of nationalisation loomed large over the bus industry in the immediate post war years. Vociferous resistance emanated from many municipal undertakings, the BET Group as well as most independents. City Coach Company's Daimler CVD 6 no. D 3 carries the slogan 'Don't let Nationalisation take you for a ride – You would find it very expensive' in this 1949 view at Woodford Waterworks. A full passenger load Southend bound is evidenced by the Roberts lowbridge body being forced hard down on the suspension. C Carter

British Transport Commission

The Labour Government which came to power in July 1945 had been elected with a manifesto which included the transfer to state ownership of many of the nation's key industries, including transport. That Government created the British Transport Commission to manage state-acquired transport interests which came to include the main-line railways, many docks and harbours, cross-channel ferries and much long-distance road haulage. From 1 January 1948 the BTC assumed responsibility for London Transport. On 5 November 1948 Thomas Tilling Ltd, a dominant holding company in the country's bus and coach industry, operating around 8,000 vehicles, sold out to the BTC. Three Tilling group companies – Eastern National, Thames Valley and Westcliff – operated bus services into or bordering the LPTA.

The introduction on 18 February 1948 by London Transport of Route 383 between Hitchin and Weston focused the attention of the nation's bus industry because of its threat to the licensing system. The route had been introduced without obtaining a road service licence. London Transport considered it was entitled to so do under delegation to it of such powers granted to the BTC by the 1947 Transport Act. A small independent, W H Smith, covered the same road and, backed by the Passenger Vehicle Operators' Association, Smith challenged the matter in court. The court, and subsequent appeals, found in favour of London Transport. Although the trial judge thought the position 'obscure' it had the effect of confirming London Transport's legal power to operate anywhere within the LPTA, without a road service licence. In practice the proceedings attracted much opprobrium upon London Transport which appeared to inhibit the organisation from attempting to implement this power again.

The Chambers Report

The 1953 Transport Act, promoted by a Conservative Government, removed the threat of further nationalisation from the bus industry. It also abolished the BTC's exemption from road service licence provision.

From the late 1940s onwards, changing social patterns and economic pressures had been having an increasingly adverse effect on London Transport's finances. Private car numbers were starting to increase, television became more common meaning people tended to stay at home and travel less in the evenings, and half-day working on Saturdays became less usual. All these factors, combined with increases in wage rates for London Transport staff, meant that London Transport's finances veered from a healthy £5.9million surplus traffic receipts in 1948 to a deficit of £1.5million in 1951. This worrying state of affairs led the then Minister of Transport, the Right Hon A T Lennox-Boyd, to appoint a Committee of Inquiry into London Transport on 28 April 1953. The Committee's findings, dubbed the Chambers Report after its Chairman, S P Chambers, were published in January 1955.

Amongst many aspects of London Transport's operations investigated, the Committee had examined unremunerative bus services in considerable detail and as a result had recommended:

'It is possible that for such (unremunerative) routes, where it is not practicable for London Transport to provide or continue a service, it might be advantageous in appropriate cases, where it would be reasonable to do so and where London Transport's economics and efficiency would not be affected adversely, to allow an independent operator to undertake the service at what might be the same or a higher scale of fares. The independent operator, though subject of course to the requirements of the Licensing Authority, may be freer than London Transport to adopt measures to make the route profitable'.

The Committee accepted that the boundaries of the LPTA were, in their view, correct but did recognise the difficulties caused by the lack of through facilities in the 'border' towns. Chambers suggested 'a more convenient arrangement would be to include the whole of these towns within the London Passenger Transport Area, and also to allow other undertakings to operate throughout these towns with suitable inter-running arrangements. We suggest that a detailed examination in this matter should be made for each of the towns in question'.

The distinction of introducing the first post-Chambers Report independent bus service fell to West London Coachways. 1948 Mulliner-bodied Bedford OB reg.no. JXH 634, acquired from airline BOAC, is seen departing Feltham Station with a good passenger load shortly after the route's introduction in September 1955. C Carter

During the 1958 LT bus strike, until able to obtain the necessary licences, The People's League for the Defence of Freedom ran services offering passengers 'Free Rides At Your Own Risk'. The tattered 'Shop at Binns' advertisement indicates that Weymann-bodied AEC Regent II reg.no. FT 5702 hailed from the North East, originating with Tynemouth & District in 1947. Seen in Oxford Street the legend on the body side proclaims 'This would not be the only bus running in London if there had been a secret ballot of the busmen'. M J Dryhurst

In Crawley LT experienced significant rivalry over town service provision – first from independent Hants & Sussex and then from BET Company Southdown. Between 1956 and 1959 Southdown obtained licences for four town services in the process of which the almost unthinkable happened when LT withdrew their original town Route 483 in favour of Southdown. For several years Southdown's Crawley based services were worked by Park Royal Guy Arab IVs such as no. 531 seen in Crawley Bus Station on a bleak Sunday in February 1962 working town Route 79 to Gossops Green. M J Dryhurst

Effect of the Chambers Report

The Chambers Report recommendations hardly opened a floodgate for independently operated bus services in London. It did however allow a small trickle of independent operators to emerge over subsequent years on what were certainly marginally profitable routes.

One consequence of a six week long strike by London Transport bus crews in May/June 1958, during which interesting emergency services were worked by the People's League and some independents, was the withdrawal later in that year of a significant number of London Transport bus services. These withdrawals triggered a handful of new independent services, five new operators taking to the roads between late 1958 and the end of 1959. Not all prospered. Sunnymede Coaches service introduced on 19 October 1958 between Grange Hill and Chigwell Row, to replace facilities formerly provided by London Transport Route 26, was abandoned within two months. Others such as Banstead Coaches service to Chipstead Valley, introduced in March 1959, proved more successful.

The Orpington Rural Transport Association was the precursor for significant independent bus activity in the Orpington area. First vehicle operated by ORTA was a British Motor Corporation (BMC) Austin J2 Omnicoach reg.no. NPV 828. The now widely used generic name 'minibus' for small buses originated from the model designation of BMC's Morris version of this vehicle. The minibus is seen at Berry's Green in 1963 driven by ORTA's Honorary Manager John Wylde whose name was to become synonymous with independent bus operations in that area.
North Downs Collection

The 'detailed examination' suggested by Chambers to improve facilities in the border towns resulted in minimal action by London Transport. Only in Crawley did significant progress occur – ironically spurred by competitive pressure from British Electric Traction group controlled company Southdown. Virtually no progress was evident in improving facilities where Tilling Group companies met up with London Transport despite the fact that both Tilling and London Transport were ultimately controlled by the BTC.

The Turbulent 'Sixties

Housing development in suburban areas was proceeding apace and often London Transport's inability or unwillingness to provide services led to independent initiatives. The Orpington Rural Transport Association started operations in June 1963 replacing a failed London Transport trial service 479. Super Coaches – whose first bus service had started in 1959 – built up quite a network of local bus services in the Hornchurch/Upminster areas.

For bus operators the 1960s, particularly so in London and the South, were characterised by chronic staff shortages, increasing traffic congestion and falling passenger numbers. In 1964 this led to two of the always rare joint services operated by London Transport passing fully into independent hands. Rover Bus Services took up all workings on the 316 between Hemel Hempstead and Chesham, whilst Tillingbourne Valley became responsible for all journeys on the 448 Guildford to Ewhurst route. A third joint working disappeared in the same year, although in this instance London Transport replaced United Counties workings on Route 359 between Aylesbury and Amersham.

Belatedly some improvements in co-ordination between London Transport and Tilling companies were implemented. From May 1963 Easter National services on the Warley – Brentwood – Ongar corridor were co-ordinated

Redundant ex London Transport 26-seat GS class Guy Specials proved ideal buses for Tillingbourne Valley. Maroon coloured former GS 76 (MXX 376) is seen in September 1964 entering Ewhurst following its descent from Hurtwood Common replacing a LT working on the formerly jointly operated Route 448 from Guildford. Such replacement journeys to Ewhurst were short-lived being withdrawn in November 1965 after which all journeys terminated at Peaslake. P R Wallis

Golden Miller emerged as a London bus operator in January 1967 quickly building up a network of routes around Feltham. The company had a penchant for Bristol chassis which had only become available again on the open market in 1965. Reg.no. CJJ 44H was a 1968 Bristol LHX chassis originally used for development work and later fitted with a 49-seat Plaxton bus body. It is seen on 2 March 1970 approaching Feltham Station terminus from Bedfont Green on Route 601 which originated with West London Coachways.
P R Wallis

with London Transport Route 339. In January 1966 quite a significant improvement occurred in Slough when Thames Valley buses on routes 60/69 from Maidenhead were extended eastwards across Slough to Langley and became co-ordinated with London Transport buses on routes 407/407A between Langley and Cippenham. An overtime ban and work to rule by London Transport crews in January 1966 led to the Board giving consent for a number of independent operators to run 'substitute services' over withdrawn London Transport facilities. Two of these, routes 98B and 235, subsequently remained in independent hands.

Meanwhile the Labour Government of the day with its pugnacious Minister of Transport, Barbara Castle was becoming increasingly involved in a political way with London Transport. This culminated in an agreement with the Greater London Council, the new unitary authority for the London area formed in 1965, to take over responsibility for London Transport from 1 January 1970. More or less coincidentally with these negotiations BET's bus operating interests in the United Kingdom were acquired by the

North Downs, formed by former ORTA Manager John Wylde, claimed a number of firsts:
first direct bus link between Orpington and Croydon introduced on 8 April 1969;
first intensive use of minibuses in the United Kingdom;
first operator to use the new Ministry of Transport standard design bus stop. High roof Strachan bodied 16-seat Ford Transit no. 8 is seen at Keston Park, the last permitted picking up point on Orpington bound journeys in order to protect LT Route 61.
North Downs Collection

Transport Holding Company on 1 March 1968. The THC's interests, which now included the former rival BET and Tilling bus groups, were transferred to the newly created National Bus Company on 1 January 1969 under one of the provisions of the massive Transport Act 1968. Arrangements for the transfer of London Transport to GLC control were contained within the Transport (London) Act 1969. This latter Act also contained the necessary legislation to transfer the assets and services of London Transport's Country Bus Department and Green Line Coaches to the NBC from 1 January 1970.

Another significant independent London area bus operator, Golden Miller, emerged in January 1967. Elsewhere, though, difficulties were being experienced. The London area's oldest independent bus operator, Birch Bros, succumbed to the pressures the industry was facing at the time, abandoning its bus services between October 1968 and September 1969.

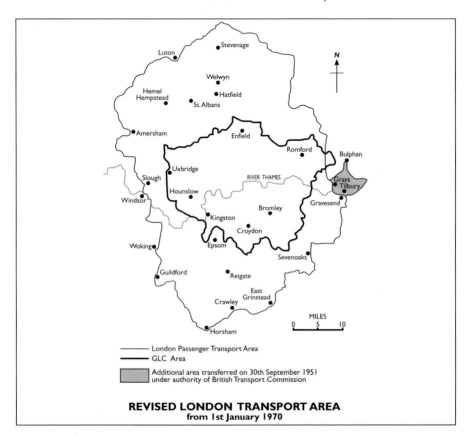

—— London Passenger Transport Area
—— GLC Area

Additional area transferred on 30th September 1951 under authority of British Transport Commission

REVISED LONDON TRANSPORT AREA
from 1st January 1970

The GLC Era

The effects of the Transport (London) Act 1969 had profound ramifications upon both the status of operators and licensing requirements in the London area. London Transport moved from its former nationalised industry status, upon being reconstituted as the London Transport Executive, under Greater London Council control, on 1 January 1970. The 1969 Act abolished both the London Passenger Transport Area and the Special Area. Henceforth London Transport became responsible for providing transport in the 600 square mile GLC area, which approximated to the former Central Area. Within the GLC area London Transport was still absolved form the necessity of obtaining road service licences, London Transport also retaining the power of veto over other operator's bus services within that new area – although the nomenclature changed from 'consent' to 'agreement' in respect of new applications. The previous need for such operators to obtain a road service licence was dispensed with.

The former London Transport Country Bus Department and Green Line were transferred to a new NBC subsidiary, London Country Bus Services Ltd, also on 1 January 1970. London Country and Green Line services continuing within the Greater London Area were protected under the terms of the 1969 Act, becoming the subject of an extensive fares and service agreement between London Transport and London Country Bus Services Ltd. The coincident abolition of the Special Area meant that bus services in the extensive zone between the boundaries of the GLC Area and those of the former Special Area became subject to normal road service licensing procedures. The constraints on the former 'provincial operating companies', as defined in the 1933 Act, on providing services in the outer part of the former LPTA were also removed. By now they were, like London Country, all owned by the NBC. Effectively these former restricted areas became subject to normal licensing procedures as applicable elsewhere in the country. This meant that bus operations therein lost any special link with London Transport and hence became removed from the scope of this volume.

The Greater London Council's period of control over London Transport saw little emerge in the way of fresh initiatives by other operators. In general London Transport's policy continued to seek to operate services itself, only occasionally allowing other operators to take up bus routes. Such operators were rarely allowed the opportunity to build up a local network of routes which would have allowed them more economical use of their vehicles and spread their overhead costs. In an article in the 5 January 1971 edition of the EVENING STANDARD about the then burgeoning Thamesmead Motor Services – at that time developing a small network of mostly Sundays-only bus routes around Bexleyheath replacing sections of London Transport routes not running on that day of the week – journalist Simon Jenkins asked '. . . would it be really disastrous for London Transport's profitability or its prestige if it withdrew altogether from certain suburbs in which its service is already sparse – provided a private operator was ready to step in with a more comprehensive pattern of routes?' Private operator Thamesmead Motor Services was indeed prepared to 'step-in'. They submitted two separate applications to London Transport, in 1971 and 1972, seeking to introduce bus routes between the developing Thamesmead area and Woolwich – which if approved would have spread the small concerns overheads across a 7-day a week operation. London Transport declined to grant Thamesmead Motor Services an 'agreement' for these proposals. Belatedly, in 1973, London Transport itself introduced bus routes between Thamesmead and Woolwich through an extension of existing Route 177 along with the introduction of new Route 198 – both of which followed routeing identical to the original Thamesmead Motor Services applications.

The only major exception to London Transport's general desire to retain direct operation of networks itself was evidenced in that triangle of suburbia bounded by Croydon, Orpington and Biggin Hill. Here London Transport seemed content to leave much bus operation in independent hands. Perhaps the biggest drama of post-war independent bus operation in the London Transport area was enacted in this area when the emergence of Orpington and District in December 1971 led to four years of rivalry between that undertaking and the already-established Orpington Rural Transport Association and North Downs operations. The latter two operators finally succumbed to financial pressures, thereby allowing Orpington and District

North Downs and ORTA's operations both succumbed to financial pressures leaving Orpington & District to mop up their services in 1975/6. Success may have been sweet but was relatively short-lived with Orpington & District soon experiencing similar difficulties before folding in 1981. Former West Riding Roe-bodied Leyland Atlantean reg.no. FHL 774D, acquired in 1979, is seen with blind set for the operator's original Forestdale route. The symbol above the fleet name was a likeness of a London General 'B' type double decker.
J Winter courtesy North Downs Collection

to take up their routes. From its zenith as the operator of seven bus routes between 1976 and mid 1977, Orpington and District too went into a financial decline, finally ceasing operations on 27 February 1981. A phoenix did arise from the ashes of previous independent operation in that area with the formation of Metrobus Ltd in September 1983 following two prior years of operation by Tillingbourne (Metropolitan) Ltd.

The election of a Conservative government in 1979 under Prime Minister Margaret Thatcher heralded an increased emphasis on commercial competition and privatisation. That government's Transport Act of 1980 was notable for the abolition of express service licences. The 1980 Act also sought to make it easier for new entrants to come into the bus industry. A provision in the Act required London Transport, as the licensing authority for the GLC area, to presume in favour of applicants unless it could be shown that a proposal was against the public interest. London Transport appeared reluctant to make such presumptions and was overruled by the Minister of Transport on appeal after rejecting applications from Lightgray Ltd for a Gloucester Road to Heathrow Airport service and Woodside Coaches for a New Addington to East Croydon service in 1981 and 1982 respectively.

Whilst this volume concerns itself with bus services which actually operated, mention must be made of an application submitted in late 1982 by a firm called Associated Minibus Operators Ltd (AMOS) to operate up to 500 franchisee owned minibuses on four high frequency routes which would have crossed central London. At a public enquiry, set up by London Transport as the licensing authority, the AMOS scheme was shown to have serious flaws with regard to projections used on costings and vehicle utilisa-

tion as well as revealing deficiencies in operational planning and control systems. Following the issue of an independent Inspector's report, which was highly critical of the AMOS proposals, London Transport rejected the application. The Government, keen to advance the cause of free enterprise in the provision of London's transport, allowed AMOS to appeal, a procedure in which AMOS was ultimately unsuccessful.

These politically inspired interventions augured further profound changes. The London Regional Transport Act 1984 wrested control of London Transport away from the GLC and put it into the hands of Central Government from 29 June 1984. The old mould of bus service provision under London Transport, which had remained substantially unchanged for over 50 years since 1933, was about to be broken. The bus operating assets of London Transport were transferred to the newly created London Buses Limited which commenced trading on 1 April 1985. On 13 July 1985, the first tranche of 13 London Transport suburban and peripheral services, which had been offered to operators under competitive tender, were taken up by the successful bidders. A watershed had been reached.

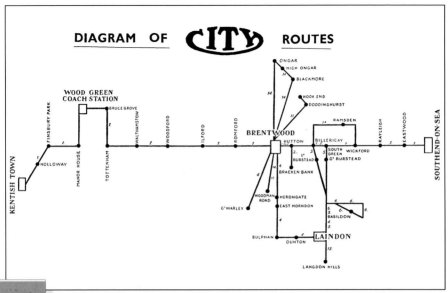

DIAGRAM OF (**ITY**) ROUTES

CHAPTER 2

Essex

Independents

City Coach Co Ltd

725 Lordship Lane, Wood Green, London N22

This company, which operated a lengthy and profitable route from North London to Southend as well as local services based on Brentwood, was the very essence of bus operating legend. Originally formed as the City Motor Omnibus Co Ltd in 1923, City began life as a London 'pirate' operator. Following the 1924 London Traffic Act, which curtailed such freelance services, City became 'respectable', developing a number of profitable bus services in London under the new regime until compulsorily acquired by London Transport on 7 November 1934. In the meantime the Directors of City had formed a new company in 1928, New Empress Saloons Ltd, which ultimately purchased control of the service from Wood Green to Southend previously worked by independent A H Young. The London terminal was extended to Kentish Town in 1929. New Empress was reconstituted as the City Coach Co Ltd in 1936. That same year saw the beginning of steady expansion by acquisition of other operators in the Brentwood area which continued until 1945 by which time City covered 148 route miles operating about 100 buses and coaches. City was a well-respected independent operator and the announcement that it had agreed to sell its business to the British Transport Commission on 17 February 1952 saddened many enthusiasts.

Latterly the City Coach Company standardised on Insert Setright tickets. The centre ticket has been pre-printed for punching at transfer points. Bell Punch New Empress Saloons Ltd tickets were issued to conductors for emergency use in the event of Setright machine failure.
D Seddon Collection

In the 1930s City purchased 30ft-long 3-axle Leyland saloons to maximise capacity on the Southend route. These included 24 Tiger TS7Ts with twin rear axles as well as six examples of the extremely rare twin steer Leyland Gnu received in 1938/9. The Gnu's design eliminated the rear bogie arrangement needed with the Tigers as well as offering claimed savings in tyre wear and fuel consumption.
Gnu no.G6 fitted with Duple 39-seat coach work is seen in Brentwood High Street, bound for Wood Green in 1951. C Carter

ROUTE PROFILE

Route 1	**Southend** (Tylers Avenue) – **London** (Kentish Town) via Billericay, Brentwood, Romford, Gants Hill, Woodford, Walthamstow, Tottenham, Bruce Grove, Wood Green, Finsbury Park, Holloway.
Note:	Whilst passengers could be conveyed for journeys entirely within the London Transport area, restrictions on boarding and alighting points applied as did a minimum fare for such journeys.
At 8 May 1945	Due to wartime exigencies had been split in September 1942 to operate in sections. At date reviewed operated: Southend – Wickford, Wickford – Brentwood, Brentwood – London (Wood Green). Frequency over latter section: Brentwood – London (Wood Green): Monday–Friday, Sunday = 1 hour. Saturday = 30 minutes. Romford – London (Wood Green): Monday–Friday, Sunday = 20 minutes, Saturday = 15 minutes.
1 Feb 1946	Through service restored:Southend – London (Kentish Town) Daily = 15 minutes (30 minutes Wood Green – Kentish Town)
30 Sep 1947	Kentish Town terminal abandoned. Service now operated: Southend – London (Wood Green). Daily =15 minutes.
16 Feb 1952	Service passed to Westcliff-on-Sea Motor Services Ltd.

Although still looking resplendent in City Coach Company livery by the time this August 1953 view was taken at Wickford Broadway (Castle Hotel) 1949-built Roberts lowbridge bodied Leyland Titan PD1A no. LD 5 (NVX 302) had passed into the ownership of BTC controlled Westcliff-on-sea Motor Services Ltd. Surviving City vehicles retained their City fleet numbers with Westcliff until renumbered on 18 July 1954 as part of a massive Eastern National fleet re-numbering exercise which also integrated the Westcliff fleet as well as vehicles owned by Hicks Bros.
Essex Bus Enthusiasts Group (Frank Church Collection)

One of the most tenuous of all connections between a London Transport bus route and that of another operator is illustrated in this view taken at Shell Haven (Shell Cottages) – at just 9 miles distant from Southend-on-Sea the most easterly point ever served by a London Transport bus route. London Transport RT 3636 (MXX 151) is working Route 349 from Grays which was amongst local Grays area bus routes acquired by London Transport from Eastern National on 30 September 1951. To the right stands Campbell's 1946-built Strachans-bodied Albion CX13 bus reg.no. LTW 470 on that operator's works service to Pitsea Station. The photograph dates from 9 January 1956, shortly before Campbell's operations were acquired by Eastern National on 19 February 1956.
Essex Bus Enthusiasts Group (Frank Church Collection)

J W Campbell & Sons Ltd.

Station Garage, Pitsea, Essex

Campbell's Motor Services operated several bus routes from Pitsea. Latterly Campbell's 10 vehicle-strong fleet, in which Albion chassis predominated, included two double-deckers – a 1942 Northern Coach Builders bodied AEC Regent and a 1949 Weymann bodied Albion CX37.

Dix Luxury Coaches Ltd

Heath Garage, Wood Lane, Dagenham, Essex

ROUTE PROFILE

Becontree Heath (Merry Fiddlers) – **Marks Gate Cemetery** via Whalebone Lane South and North.

This Sundays-only route offered Becontree Heath residents a direct bus service to the Cemetery at Marks Gate, a journey which was only otherwise possible by interchanging between buses on London Transport routes 139 and 62. Introduced on 2 June 1963 with an hourly frequency the route only survived for one month, last operation taking place on 30 June 1963.

Elm Park Coaches Ltd

2 Oldchurch Road, Romford, Essex

ROUTE PROFILE

	Romford (Station) – **Chadwell Heath** (Station) via Crow Lane.
15 June 1964	Introduced. Mondays–Fridays = 9 journeys.
6 July 1964	Increased to 13 journeys.
June 1965	Saturday service introduced = 4 journeys.
Sept 1965	Saturday service abandoned.
August 1966	Mondays–Fridays reduced to 8 journeys.
21 April 1967	Withdrawn*.
6 Nov 1967	Re-introduced. Mondays–Fridays = 7 journeys.
19 July 1968	Withdrawn .
*	Was to have been withdrawn after 21 April 1967 but it was decided to continue 'for a further period of one month'. London Transport records suggest that the service may have continued until 22 September 1967.

Elm Park Coaches' route from Romford to Chadwell Heath Station via Crow Lane mostly covered roads not served by LT. Introduced on 15 June 1964 the route peaked at 13 journeys on Mondays to Fridays as well as enjoying three months Saturday operation during 1965 before final withdrawal after operation on 19 July 1968. Seen in Romford South Street in 1965 reg.no. MHW 985 was a 1950 Bristol L5G whose 35-seat ECW body had been converted to front entrance for one man operation by former owner Bristol Omnibus Company.
T K Brookes

Hicks Bros Ltd

Fairfield Road, Braintree, Essex

Hicks were a vigorous independent operating about 40 buses on a 264-route mile network of services based on Braintree. Connections with London Transport were made at Bishop's Stortford as well as by the company's twice daily Route 22 from Braintree to London (King's Cross) via Harlow and Epping.

The fare paid on this Hicks Bros Willebrew ticket was 10d i.e. the value remaining immediately above the cut off portion. Use of the Willebrew system was uncommon in the London Area.
D Seddon Collection

Hicks Bros succumbed to nationalisation pressures selling out to the BTC on 1 January 1950. Operational control passed to Eastern National but Hicks' separate identity was retained until 2 January 1955. Seen

departing Judd Street Coach Station, King's Cross is no. 90, a 1949 Strachans lowbridge bodied Guy Arab III. The vehicle behind, apparently using a trade plate, is Scottish Motor Traction no. B 422, one of a

batch of Alexander bodied AEC Regal IVs bought for that operator's Edinburgh – London services and so probably dating this view to summer 1951 during Eastern National ownership.
P J Snell collection

BUS ROUTES IN THE ROMFORD & HORNCHURCH AREA 1965

EN - Eastern National Omnibus Co. Ltd.
EP - Elm Park Coaches Ltd.
U - Super Coaches (Upminster) Ltd.
    trading as Upminster & District
Other routes London Transport

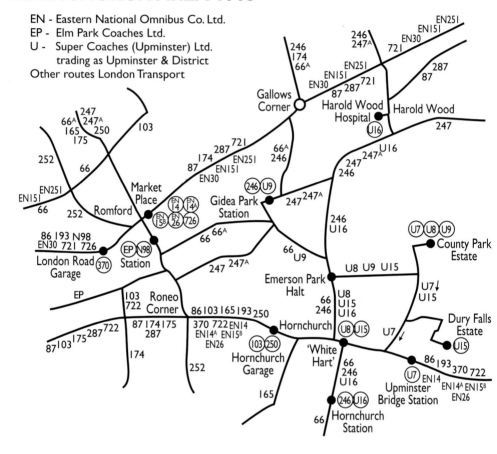

Inner South West Essex

The year 1959 saw the emergence of independent bus services in this area with both Sterling Bus Service and Super Coaches introducing facilities to replace London Transport routes withdrawn as an economy measure following the 1958 strike. From these tentative beginnings Super Coaches went on to develop a significant a network of services in the area, filling a void in the London Transport network.

Frequent, and sometimes rather complicated, changes in ownership followed from 1968 onwards, which are chronicled. The various routes, in so far as they continued to operate, changed hands in line with the changes in ownership. New route introductions followed a similar chronology.

A G Sterling (t/a Sterling Bus Service)

Cambridge Avenue, Gidea Park, Essex

The withdrawal of London Transport Route 238 on 20 August 1958, as an economic casualty of that summer's London Bus Strike, left the Emerson Park Area without a bus service. Protests from residents about this loss of facilities led to the emergence of the Sterling Bus Service who introduced a 60-minute frequency weekday route between Emerson Park Halt and Hacton Lane, Hornchurch on 5 August 1959. This shot shows Sterling Bus Service's ex London County Council 1949 built 30-seat Mulliner bodied Bedford OB reg.no. KJJ 315 at the Emerson Park terminal in Parkstone Avenue (junction Butts Green Road) working a projection of the route to Hornchurch Station introduced at an uncertain date in Autumn 1959. Sterling Bus Service's operation was discontinued after 26 February 1960. Super Coaches (Upminster) Ltd covered the route with one morning peak hour journey from 29 February 1960. P J Snell Collection

Following cessation of the Sterling Bus Service's operation the Seabrook Residents Assocation stepped in to work a private, members only service between County Park Estate (Essex Gardens) and Hornchurch (White Hart) via Wingletye Lane and Parkstone Avenue. This operated on Tuesday and Friday mornings, starting on 15 March 1960 and using coach hired from Super Coaches (Upminster) Ltd. A Tuesday evening 'cinema' service also ran. This operation was so successful that it encouraged Mr R W Wordsworth of Super Coaches to seek and obtain London Transport's 'consent' to introduce 3 new local bus routes.

Super Coaches (Upminster) Ltd

168/170 Upminster Road, Upminster, Essex

Originating as a coach operator before World War II the limited company was formed about 1950 with D M and R W Wordsworth as Directors. Expansion really got under way from 20 February 1961 when three new services based on County Park Estate and Emerson Park were introduced. The fleet name 'Upminster and District' for bus routes was adopted from 1962 whilst in 1964 another fleet name, 'Redbridge and District', was adopted for new Route 19 from Chadwell Heath to Woodford Bridge, at the time of its introduction the longest independent bus route wholly within London Transport's Central Area. Super Coaches erected their own bus stops along the line of this route, a practice not followed by them for their Upminster area services.

SCHOLARS TICKET

Redbridge & District Omnibus Co.
Upminster & District Omnibus Co.
Super Coaches (Upminster) Ltd.

168/170 Upminster Road
Upminster, Essex
Telephone: Hornchurch 49797

AVAILABLE FOR ONE RETURN JOURNEY
PER SCHOOLDAY ON SERVICE

BETWEEN

7.30 a.m. - 9.30 a.m. and 3.45 p.m. - 5 p.m.

DATE OF ISSUE:

This un-issued Scholar's ticket details the various fleetnames used by Super Coaches (Upminster) Ltd. D Seddon Collection

SUBSEQUENT CHANGES IN OWNERSHIP

Date	Owner/Address
19 Nov 1968	R W Wordsworth (t/a Upminster & District Services) 168/170 Upminster Road, Upminster, Essex.
Commentary	Title for bus services changed.

Super Coaches fleet was full of variety and interest as may be seen from this shot taken in the garage yard on 5 August 1965. From left to right are seen:

201 AOU – 1960 Plaxton dual purpose-bodied AEC Reliance ex Creamline, Bordon, Hampshire.

LOU 40 – 1954 East Lancs lowbridge bodied Dennis Lance K4 ex Aldershot & District.

SMU 599 – acquired for spares was 1951 Yeates coach bodied AEC Regal IV ex Taylor's Coaches, London SE1, originally new to Valliant Direct Coaches of Ealing.

LUC 222 – 1951-built Metro-Cammell bodied 'short' 27ft 6in long AEC Regal IV, originally in London Transport's private hire fleet.

XMW 706 – 1961 built Weymann lowbridge bodied coach seated Leyland Atlantean ex-Silver Star, Porton Down, Wiltshire.

150 AOU – AEC Regent III chassis built in 1949 and used by the manufacturer as a test-bed. By February 1961 it had been fitted with a new full fronted, front entrance double deck Roe body and entered service with Liss & District – an associate company of Creamline, Bordon.

J C Gillham

Date	Owner/Address
25 Feb 1969	City Coach Lines (Upminster) Ltd 168/170 Upminster Road, Upminster, Essex.
Commentary	Consequent upon the retirement of Mr R W Wordsworth due to ill health the business was acquired by Passenger Vehicle Sales (Holdings) Ltd dealer group which formed City Coach Lines to absorb the operation.
8 July 1971	Blue Line Coaches Ltd, Station Approach, Upminster Bridge Station, Hornchurch, Essex.
Commentary	Mr B F Lemprière, a local shopkeeper as well as an existing coach operator, formed Blue Line Coaches Ltd to acquire 26 vehicles and services from City Coach Lines (Upminster) Ltd.
1 August 1974	W R Thompson (t/a Coppin's Coaches), Havering-atte-Bower.
Commentary	The bus services were acquired by W R Thompson but passed back again to Blue Line Coaches Ltd on 27 August 1974 due to complications with the sale. On 9 December 1974 the sale to Thompson was completed.
1 June 1976	M J Williams (t/a Coppin's Coaches), Hutton, Brentwood, Essex and G F Stubbington (t/a Dorayme Travel), 4 Highview Road, Thundersley Common, Benfleet, Essex.
Commentary	Coppin's Coaches was acquired by M J Williams and the bus services became jointly operated with G F Stubbington. On 23 August 1976 a partnership was formed between M J Williams and G F Stubbington (t/a Dorayme Travel). M J Williams left the partnership on 11 May 1977, the title then became G F Stubbington (t/a Dorayme Travel).
13 April 1981	G F Stubbington (t/a Dorayme Travel) and Lewington Coach Hire Services Ltd, Patch Park, Ongar Road, Abridge, Essex. Fleetname: Bordabus
Commentary	An association between these two operators led to the introduction of new service 6 (Abridge-Brentwood). Thereafter Dorayme Travel and Lewingtons were named as joint operators with local routes having Bordabus titling.
1 March 1982	Bordabus Ltd, 4, Highview Road, Thundersley Common, Benfleet,. Essex.
Commentary	Lewington Coach Hire Services Ltd went into liquidation and so ceased trading. Bordabus Ltd was formed with G F Stubbington as Director. The former Lewington depot at Patch Park, Abridge continued as the main operating base.

Super Coaches first bus routes were mostly short peak hour only links from residential areas to railway stations at Gidea Park, Hornchurch and Upminster Bridge. Former Tillings Transport (BTC) Ltd 1951 AEC Regal IV reg.no. LYM 731 was re-bodied by Eastern Coachworks in 1960. It is seen loading for Emerson Park at Gidea Park Station on a wet evening in 1964. Sunday and late evening workings were trialled on some routes from September 1963 but quickly abandoned.
A J Douglas / courtesy C Stewart

Dorayme Travel and Bordabus Ultimate tickets. Control Systems Ltd was a new title adopted by Bell Punch Co.Ltd from 1 April 1976. The Ultimate ticket system, originally developed in 1944, was extensively used by London Transport on one man operated buses.
J M Aldridge & D Seddon Collections

For several years Geoff Stubbington owned just one vehicle to maintain his Hornchurch area bus routes. 1969-built Eastern Coach Works-bodied AEC Swift reg.no. YRT 897H, originally supplied new to the small Lowestoft Corporation Transport fleet, served in this role for several years from 1978 onwards. With a musical clue to the origins of the Dorayme fleet name, the Swift is seen at the Patch Park, Abridge premises of J M Lewington (Lewington's Hire Services) on 3 November 1979.
T K Brookes

Date	Owner/Address
c January 1984	G F Stubbington (t/a Bordabus or Bordacoach), 4 Highview Rod, Thundersley Common, Benfleet, Essex.
Commentary	Bordabus Ltd ceased trading, all vehicles and services passed to G F Stubbington who continued to use the Abridge premises. The Dorayme Travel name was resurrected.
12 July 1985	
Commentary	Extant.

ROUTE PROFILE

Upminster (Station) – Corbets Tey (Huntsman & Hounds).	
23 Feb 1959	Introduced. Monday–Friday peak hours, 20 minutes.
15 May 1959	Withdrawn.
Note:	This service operated without London Transport's consent so no fares were charged although passengers could make 'donations' if they so wished. It was introduced after protests following the withdrawal of London Transport Route 249 after operation on 20 August 1958. Although London Transport introduced a new Route 248A over this route on 6 April 1959 the Super Coaches service continued until intervention by the Metropolitan Traffic Area Commissioner led to its withdrawal.

1962 Weymann-bodied AEC Reliance reg.no. TRJ 109 originated with Salford City Transport subsequently passing to SELNEC PTE before sale to Colchester Corporation. When seen on 18 March 1978 it was on hire to G F Stubbington's Dorayme Travel from Lewington's Hire Services. The bus has just turned into Curtis Road on the Emerson Park Estate whilst working Route 2. D M Persson

ROUTE PROFILE

	Emerson Park / County Park Estate – Gidea Park Station.
20 Feb1961	Introduced. Mondays – Fridays peak hours only = 2/3 journeys.
30 October 1962	Numbered 9. Circular working introduced from Gidea Park Station.
Autumn 1970	Service number no longer used.
1 June 1976	Numbered 1. Monday – Friday peak hours only = 5/6 journeys.
12 July 1985	Extant.
Note:	One source states that this route started on 3 November 1960.

ROUTE PROFILE

	County Park Estate – Hornchurch (White Hart).
20 Feb 1961	Introduced. Mondays – Fridays off peak = 3 journeys.
1 March 1963	Diverted via Emerson Park. Numbered 2. Weekdays = 5/7 journeys.
17 April 1967	Extended from Hornchurch to Hacton Lane (The Optimist). Interworked with Route 15 over this section. Weekdays = 6/7 journeys.
Autumn 1970	Route Number no longer used.
2 June 1975	Curtailed at Hornchurch (White Hart). Weekdays = 3/4 journeys.
1 June 1976	Numbered 2. Reduced to Mondays – Fridays = 5 journeys.
26 Feb 1982	Withdrawn.
Note:	Just over 23 years after abandoning the Emerson park area with the withdrawal of Route 238 London Transport re-introduced a bus service to the area when Route 256 from Romford to County Park Estate via Hornchurch commenced on 28 November 1981. This sounded the death knell for independent operation from County Park Estate into Hornchurch.

ROUTE PROFILE

	Emerson Park Halt – Hornchurch Station via Parkstone Avenue, Wingletye Lane, Hacton Lane.
Note:	This route had been worked by Sterling Bus Service between 5 August 1959 and 26 February 1960.
29 Feb 1960	Introduced. 1 journey, Monday–Friday morning peak hour.
2 Nov 1962	Discontinued.

ROUTE PROFILE

	County Park Estate – Upminster Bridge Station.
20 Feb 1961	Introduced. Monday–Friday morning peak hours = 2 journeys.
1 March 1963	Numbered 7.
Autumn 1970	Route number no longer used.
31 July 1974	Withdrawn.
18 Nov 1974	Re-introduced. Monday–Friday peak hours = 3 journeys.
1 June 1976	Numbered 3. Reduced to 2 journeys.
24 Sept 1982	Withdrawn (since May 1977 had operated schooldays only).

ROUTE PROFILE

Harold Hill Local Service:
Dagnam Park Drive – Hilldene (shopping centre).

10 Dec 1962	Introduced. Mondays–Saturdays off peak = 1 hour.
5 Jan 1963	Withdrawn.

ROUTE PROFILE

Hornchurch (Station) – **Harold Wood Hospital**.

15 Sept 1963	Introduced. Numbered 16. Sundays only = 1 journey.
by Oct 1967	Withdrawn.

ROUTE PROFILE

Dury Falls Estate – Hornchurch (White Hart).

Dec 1962	Introduced. Weekdays = 3/7 journeys.
1 March 1963	Numbered 15.
17 April 1967	Extended from Hornchurch to Hacton Lane (The Optimist). Interworked with Route 8 over this section. Weekdays = 5/7 journeys.
31 May 1975	Withdrawn (route number not used after Autumn 1970).

ROUTE PROFILE

Chadwell Heath (Wangey Road) – Woodford Bridge.

17 Aug 1964	Introduced. Numbered 19. Operated under Redbridge & District fleetname. Weekdays = 30 minutes (Monday–Friday peaks = 15 minutes, evenings = 1 hour).
31 May 1965	Extended to Claybury Broadway. Hourly.
3 Jan 1966	Curtailed at Woodford Bridge due to staff shortages. Frequency now: Mondays–Fridays = 1 hour (15–30 minutes peaks), Saturdays = 30 minutes.
2 April 1966	Acquired by D Young of Barkingside.

ROUTE PROFILE

County Park Estate – Romford (Mercury Gardens).

1 Oct 1980	Introduced. Numbered 5. Wednesdays and Fridays only = one journey.
26 Feb 1982	Withdrawn.

Former Trent Roe-bodied Leyland Atlantean PDR1/1 reg.no. RRC 74 was Geoff Stubbington's Dorayme bus for a period. With a board destination display propped up in its windscreen the Atlantean is seen at Hornchurch (White Hart) working Route 2. A Saturday service was reintroduced to Route 2 between 21 August and 18 December 1976 as well as between 29 October 1977 and 10 December 1979.
R Delahoy

Smartly presented and bearing Upminster & District fleetname Super Coaches former London Transport RT 4265 (KYY 868) is seen at Hornchurch (White Hart) on 18 July 1964 working Route 15 to Dury Falls Estate. At that period Super Coaches fleet included around a dozen double deckers, which were often to be found on temporary railway and underground replacement services.
Photobus / R Marshall

ROUTE PROFILE

	Abridge (Patch Park) – Brentwood (Station)
	via Chigwell Row, Collier Row, Chase Cross, Harold Hill, Noak Hill, South Weald.
Note:	Until 1 March 1982 passengers could not be carried for local journeys between: i) Abridge – Collier Row ii) Collier Row – Chase Cross
13 April 1981	Introduced. Numbered 6. Abridge – Collier Row: Frequency: Mon–Fri = 6–8 journeys Sats = 9/10 journeys Suns = 2 journeys Collier Row – Brentwood. Frequency: Mon–Fri = 20/60 minutes Sats = 40/60 minutes Suns = 6 journeys
19 July 1981	Sunday service discontinued.
25 July 1981	All journeys bar one diverted between Abridge and Chigwell Row to operate via Debden Broadway, Chigwell Station and Grange Hill. Frequency now: Mon–Sats = 20/30 minutes peak, = 1 hour off-peak.
20 Feb 1982	Saturday service discontinued.
1 March 1982	Frequency now: Mondays – Fridays = 1 hour peak, 2 hours off-peak.
20 June 1982	Peak hour extras Abridge – Harold Hill withdrawn.
12 July 1985	Extant.

The Bordabus name originated as route branding for the Abridge – Brentwood service reflecting its operation along the GLC/Essex border. Lewington Coach Hire's reg.no. LJB 421E, a 1967 Bristol RELH6G with ECW dual purpose bodywork originally new to Thames Valley's South Midland subsidiary, passes along Brentwood High Street just six days into operation of Route 6 on 18 April 1981.
D M Persson

In 1981/2 Bordabus introduced a number of once weekly single return journey routes from the Waltham Cross area to far distant destinations including Clacton, Maidstone, Southend and Walton-on-the-Naze. Intended for passengers to the outer destination, carriage within the LT area was restricted. Lewington's former Western SMT Alexander-bodied Daimler Fleetline reg.no.BCS 942C, passes over the River Lea Navigation in Station Road, Waltham Abbey making the Thursday return journey from Southend on Route 9. Passengers are conspicuous by their absence. M J Dryhurst

The Romford Market service often achieved good passenger loadings, sometimes leading to duplication. Seen in Eleanor Cross Road, Waltham Cross on 29 June 1985 is former East Kent 1966-built Park Royal-bodied AEC Regent V reg.no. GJG 752D which Geoff Stubbington had hired from Mac's Bus Hire of Hamlet Hill, Roydon, Essex to work the route on that day. D M Persson

ROUTE PROFILE

	Emerson Park – Harold Hill (Gooshays Drive) via County Park Estate.
25 July 1981	Introduced. Numbered 7. Mondays– Saturdays = 40/60 minutes.
Mid Aug 1981	Withdrawn.
8 Sept 1981	Reintroduced. Schooldays only = 5/6 journeys.
25 Sept 1981	Abandoned.

ROUTE PROFILE

	Cheshunt – Waltham Cross – Romford (St Edwards Way) via Waltham Abbey, Debden, Chigwell, Chigwell Row.
Note:	Passengers carried to/from Romford only.
28 Oct 1981	Introduced. Numbered 8. Operated Waltham Cross – Romford. Wednesdays and Fridays, one journey
18 Nov 1981	Increased to Wednesdays, Fridays, Saturdays, five journeys
22 April 1983	Reduced to one/four journeys. One journey Wednesdays/Saturdays extended from Waltham Cross to Cheshunt
27 Aug 1984	Fridays (except in school terms) and Saturdays service withdrawn
12 July 1985	Extant

Mrs J M Lemprière, trading as:

L and A Coaches

156 Upminster Road, Hornchurch, Essex

ROUTE PROFILE

	Rainham Station – Rainham Ferry (Murex works)
8 July 1971	Former works service transferred from City Coach Lines (Upminster) Ltd to Blue Line Coaches Ltd. Numbered 12. Became available to general public.
Unknown date	Acquired by Mrs J M Lemprière.
c 1977	Ceased to be a public service.
Note:	This service replaced an original facility provided by London Transport Route 375.

This 1½d Our Bus Service Bell Punch style ticket was actually printed by Punch & Ticket Co.Ltd of London N1. Whilst there is evidence of commercial co-operation between Punch & Ticket Co.Ltd and Bell Punch Co.Ltd the exact relationship between the two companies remains obscure. Punch & Ticket Co.Ltd closed down in 1968.
D Seddon Collection

Our Bus Service was the sole surviving independent from a host which had existed in the Grays area before the 1933 Act. Our Bus worked two short daily town services to Nutberry Corner and Fairway jointly with Eastern National routes 32A and 32B respectively. As a prelude to the Grays scheme Our Bus, under pressure, sold its bus routes to Eastern National on 15 September 1951. Guy Vixen no. 19 is seen in Grays on 29 September 1951 technically on hire to Eastern National on that concern's last day of operation on routes 32A and 32B. The next day they became a London Transport responsibility. C Carter

Elias Benjamin and Esther Brandon, trading as:

Our Bus Service

17, Nutberry Avenue, Grays, Essex

F Rogers

(address unknown)

ROUTE PROFILE

	Romford Station – Crow Lane.
	In September 1970 F Rogers introduced a service between Romford Station and Crow Lane with five journey on Mondays, Tuesdays, Thursdays, and Fridays. This service, which followed part of the line of route of the former Romford – Chadwell Heath service of Elm Park Coaches, operated without a licence for about three months until abandoned in December 1970.

Sunnymede Coaches Ltd

Registered office: Rear of 15–16 Rathbone Place, Oxford Street, London W1

ROUTE PROFILE

Grange Hill (Bald Hind) – Chigwell Row (Maypole)
via Manor Road, Lambourne Road.

Sunnymede's service was introduced on 19 October 1958 to replace a section of London Transport Route 26 (Ilford – Lambourne End) withdrawn after 20 August 1958 as a economic consequence of that summer's London Bus Strike. Sunnymede's 8-minute journey time route was scheduled for eleven weekday journeys with five on Sundays. Clearly the route's patronage did not live up to expectations, being abandoned after two months operation, the last day of service being 11 December 1958.

Automaticket Ltd, a subsidiary company of Bell Punch Co.Ltd, produced tickets similar to the Ultimate. The Breach Barns examples illustrated were issued on 1 September 1972.
D Seddon Collection

Breach Barns Service

The service between the residential mobile home park at Breach Barns and Waltham Abbey was initiated by site residents Mr and Mrs Turner. Subsequently operation was maintained by successive owners of the park.

A daily service, which peaked at 17 journeys on Mondays to Fridays, 10 on Saturdays and 5 on Sundays, was operated over the Breach Barns route from inception until October 1968 when Sunday operation ceased. Throughout its existence the route was usually worked by small vehicles. J C and S M Turner's Commer 1500 reg.no. 9859 PU is seen at Breach Barn's caravan park on 18 July 1964.
Photobus / R Marshall

On 27 September 1972 Greens (Breach Barns) Ltd was using this anonymous looking white Ford Transit crew bus reg.no. NXJ 792H. It had just arrived at Waltham Abbey from Breach Barns and had stopped to set down passengers opposite 'The Green Man'. From October 1968 twenty Monday to Friday and ten Saturday journeys were operated over the route. By 14 July 1980 frequency had reduced to just eight peak hour journeys on Mondays to Fridays, supplemented by two off peak 'shopping' journeys on Tuesdays, Fridays and Saturdays. Circa February 1981 the Waltham Abbey terminus was changed to the Market Place. Photobus / R Marshall

Possibly the largest size vehicle ever used on the Breach Barns route was this 1950-built Duple Vista bodied Bedford OB coach reg.no. VMF 745. Operated by site proprietors, Mr and Mrs Turner, it is seen at The Cottage, Breach Barns on 18 July 1964 still sporting the livery and motif of its former owner, Evan Evans Tours. R Marshall

ROUTE AND OPERATOR PROFILE

	Breach Barns (Caravan Park) – **Waltham Abbey** (Green Man).
March 1959	Introduced by J C and S M Turner. Operated without licence until May 1959.
25 April 1965	Acquired by E J Green (Breach Barns) Ltd, Breach Barns Farm, Waltham Abbey, Essex.
By Dec 1968	Title became: Greens (Breach Barns) Ltd.
1974	Acquired by Godfrey Davis (Parks) Ltd, 77 High Street, Epping, Essex..
Nov 1978	Title became: Godfrey Davis (Home Estates) Ltd.
26 April 1985	Withdrawn. Replaced by new Waltham Abbey minibus network operated by Sampson Coaches and Travel Ltd (Detailed in Chapter 9).

West's Coaches Ltd

198/200 High Road, Woodford Green, Essex

ROUTE PROFILE

	Chigwell (Station) – Grange Farm Leisure Centre.
15 June 1973	Seasonally introduced. Daily 15 minutes (08.30–11.00 and 16.30–19.30 hrs only).
31 Aug 1973	Seasonally withdrawn.
1974	Re-introduced for Summer 1974. Exact dates of operation not known.
Note:	This service did not operate in 1975. From 31st January 1976 London Transport Route 235 from Chingford Station was extended to Grange Farm Leisure Centre throughout the year.

ROUTE PROFILE

	Chigwell (Station) – Romford (Station) via Chigwell Row, Lambourne End, Chase Cross.
15 Nov 1977	Introduced. Tuesdays, Wednesdays, Thursdays, Fridays only. 2 journeys.
10 Feb 1978	Reduced to operate Wednesdays and Fridays only.
26 May 1978	Withdrawn due to poor patronage.
Note:	This route replaced the section of London Transport Route I50 between Chigwell Row and Lambourne End withdrawn after 14 October 1977. London Transport had intended to introduce a replacement Route 247C from Romford to Chigwell but this proposal was frustrated by the refusal of crews at Romford Garage to drive buses along Bournebridge Lane, which they considered to be unsafe for buses.

D Young, trading as:

Redbridge and District Motor Services

28 Bysouth Close, Clayhall, Ilford , Essex

D Young took up operation of former Super Coaches Route 19 (Chadwell Heath – Woodford Bridge) from 2 April 1966 using Super Coaches road service licence. Retaining use of route number 19, an hourly service was scheduled on Mondays to Fridays, with some additional peak hour journeys, whilst on Saturdays the scheduled frequency was increased to 30 minutes.

Quite fortuitously Derek Persson recorded the last journey on Route 19 before abandonment during the afternoon of 14 May 1966. Although operator D Young is recorded as having owned former Eastern National Bristol K5G reg.no. NNO 95 and Leyland Titan PD2/12 reg.no. FJN 204 (originally ordered by City) this journey was worked by former London Transport RLH 15 (KYY 515) on hire from Super Coaches. The bus is seen at Fulwell Cross, Barkingside. D M Persson

Group Companies

Eastern National Omnibus Co Ltd

New Writtle Street, Chelmsford, Essex

This Essex territorial operator looms large throughout the period reviewed since the close physical interface between East London and neighbouring parts of Essex led to significant services working across the LPTA boundary. A Tilling Group company, with around 450 vehicles in the immediate post war years, operations in Essex formed the company's Eastern Section. The almost entirely separate Midland Section, centred on Bedford, is discussed in Chapter 3.

Following its acquisition of the Tilling Group in November 1948, the British Transport Commission sought to rationalise operations between

Buses loaned by Eastern National to London Transport comprised Bedford, Bristol and Dennis single deckers as well as Guy Arab I double-deckers – although the Dennis Lancet Is and Bedford OBs involved were mostly not used by LT. The buses received LT fleetnames and garage stencils although all retained Eastern National fleet numbers. No. 3905 was one of five ECW-bodied Bristol L5Gs involved. It is seen in November 1951 at Grays working Route 32A to Nutberry Corner. All the Eastern National buses were returned to their original owner by 2 January 1952.
V C Jones / courtesy Ian Allan Publishing Ltd

constituent undertakings in various part of the country. London Transport, at the time ultimately controlled by the BTC, had been drawn into one such scheme, which resulted in the transfer of Eastern National's local bus operations in the Grays/Tilbury area to London Transport on 30 September 1951. On that date 13 local bus routes, the company's garage in Argent Street, Grays and 200 staff became the responsibility of London Transport. London Transport continued to work the Eastern National routes unchanged for three months, supplementing loaned Eastern National buses with increasing numbers of its own STL – and (later) RT-class double-deckers. The main stage of the scheme was implemented on 2 January 1952 when a completely revised route network was introduced. The former Eastern National garage was closed for operational purposes, as all buses now worked from London Transport's garage in Hogg Lane, Grays.

REVISED ROUTE PATTERNS IN GRAYS

Pre-existing Routes. All operated by London Transport from 30 September 1951.		New or Revised London Transport Routes from 2 January 1952.	
EN31	Grays – Tilbury (Feenan Highway)	Linked to form 2 new routes;	
LT 371	Grays – Rainham	371	Tilbury (Feenan Highway) – Rainham
LT371A	Grays – Purfleet	371A	Tilbury (Feenan Highway) – Purfleet.
EN32	Grays – Orsett (section only)	Combined as new route: 323	
EN44	Grays – Bulphan	Grays – Orsett – Bulphan.	
EN32A	Grays – Nutberry Corner	323A	Grays – Nutberry Corner.
EN32B	Grays – Fairway	323B	Grays – Fairway.
EN35	Grays – Shell Haven or Coryton	349	Grays – Shell Haven or Coryton.
EN37A	Grays – Tilbury Ferry	Linked to form two new routes;	
LT 370	Grays – Romford	370	Tilbury Ferry – Grays – Romford
		370A	Tilbury Ferry – Grays – Purfleet.
EN37B	Tilbury Docks – Chadwell St Mary	379	Tilbury Docks – Chadwell St Mary.
EN45	Grays – Linford (section only)	380	Grays – Linford.
EN57	Tilbury Docks – Nutberry Corner	357	Tilbury Docks – Nutberry Corner.
EN81	Tilbury Docks – Bata Shoe Factory	367	Tilbury Docks – Bata Shoe Factory.
EN82	Grays – Bata Shoe Factory	368	Grays – Bata Shoe Factory.

Pre-existing Routes. All operated by London Transport from 30 September 1951.		New or Revised London Transport Routes from 2 January 1952.
EN85 LT370A	Grays – Woodside Estate South Ockendon station – Grays or Purfleet	Linked to form two new routes; 328 South Ockendon – Woodside Estate, 328A Purfleet – Woodside Estate (direct).
LT374	Grays – Aveley (Tunnel garage) – Rainham	Remained unaltered; 374 Grays – Aveley (Tunnel garage) – Rainham.
LT375	Rainham Ferry – White Post Corner	Remained unaltered; 375 Rainham Ferry – White Post Corner.

Note: Routes 323/A/B had special journeys extended to Purfleet for works traffic.

Key: EN – Eastern National   LT – London Transport

Following the transfer of Eastern National's Midland Section to United Counties on 1 May 1952, control of fellow Tilling company Westcliff-on-Sea was passed to Eastern National in the same month. Westcliff's licences and vehicles were formally transferred on 2 January 1955. This brought the former City Coach Company Southend – London (Wood Green) service under Eastern National control.

On 22 May 1963 London Transport replaced its garage in Epping with a new facility at Harlow, at the same time extending its Route 339 to operate Harlow – Brentwood – Warley. The location of the new garage at this route's western extremity made operation of short workings on the 339 from Warley to Coxtie Green via Brentwood difficult so these short workings were incorporated into Eastern National Route 260. The 260 also had occasional journeys working direct between Ongar and Brentwood co-ordinated with London Transport's Route 339 timetable. On the same date a new bus link between Brentwood and Upminster was created by the extension of Eastern National Route 253 to work Shotgate – Brentwood – Upminster.

On 1 January 1969 Eastern National became a subsidiary of the newly

Although eclipsed by the opening of the Dartford Tunnel in 1963 Tilbury Ferry, with its passenger link across the Thames to Gravesend, was an important terminal whose origins go back to an ancient pilgrim route. Long distance Eastern National routes remained unaffected by the Grays area transfer to London Transport. Colchester based 1953 Bristol LS5G no.384 is seen at Tilbury Ferry in October 1962 before setting off on a 4-hour journey bisecting Essex to Clacton. Beside is Green Line liveried RT 4503 awaiting departure for London (Aldgate) on Route 723B. D J Bubier

Eastern National's Chelmsford – London (Bow) route was acquired in November 1933 from Edward Hillman's Saloon Coaches. Through workings were resumed following wartime disruption on 7 April 1946 as Route 10 with a 30-minute headway. The route was re-numbered 30 on 2 January 1955. Seen beneath LT trolleybus wires at Stratford Broadway in March 1958 is 1952-built ECW-bodied Bristol LWL5G no. 348. By 1965 through journeys had been reduced to every two hours and the route was withdrawn after operations on 6 January 1968. M J Dryhurst

created National Bus Company. The next decade witnessed a gradual erosion in frequency and scope of the London services. The more competitive environment engendered by the Transport Act of 1980 led to the Dartford service 402 being extended to operate through to London (Victoria) from November 1980 (detailed in Chapter 6).

Introduction by Bordabus of their new Route 6 (Abridge – Collier Row – Brentwood) prompted Eastern National to project their existing Route 261 (Blackmore – Brentwood – Brook Street) beyond Brook Street across the Essex border to terminate at Collier Row, within the GLC area. Eastern National even instigated the publication of a joint Eastern National / Bordabus timetable for the new services, which during weekday daytimes offered a combined 20-minute frequency of departures between Collier Row and Brentwood. The Eastern National route extension was certainly a tactical move to safeguard the company's interests should the Bordabus initiative prove successful.

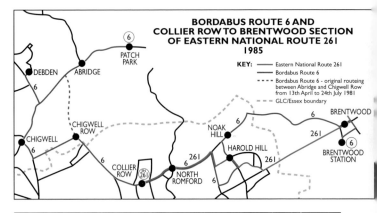

BORDABUS ROUTE 6 AND COLLIER ROW TO BRENTWOOD SECTION OF EASTERN NATIONAL ROUTE 261 1985

KEY:
— Eastern National Route 261
— Bordabus Route 6
- - - Bordabus Route 6 - original routeing between Abridge and Chigwell Row from 13th April to 24th July 1981
– – GLC/Essex boundary

ROUTE PROFILE

Route 322	**Sudbury – Braintree – London** (King's Cross/Euston Square) via Dunmow, Harlow, Epping, Walthamstow, Tottenham.
Note:	No local passengers carried Epping – London.
2 Jan 1955	Licence acquired from Hicks Bros Ltd. Daily = 1/3 journeys. Operated Braintree – London.
11 April 1965	Extended to start from Sudbury.
19 June 1971	Withdrawn.

Routes to London (Wood Green)

Whilst passengers could be conveyed for journeys entirely within the London Transport area, restrictions on boarding and alighting points applied as did a minimum fare for such journeys.

ROUTE PROFILE

Route 251	**Southend – London** (Wood Green) via Rayleigh, Billericay, Brentwood, Romford, Gants Hill, Woodford, Walthamstow, Tottenham.
17 Feb 1952	Acquired from City Coach Company Ltd by British Transport Commission. Operation transferred to Westcliff-on-Sea Motor Services Ltd. Daily = 15 minutes.
2 Jan 1955	Operation passed to Eastern National Omnibus Co. Ltd.
25 June 1961	Re-routed to direct route between Rawreth and Wickford after lowering of the road at Blue Brick Bridge, Shotgate allowed double-deck buses to pass underneath the bridge
19 April 1964	Frequency reduced to: Weekdays = 20 minutes, Sundays = 30 minutes. Interworked with new route 151 to give a combined 10-minute frequency Southend – Wood Green at Monday–Friday peak hours and all-day Saturdays and between Southend – Romford at Monday–Friday off-peak hours. Combined 15 minute frequency between Southend – Wood Green on Sundays.
22 May 1966	Frequency reduced to: Daily = 30 minutes. Interworked with Route 151 to give a daily, combined frequency of 15 minutes between Southend and Wood Green.

Eastern National's Wood Green routes represented the most intense bus services operated other than by London Transport in the Special Area. With a 15-minute headway for many years frequencies reached their zenith between 19 April 1964 and 21 May 1966 when at peak hours and on Saturdays routes 151/251 combined gave a departure from Wood Green every 10 minutes. Although operated as limited stop within the Special Area much local traffic was carried as evidenced by passengers both alighting and waiting to board 1967 Bristol FLF6LX no. 2899 in Romford Market Place in February 1968. Overtaking is London Transport's RT 3787.
P R Wallis

The last double decker to retain City Coach Company's brown and cream livery was former no. LD8 (NVX 305), one of six Roberts lowbridge-bodied Leyland Titan PD1As which entered service with City in 1949. By the time this view was taken in Brentwood High Street on 28 February 1955 this bus had spent approaching three years with Westcliff-on-Sea Motor Services before being transferred, along with the rest of the Westcliff fleet, to Eastern National ownership on 2 January 1955. By then re-numbered 1125 the bus is seen parked ahead of one of six Leyland Farington style lowbridge bodied Leyland Titan PD2/12s originally ordered by City but delivered to Westcliff after City's sale to the BTC.
K Taylor Collection / courtesy C Stewart

7 Jan 1968	Re-routed via West Green Road, Tottenham in lieu of Bruce Grove.
5 Sept 1971	Frequency now: Weekdays = 30 minutes, Sundays = 1 hour.
14 June 1981	Section of route Walthamstow – Wood Green withdrawn. Now operated Southend – London (Walthamstow Central Station). Daily = 30 minutes.
12 July 1985	Extant.

ROUTE PROFILE

Route 151	**Southend – London (Wood Green)** via Basildon, Billericay, Brentwood, Romford, Gants Hill, Woodford, Walthamstow and Tottenham.
19 April 1964	Introduced. Daily. 20 minutes frequency Monday to Friday peak hours and all-day Saturday between Southend – Wood Green. Monday–Friday off-peak hours 20 minutes frequency between Southend and Romford. 30 minute frequency on Sundays between Southend and Wood Green. Some Monday–Friday peak-hour journeys operated via Chesnut Road, Tottenham to avoid traffic congestion in Broad Lane area. Interworked with Route 251.
22 May 1966	Frequency altered to: Daily, 30 minutes over entire route. Journeys via Chesnut Road, Tottenham withdrawn. (Continued to be interworked with route 251).
7 Jan 1968	Re-routed via West Green Road, Tottenham in lieu of Bruce Grove
5 Sept 1971	Section Southend – Basildon withdrawn. Revised to operate: Canvey – Basildon , thence as original routing to Wood Green. Weekdays = 30 minutes, Sundays = 1 hour.
20 June 1976	Section Romford – Wood Green withdrawn. Revised to operate Canvey – Romford only.

Westcliff, and subsequently Eastern National, continued to use City's compact 1930s built bus garage-cum-station at Lordship Lane, Wood Green. Eastern National's Southend depot based ECW-bodied 1968-built Bristol FLF 6X no. 2920 (AEV 814F) is seen at Wood Green waiting time to return to Southend. The premises, which had gained a rather run down appearance by the time this April 1981 view was taken, were by then destined to remain open for only another two months. After operation on 14 June 1981, following which surviving Southend Route 251 was truncated to terminate at Walthamstow Central, it was closed. From 1969 into the early 1970s the premises were used as a location for filming episodes of the popular London Weekend Television series 'On the Buses' starring Reg Varney with Stephen Lewis as the beleaguered Inspector Blakey. C Stewart

ROUTE PROFILE

Route 351	**Chelmsford – London (Wood Green)** via Ingatestone, Brentwood, Romford, Gants Hill, Woodford, Walthamstow, Tottenham.
7 Jan 1968	Introduced (coincident with the withdrawal of route 30 Chelmsford – Bow). Mondays–Fridays and Sundays = 2 hours, Saturdays = 1 hour.
3 April 1971	Section Romford – Wood Green withdrawn on weekdays.
12 March 1973	Section Romford – Wood Green withdrawn on Sundays. Service now operated Chelmsford – Warley via Brentwood.

ROUTE PROFILE

	Southend – London (King's Cross and **Victoria)** via Basildon, Gidea Park, Romford, Leyton, Islington.
Note:	No local passengers carried Laindon – London.
1 Oct 1963	Former express route D became limited stop with conductors issuing tickets. Numbered X10. Daily = 1 hour.
18 April 1971	Re-numbered 400.
26 May 1973	All journeys now terminate at Kings Cross.
12 July 1985	Extant.

ROUTE PROFILE

Route 347	**Brentwood – Romford** via Warley, Harold Wood, Gidea Park.
25 July 1981	Introduced. Partly replaced London Transport Route 247 (Epping – Romford – Brentwood) which, at the time, was the Executive's longest bus route at 25 miles. Jointly operated with London Transport but no inter-availability of tickets. This was the first post-war Central Area to be numbered above 299. Eastern National operated 4 journeys Mondays–Fridays, off-peak hours and 2 journeys Saturday mornings only. London Transport operated 4 journeys Mondays–Fridays, peak hours and 2 journeysSaturday afternoons.
23 Jan 1982	Saturday operation now entirely by London Transport.
4 Sept1982	London Transport operation withdrawn. Eastern National now operated entire service Mondays–Fridays = 4/5 journeys.
12 July 1985	Extant.

Westcliff's 1934-built Weymann lowbridge-bodied AEC Regent reg.no. JN 4746 overtakes London Transport 1938-built 10T10/3 Class AEC Regal no. T576 in South Street, Romford on 26 June 1952. The, by then, ageing Westcliff double-decker was working on that operator's lengthy 1¾-hour journey time Route 2A from Southend-on-Sea to Romford. T576, about to set off on short local Route 252, originally entered service in 1938 as a 10T10 Class Green Line coach. On the outbreak of the Second World War it was converted for use as an ambulance. Converted back for Green Line use in 1946 T576 was amongst a batch of forty 10T10 Class coaches adapted in 1951/1952 for use as Central Area buses.
A B Cross

Westcliff's fleet almost doubled in size to 200 vehicles on 17 February 1952 when City's operations were absorbed. Six lowbridge all Leyland Titan PD2/12s ordered by City were delivered to Westcliff after the take-over. Bearing a fleet number in the City sequence no. LD 21 of this batch is seen leaving Southend for Wood Green.
A B Cross

Westcliff-on-Sea Motor Services Ltd

17/21 London Road, Southend-on-Sea, Essex

This Tilling Group company operated services focused on Southend. From that town Route 2A extended into the London Passenger Transport Area to terminate at Romford. Westcliff-on-Sea routes 2/2B interworked with Eastern National Route 70 between Southend and Grays. Westcliff's operations were absorbed by Eastern National on 2 January 1955.

From 1975 Southend began working a Boxing Day service on Eastern National Route 400 from Southend to King's Cross whilst from 1976 this operation was extended to include a single return journey on Christmas Day. That pattern on Route 400 was repeated until Christmas 1981 after which Christmas and New Year operation switched to Route X1. 1975 Northern Counties bodied Daimler Fleetline no. 386 is seen at the EN stop in Pentonville Road, Kings Cross. The prospective passenger appears more startled by the photographer than by the actual appearance of a bus on Route 400 on Christmas Day 1978.
R Delahoy

Municipal

Southend Transport

Civic Centre, Southend on Sea, Essex

Municipally owned Southend Transport's origins dated back to tramway operation started on 19 July 1901. Subsequently trolleybus and motorbus operation followed, the undertaking becoming solely a motor bus operator following withdrawal of the last trolleybuses on 28 October 1954. A co-ordination agreement with BTC company Eastern National, covering 98 square miles around Southend, came into effect on 2 January 1955.

Eastern National's decision to withdraw from Boxing Day operation in 1971 led to Southend Transport covering certain Eastern National routes on that day. The precedent thereby set expanded to include Christmas Day and New Year's Day workings in 1976 and 1981 respectively. Express service Deregulation Day, 6 October 1980, saw Southend Transport introduce, jointly with fellow municipal undertaking Reading Transport, a marathon 3¾ hour journey time Route X1 which travelled across London to link the respective towns. Passenger loadings on the X1 were bolstered by a series of rail strikes in 1982. Differences in emphasis between two partners – Reading Transport favoured a fast motorway service whereas Southend Transport

Southend Transport's Duple-bodied Leyland Tiger no. 209 is seen at Aldgate Minories Bus Station on 18 February 1982 working a through journey on Route X1 from Southend to Reading. Behind is Southend's Leyland Fleetline no. 235 one of up to eleven double-deckers needed at peak hours to cope with a surge in traffic due to industrial disputes on the Shoeburyness – Fenchurch Street 'Misery Line' Railway. That rail dispute together with another in the summer of 1982 transformed the fortune of the X1 by increasing public awareness of the cheap, frequent and reliable service. R Delahoy

saw more potential for intermediate traffic – led to dissolution of joint working from 17 May 1982. Thereafter Southend Transport concentrated on developing its section of the X1 between Southend and London, with some journeys continuing onwards to Heathrow Airport. Growth proved explosive, Southend initially supplementing its own relatively small coach fleet with hired in vehicles. This policy was soon superseded by the purchase of substantial quantities of second-hand Leyland Leopard coaches. At the end of the period reviewed in this book – 12 July 1985 – Southend Transport's coach fleet comprised 62 vehicles – by then larger than its municipal bus fleet.

ROUTE PROFILE

	Southend-on-Sea – Reading via Basildon, Dagenham, Canning Town, Aldgate, Blackfriars, Trafalgar Square, Hyde Park Corner, Hammersmith, Heathrow Airport Central, Slough, Maidenhead.
6 Oct 1980	Introduced. Express service. Operated jointly with Reading Transport. Numbered X1. Daily = 2 hours.
26 Feb 1981	Stage carriage licence granted.
16 Jan 1982	London Transport Bus Agreement granted. Although still subject to some restrictions passengers could be carried for journeys wholly within the London Transport area.
17 May 1982	Joint operation with Reading Transport ceased. Now operated Southend – London Heathrow Airport. Daily = 2 hours. Extra peak hour journeys to London (Green Park).
1982/3	Service enhancements develop to give approximate 10 minute frequency Monday–Friday peak hours between Southend and London (Green Park). Off-peak = 1 hour to London (Green Park).
1983 – 1985	X11 (fast, omitting Basildon) X21 (Shoeburyness) X31 (Canvey) X41 (Prittlewell) peak hour variants introduced to London (Green Park). With X1 combined frequency about every 2½ minutes in peaks, requiring 45 coaches. Summer Sunday extension to Windsor or, during 1984/5, Thorpe Park.
12 July 1985	Extant.

As traffic demand on Route X1 grew Southend Transport purchased three high capacity Van Hool Astromega integral double deck coaches powered by Mercedes engines. These massive 40ft long 3-axle 84-seat vehicles, which entered service from April 1983, were intended to reduce duplication requirements on the X1. No. 243 (JEV 243Y) is seen traversing Hyde Park Corner in August 1983 accompanied by 27ft 6in long London Transport RM 1676 working Route 73 (Stoke Newington – Hammersmith). C Essex

The three Astromegas alone were quite unable to cope with ever increasing passenger demand on route X1 and its derivatives, which led Southend Transport to hire in additional coaches. No. 212 (CHA 443K), a former Midland Red 1971 built Willowbrook dual purpose bodied Leyland Leopard, was on hire to Southend Transport from dealer Ensign of Purfleet when seen at Hyde Park Corner in August 1983. By December 1983, when Southend had 13 coaches on hire, a policy decision was made to switch from hire to purchase of second hand coaches which resulted, inter alia, in number 212 being bought by Southend Transport in early 1984. C Essex

CHAPTER 3

Hertfordshire and the Chiltern Hills

North Hertfordshire and South Bedfordshire

Independents

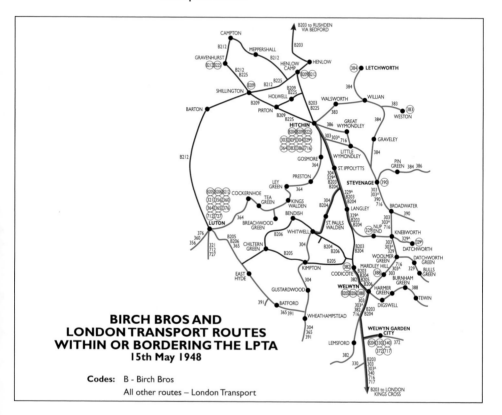

**BIRCH BROS AND
LONDON TRANSPORT ROUTES
WITHIN OR BORDERING THE LPTA**
15th May 1948

Codes: B - Birch Bros
All other routes – London Transport

Birch Bros Ltd

Royal Mail Yard, Cathcart Street, London NW5

Family owned Birch Bros were true pioneers in the road passenger transport industry, starting off with the operation of cabs in London in 1836 which was followed by the introduction of horse bus services in 1847. The limited liability company was formed in 1899 shortly after which, in 1904, Birch became one of the earliest operators of motor buses in London.

Birch Bros Central London bus services were compulsorily acquired by London Transport on 21 February 1934. Anticipating this eventuality Birch pioneered a London – Bedford route in 1928, subsequently extended to

Seen at Henlow Camp 'Bird in Hand' in the early post war years, awaiting departure for Luton on the then hourly Route 212 is no. K104, a 1945 Weymann utility-bodied Guy Arab II. The batch of four buses, K101–K104, only remained with Birch for six years before sale to Essex independent Moore Bros of Kelvedon in 1951. Subsequently re-bodied by Strachans, they survived Moore's acquisition by Eastern National in 1963 before withdrawal in 1965/6. DWK Jones / courtesy J C Gillham

Birch Bros. five day weekly ticket printed by Bell Punch and 3/- Bellgraphic. Conductors wrote fare details onto Bellgraphic tickets which provided carbon copies for auditing by operators.
D Seddon Collection

Rushden. In another shrewd move, which displayed the commercial acumen of the company, Birch acquired a number of small operators in North Hertfordshire / South Bedfordshire in 1939 supplementing these acquisitions with further purchases in 1944 and 1949 to build up a comprehensive network of bus services substantially within the LPTA.

Birch's services reached their zenith in the mid-1950s. The fuel crisis which arose as a result of the aborted British and French invasion of Suez in late 1956 saw the beginning of a contraction in services which continued relentlessly thereafter. The company's fortunes were further frustrated by London Transport's sustained objections to Birch's proposals to further extend services into Welwyn Garden City. By the second half of the 1950s London Transport itself was experiencing significant passenger erosion and, understandably, wanted to protect its own position. Nevertheless Birch Bros still retained their pioneering spirit, introducing an express version of the London – Rushden service, 203M, on 2 November 1959 – the very first day the M1 motorway opened..

After operation on 12/13 October 1968 Birch's remaining bus routes, apart from the Rushden services, were abandoned, operation passing to:

Route 204	Hitchin – Whitwell:	Incorporated into London Transport Route 304 (Hitchin – St Albans)
All outside LPTA		
Route 209	Hitchin – Holwell:	Acquired by United Counties: re-numbered 89
Route 211	Harrold – Bedford:	Acquired by United Counties: re-numbered 123
Route 212	Luton – Henlow Camp:	Acquired by United Counties: re-numbered 146/7/8

Birch's remaining routes 203 and 203M continued for less than a year longer being acquired by United Counties on 14 September 1969. Birch Bros continued as a coach operator for just over another year before selling out to George Ewer (Grey Green) on 1 February 1971, thereby ending 136 years of a family service.

Route profiles

Birch Bros. Bus routes which operated substantially within the London Passenger Transport Area and Express Route 203M.

ROUTE PROFILE

Route 203	London (King's Cross) – Rushden
	via Highgate, Barnet, Potters Bar, Hatfield, Welwyn, Hitchin, Bedford.
Note:	No local passengers carried south of Barnet to / from London.
At 8 May 1945	Extant. Operated Hatfield – Bedford as route 203A . Daily = 1 hour. Hitchin – Rushden as route 203B. Daily = 1 / 2 hours.
Note:	Section of route London-Hatfield had been withdrawn as a result of wartime exigencies after 29 September 1942.
11 March 1946	Through service restored London – Rushden. Daily = l hour. London terminus Crestfield Street Coach Station, King's Cross.
30 Sept 1947	London terminus changed to Judd Street Coach Station, King's Cross.
Dec 1953	London terminus changed to Pancras Way, King's Cross.
1 Nov 1962	London – Welwyn section reduced to every 2 hours.
11 Oct 1964	Diverted to serve Bedford Bus Station instead of St Peters.
By 20 June 1965	London – Welwyn section reduced to: Mondays–Fridays = 4 journeys, Saturday = 2 /3 hours, Sunday = 3 hours.
7 Jan 1968	London – Welwyn section reduced to: Mondays–Fridays = 1 return journey: Saturday = 3 / 4 hours. Sunday = no service.
16 June 1968	London – Welwyn section further altered to: Monday–Fridays = no service. Saturday and Sunday = 2 journeys.
16 Feb 1969	London – Welwyn section suspended. Now operated Welwyn – Rushden only. Weekdays = 1 hour. Sunday = 1 / 2 hours.
13 Sept 1969	Acquired by United Counties Omnibus Co. Ltd. Route number 203 retained.

In 1951 Birch purchased ten double deckers with distinctive full fronted Willowbrook bodywork – six based on Guy Arab III and four built on Leyland Tiger PS1/4 chassis. Number K 211, one of the Arab IIIs, is seen leaving Kings Cross Coach Station in Judd Street during Festival of Britain year 1951. The absence of passengers in the front upper deck is explained by the use of that area as a luggage pen. Also visible is reg.no. LPU 940, a 1947 Duple-bodied Guy Arab III saloon of Moore Bros on hire to George Ewer & Co Ltd probably to duplicate a Grey-Green Express journey. C Carter

Birch's 1959 Willowbrook bodied Leyland Tiger Cub no. K50 is seen in 1960 at speed on the M1 Motorway near Leavesden working a 203M journey to Rushden. The success of Route 203M eclipsed traditional Route 203 which suffered progressive reductions in through journeys to London from November 1962, finally being truncated to operate Welwyn – Rushden only from 16 February 1969. The absence of traffic provides a stark contrast with today's M1 conditions.
NA3T / Arthur Hustwitt

ROUTE PROFILE

Route 203M	**London** (King's Cross) – **Rushden** via Highgate, Barnet, M1 Motorway, Bedford.
2 Nov 1959	Introduced. Daily = 3/6 journeys.
By 3 Dec 1959	Main service operated London – Bedford. Daily = 5/8 journeys, 2 of which were extended to Rushden. Other journeys offered connections and through fares with Route 203 between Bedford and Rushden.
By 3 Sept 1961	Frequency now Monday–Fridays = 1/2 hours, Saturdays / Sundays = 1 hour. Most journeys advertised as operating through from London to Rushden, although in practice a change to a Route 203 bus was often necessary at Bedford.
By 21 Feb 1962	'Nonstop' section diverted to serve Ampthill.
11 Oct 1964	Diverted to serve Bedford Bus Station instead of St Peters. Additional stops introduced as Flitwick and Westoning.
7 Jan 1968	Most journeys now operated London – Bedford only. Frequency now: Mondays–Fridays = 2 hours. Saturday–Sunday = 1/2 hours.
8 June 1968	Saturday and Sunday service increased to hourly over full route.
13 Sept 1969	Acquired by United Counties Omnibus Co. Ltd. Route number 203M retained.

Below **Birch Bros 1961-built Willowbrook coach-bodied AEC Reliance no. K45 stands at Whitwell Gravel on the last day of operation of Route 204 Saturday 12 October 1968. Alongside is LT RF 33 on Route 304 from the St Albans direction. Virtually all 304 journeys terminated at Whitwell and LT timetables publicised connections by Birch Bros thence to Hitchin. However occasional long established weekend evening journeys on LT's 304 extended beyond Whitwell into Hitchin paralleling Birch's 204. K45 later worked the final evening journeys on routes 204 and 209 (Hitchin – Henlow Camp).** G Smith

Bottom **Birch Bros K62 (PYK 62) was a Beadle-Commer TS3 with 41-seat Beadle coachwork. Manufacturer John C. Beadle (Coachbuilders) Limited of Dartford, Kent**

ROUTE PROFILE

Route 204	Hitchin – Whitwell via St Paul's Warden.
At 8 May 1945	Extant. Mondays–Fridays =1/4 hours. Saturday = 2/3 hours. Sundays = 4 journeys. Certain journeys on Thursday. Saturdays and Sundays projected beyond Whitwell to Luton via Bendish and Chiltern Green. Weekday peak hour journeys projected beyond Whitwell to Welwyn Garden City (Terwin Road) via Codicote and Welwyn.
31 May 1945	Mondays–Fridays frequency increased to 1/2 hours.
31 Jan 1946	Whitwell – Luton journeys replaced by new Route 206. Frequency now: Mondays–Saturdays = 1/2 hours, Sundays = 2 hours.
30 Sept 1946	Frequency now: Daily = 1 hour.
12 Jan1948	Frequency reduced to: Daily = 2 hours.
By Nov 1954	Frequency now: Mondays–Fridays = 1/2 hours, Saturdays = 1 hour, Sundays = 1½ hours.
13 April 1957	Following a reduced schedule operated from 7 January 1957 as a consequence of fuel rationing cuts associated with the Suez crisis, the following changes were implemented. Welwyn Garden City projection withdrawn on Saturdays. On Thursdays, Fridays and Saturdays certain journeys projected beyond Whitwell to Bendish as partial replacement for Route 206. Frequency now: Daily = 1/3 hours.
7 April 1958	Projections to Bendish and to Welwyn Garden City withdrawn. Sunday service withdrawn. Frequency now: Weekdays = 1/3 hours.
12 Oct 1968	Route abandoned by Birch Bros. Ltd.
Note:	From 14 October 1968 London Transport provided additional journeys between Hitchin and Whitwell on existing Route 304 (Hitchin – St Albans).

had first developed its semi-chassisless design in 1945. Many earlier examples built used running units from older, scrapped vehicles but latterly use of new Rootes TS3 two stroke engines became usual. The batch of six similar vehicles (K60 – 65) delivered to Birch Bros in 1955 was the first to incorporate the more powerful 105bhp version of the distinctive sounding TS3 diesel engine. When photographed on 27 April 1963 K62 was parked in Luton between turns on Route 205 (Luton – Kimpton). P R Wallis

ROUTE PROFILE

Route 205	**Luton – Welwyn Garden City**, via Chiltern Green, Kimpton, Codicote, Welwyn.
At 8 May 1945	Extant. Operated Luton – Welwyn. Daily = 2/7 journeys.
31 May 1945	Frequency increased to: Mondays–Fridays = 6/7 journeys, Saturdays = 2 hours, Sunday = 4 hours.
31 Jan 1946	Frequency increased to: Daily = 2 hours.
12 Jan 1948	Frequency reduced to: Daily = 6/10 journeys.
18 June 1955	Route projected beyond Welwyn to Welwyn Garden City Station (with restriction on carriage of local passengers between these points). Frequency now: Mondays–Fridays = 1 hour, Saturdays = 30 minutes, Sundays = 1/2 hours.
Dec 1955	Saturday afternoon service increased to 15 minutes (in co-ordination with Route 206).
May 1956	Frequency reduced to: Mondays–Fridays = approx 2 hours, Saturdays = 30/60 minutes, Sundays = 4 journeys.
13 April 1957	Following a reduced schedule operated from 7 January 1957 as a consequence of fuel rationing cuts associated with the Suez crisis, the following changes were implemented: On Saturdays and Sundays only certain journeys diverted at Kimpton to Whitwell and Bendish (Saturdays only) to cover withdrawal of route 206. Frequency now: Mondays–Fridays = 6/7 journeys, Saturdays = 1 hour, Sundays = 4 journeys (Luton – Whitwell only).
7 April 1958	Section of route from Kimpton to Welwyn Garden City abandoned. Now operated Luton – Kimpton only with first and last journeys on Mondays-Fridays extended beyond Kimpton to/from Codicote. Frequency now: Mondays–Fridays = 9 journeys, Saturdays = 1 hour.
Note:	London Transport route 315 provided peak hour replacement between Welwyn Garden City and Kimpton.
15 May 1961	Mondays–Fridays: Codicote journeys and evening service withdrawn.
30 Oct 1965	Route withdrawn without replacement.

ROUTE PROFILE

Route 206	**Luton – Welwyn Garden City** via Chiltern Green, Bendish, Whitwell, Codicote, Welwyn.
31 Jan 1946	Introduced. Operated Luton – Whitwell, replacing route 204 journeys over this section. Frequency: Thursdays = 4 journeys, Saturdays = 2 hours, Sundays = 4 hours.
30 Sept 1946	Extended to operate Luton – Welwyn. Daily = 2 hours.
Aug 1947	Reduced to operate 3 days per week. Thursdays Luton – Whitwell only = 2/3 hours. Saturdays /Sundays Luton – Welwyn = 1½/2 hours.
c. Feb 1951	Further reduced to operate: Thurs: Luton – Whitwell only = 4 journeys. Sat/Sun: Luton – Welwyn = 3/1 jnys plus 2/4 'shorts' Luton – Whitwell.
18 June 1955	Extended to operate Luton – Welwyn Garden City. Frequency now: Mon–Fri = 3 journeys, Saturdays = 2 hours, Sundays = 3 journeys.
Note:	Restriction on carriage of local passengers between Welwyn and Welwyn Garden City.
Dec 1955	Saturday afternoon frequency increased to 45/90 minutes.
March or June 1956	Route curtailed to operate 3 days per week: Thursdays / Sundays: Luton–Whitwell only = 3 journeys, Saturdays: Luton – Welwyn Garden City = 2 /3 hours.
6 Jan 1957	Suspended as a result of fuel rationing cuts associated with Suez crisis.
13 April 1957	Route formally withdrawn. Partially replaced by diversions of routes 204 and 205.

ROUTE PROFILE

Route 215	**Luton – Stevenage**, Broadwater via Chiltern Green, Kimpton, Codicote, Tower Lodge, Knebworth.
18 June 1956	Introduced. Monday, Tuesday, Thursdays, Fridays = 4 journeys.
7 Jan 1957	Route suspended by fuel rationing cuts associated with Suez crisis.
31 May 1957	Licence formally surrendered.

Association of Public Transport Users

George E Ausden, Hon. Sec., 2 Station Cottages, Amptill, Bedfordshire

ROUTE PROFILE

Luton – Codicote via Chiltern Green, Kimpton	
6 September 1968	Introduced. Fridays only =1 journey. Operation sub-contracted to Stevenage Travel Ltd.
March 1969	Operation re-contracted to P. Blatchly (trading as Contractus). A Bristol K or KSW type lowbridge double-decker was regularly used.
By October 1969	Withdrawn Note: This route was subsequently reinstated post the 1 January 1970 transfer of London Transport's Country Area operations to London Country Bus Services Ltd.

The Association of Public Transport Users introduced a single return trip Fridays only bus route from Codicote to Luton restoring a link severed when Birch Bros withdrew Route 205 on 31 October 1965. Operation was initially sub contracted to Stevenage Travel whose Duple-bodied Bedford VAL reg.no. DME 999A is seen on the inaugural journey's arrival at Luton Park Square on 6 September 1968. Over 80 passengers were carried necessitating the duplicate Bedford SB seen behind. Sadly patronage did not remain at this level and, after changing sub contractor to Contractus in March 1969, the route was abandoned by October 1969. G Smith

Premier Travel's rapid expansion in the immediate post-war years brought that operator to Bishop's Stortford following its acquisition of Weeden's Motor Service in May 1945 and A Drayton and Sons in September 1947. No.197 (VDV 797) was one of nine former Devon General 1957-built Metro-Cammell-bodied AEC Reliances acquired by Premier Travel during 1969. Although fitted with internal cab doors, rather unusually the bodywork of this batch also featured external sliding cab doors. No.197 was photographed in Station Road, Bishop's Stortford prior to taking up a journey on the former Weeden's Motor Service route which had become Premier Travel Route 10. The packed car park visible behind the bus was symptomatic of the progressive passenger erosion being experienced by most bus undertakings. Rural operators, such as Premier Travel, were particularly adversely affected by the growth in private car usage. Photobus / R Marshall

S G & R P Biss, trading as:

Biss Bros

Sun Garage, Rye Street, Bishop's Stortford, Hertfordshire

Biss Bros started in business as an old style London independent operator based at Waltham Abbey, selling out to the London Public Omnibus Company in 1927. The family then left the bus industry for a period and established a poultry farm at Waltham Cross. Bus operations recommenced in 1950 at Bishop's Stortford with the acquisition of the old established business of H Monk. The family's links with the Waltham Abbey area led them to introduce a short lived service thence to Roydon Hamlet on 20 October 1952 but which was abandoned in February 1954.

Biss Bros routes from Bishops Stortford to Birchanger, Farnham and Furneux Pelham were rural market day (Thursday) and Saturday operations with some Tuesday and Sunday workings. Coaches were often used on these routes, but for a number of years from 1966 duties were usually covered by reg.no. HJU 339D, a Duple Midland bus Bedford SB5 seen departing Bishops Stortford on 29 April 1967. G R Mills

2½d single ticket recorded by ticket enthusiast John Cunningham as having been issued on H. Monk's service in 1950. Cut unevenly, it was most likely produced by a now unknown local printer to Bell Punch style.

Biss Bros 3d single numerical stage ticket printed by Williamson of Ashton.

'Stock' Bell Punch numerical stage Omnibus Ticket recorded by John Cunningham as having been issued on B.C. Cannon's route on 5 August 1948. 'Stock' tickets, to a standard design, were mostly sold to small bus operators who could not afford to have tickets specially printed for them bearing their name.
All D Seddon Collection

ROUTE PROFILE

The three Bishop's Stortford routes were operated by H Monk of Northgate Garage, Bishop's Stortford until acquired by Biss Bros in 1950.

	Bishop's Stortford – Furneux Pelham.
At 8 May 1945	Tuesdays, Thursdays, Saturdays, Sundays = 2/4 journeys.
1950	Frequency increased to: Daily = 5/6 journeys.
1965	Sunday service withdrawn.
31 Dec 1969	Extant.
	Bishop's Stortford – Birchanger.
At 8 May 1945	Thursdays, Saturdays = 2 journeys.
31 Dec 1969	Extant.
	Bishop's Stortford – Farnham.
At 8 May 1945	Thursdays, Saturdays = 2 journeys.
1950	Tuesday service introduced.
31 Dec 1969	Extant.
	Waltham Abbey – Roydon Hamlet via Nazeing Gate, Bumbles Green, Broadley Common.
20 Oct 1952	Introduced. Daily = 3/9 journeys.
May 1953	Frequency reduced to Fridays only = 3 journeys.
Feb 1954	Abandoned.

B C Cannon Ltd

High Street, Puckeridege, Hertfordshire

ROUTE PROFILE

Braughing – Bishop's Stortford via Puckeridge, Albury.	
At 8 May 1945	Thursdays only = 3 journeys.
31 Dec 1969	Extant. By now reduced to 2 Thursday journeys.

E C W Halls, trading as:

The Stag Bus Service

Downfield House, Hatfield Heath, Essex

ROUTE PROFILE

Bishop's Stortford – Hatfield Heath – Sheering	
At 8 May 1945	Extant. Thursdays only = 6 journeys ex Bishop's Stortford, 5 journeys ex Hatfield Heath. 1 journey in each direction projected beyond Hatfield Heath to terminate at Sheering.
At 31 Dec 1969	Extant, with only minor changes since 1945.

A quintessentially rural operation The Stag Bus Service route from Bishops Stortford to Sheering via Hatfield Heath remained substantially unchanged throughout the period reviewed with operation on Thursdays only. Duple Vista bodied Bedford OB reg. no. MMT 506, a vehicle type which provided the backbone of so many rural operations in the immediate post war years, is seen in Station Road, Bishops Stortford in March 1961.
R Marshall

Premier Travel Ltd

15 Market Hill, Cambridge

Premier Travel, founded by Arthur Lainson in 1936, had expanded rapidly in the years immediately following World War II by acquisition of smaller

Premier Travel covered a broad geographical territory meeting up with LT services at Bishops Stortford and Hitchin. Number 118 was one of the earliest built Bristol K5Gs when delivered in 1937 to West Yorkshire. It was re-bodied by ECW in 1949. The bus is seen at Bishops Stortford on 23 May 1961 working lengthy Route 26 to Royston acquired from A Drayton & Sons (Barley) in September 1947 along with Route 29 to Hitchin. R Marshall

independent operators who were fearful of the Labour Government's nationalisation plans. Two such acquisitions, F E Weeden of Chrishall in May 1945 and A Drayton & Sons (Barley) Ltd in September 1947, introduced Premier Travel bus routes to the northern fringes of the London Passenger Transport Area.

Premier Travel displayed much of the mien of contemporary larger 'group-owned' operators. For many years double-deckers, usually second-hand, were used extensively on the company's essentially rural bus network which, at its zenith, stretched across seven counties. The company was one of the earliest in the industry to introduce sick pay and pension schemes for its employees, such consideration being rewarded by a high level of staff loyalty. The expansion of Premier Travel's long-distance express service network compensated to some extent for the general contraction of the company's bus network from the 1950s onwards as, following national trends, usage of these declined.

Weeden's Motor Service 3/6d Bell Punch return ticket. Premier Travel 1/- numerical stage Bell Punch ticket.
All D Seddon Collection

ROUTE PROFILE

Route 10	**Chrishall – Bishop's Stortford** via Langley, Arkesden, Clavering, Manuden.
30 May 1945	Acquired from F E Weeden (t/a Weeden's Motor Service) of Chrishall. Thursdays, Saturdays, Sundays = 3/6 journeys.
By 1950	Revised to operate: Thursdays, Fridays, Saturdays, Sundays = 2/9 journeys.
By 1957	Revised to operate: Wednesdays, Thursdays, Saturdays, Sundays = 1/8 journeys. One Thursday journey extended beyond Chrisall to Elmdon.
By 1968	Revised to operate: Thursdays, Saturdays = 2/3 journeys.
31 Dec 1969	Extant.

ROUTE PROFILE

Route 26	**Royston – Bishop's Stortford** via Barley, Barkway, Brent Pelham, Manuden.
Sept 1947	Acquired from A Drayton and Sons (Barley) Ltd. Daily = 1/4 journeys.
By 1950	Revised to operate: Daily = 2/7 journeys.
By 1957	Revised to operate: Mondays, Thursdays, Fridays, Saturdays = 1/4 journeys. Additional service on Tuesday during summer months.
By 1968	Revised to operate: Mondays, Thursdays, Saturdays = 1/2 journeys.
31 Dec 1969	Extant.

With the general decline in passenger loadings on rural bus services Premier Travel's fleet became increasingly single deck in the 1960s. Former London Transport RF 9 private hire coach became one man operated bus no. 167 with Premier Travel. It is seen at Bishops Stortford working Route 26 on 29 June 1967. To the left is an LT Green Line RF coach refurbished in the 1966/7 modernisation programme working Route 720 to London (Aldgate). G Smith

**Premier Travel Insert
Setright return ticket.**
D Seddon Collection

ROUTE PROFILE

Route 27	**Cambridge – Little Hadham** via Barley, Nuthampstead, the Pelhams, Albury.
Sept 1947	Cambridge – Nuthampstead route acquired from A Drayton & Sons (Barley) Ltd.
By 11 Nov 1950	Extended to terminate at London Transport stop at Little Hadham (Nag's Head). Daily, except Thursdays. Connections with London Transport routes 350, 350A, 386.
By 1957	Little Hadham journeys now operate only Wednesdays in August.
End Aug 1966	Little Hadham journeys withdrawn. No longer reached LPTA.

ROUTE PROFILE

	Saffron Walden – Hitchin via Chrisall, Barley, Royston, Baldock Letchworth.
Sept 1947	Barley – Hitchin route acquired from A. Drayton & Sons (Barley) Ltd. Numbered 29. Tuesdays, Sundays = 1/2 journeys.
10 June 1950	Incorporated into new route numbered 12. Through journeys Saffron Walden – Hitchin operated Tuesdays, Sundays = 2/3 journeys.
By 1963	Tuesday service now operated summer only. Sunday service withdrawn.
Sept 1966	Royston – Hitchin section withdrawn. Route no longer reached LPTA.

ROUTE PROFILE

	Hitchin – Clothall Bury via Baldock.
10 June 1950	Introduced. Numbered 40. Tuesdays = 2 journeys.
1951	Abandoned.

ROUTE PROFILE

	Buntingford – Therfield
10 June 1950	Introduced. Numbered 41. Mondays = 2 journeys.
1951	Re-numbered 47.
1953	Revised to operate on Mondays in August only.
1957	Withdrawn as consequence of Suez-crisis fuel rationing.

Hitchin

This was another country town offering a reasonable amount of independent activity although it became much diluted following the demise of Birch Bros.

J & G Bygrave

Redhill, Baldock, Hertfordshire

ROUTE PROFILE

	Redhill – Hitchin via Baldock, Letchworth.
At 8 May 1945	Tuesday, Saturday = 1/3 journeys. Friday service later introduced.
By 1966	Acquired by Smiths (Buntingford) Ltd.

H V Richmond

The Priors, Barley, Hertfordshire

ROUTE PROFILE

	Barley – Hitchin
At 8 May 1945	Operated by A Livermore. Tuesdays = 1 journey.
1946	Acquired from A Livermore by H V Richmond. Tuesdays = 1 journey.
31 Dec 1969	Extant.

W H Smith

4 Station Road, Buntingford, Hertfordshire

Title later:

Smiths (Buntingford) Ltd.

ROUTE PROFILE

	Hitchin – Buntingford via Weston, Ardeley, Cottered.
At 8 May 1945	Tuesdays, Thursdays, Saturdays = 1/2 through journeys.
By 1960	Now operated: Tuesdays, Saturdays = 1/2 journeys.
31 Dec 1969	Extant.

ROUTE PROFILE

	Hitchin – Buntingford via Baldock, Sandon, Mill End.
By 1966	Acquired from J and G Bygrave. Operated Hitchin – Mill End. Saturdays = 2 journeys.
31 Dec 1969	Extant.

ROUTE PROFILE

	Buntingford – Letchworth via Sandon, Baldock.
At 8 May 1945	Mondays–Fridays = 1 works journey.
31 Dec 1969	Extant.

W H Smith was fated to receive national celebrity in 1948 when London Transport decided to exercise powers delegated by the BTC under the 1947 Transport Act by introducing unlicensed Route 383 between Hitchin and Weston over roads already licensed to Smith. The ensuing trials and tribulations are detailed in Chapter 1. Suffice it to say that Smith survived the rigours of court appearances to run a steady business with around a dozen coaches. One such was reg.no. TMV 597, a 1948 Duple Vista-bodied Bedford OB, seen at Hitchin (St Mary's Square) on 2 May 1959. J C Gillham

Cuffley Motor Co Ltd

Station Road, Cuffley, Hertfordshire

ROUTE PROFILE

Cuffley Station – Tolmers Park Hospital.
This short Sundays only operation was introduced on 12 October 1960 following the withdrawal of Sunday operation on London Transport Route 308 (Hertford – Cuffley Station). The facility offered one return journey on Sunday for hospital visitors with no intermediate stops between terminals.
The route did not prosper, being withdrawn by June 1961.

Albert Edward Henry Nash, trading as:

Universal Cars (Hertford)

13 Burleigh Road, Hertford

ROUTE PROFILE

Hertford – Claybury Hospital via Ware, Hoddesdon, Broxbourne. Use restricted to passengers to / from Claybury Hospital.	
5 June 1960	Introduced. Sundays = 1 journey.
2 April 1961	Diverted to serve Cheshunt.
31 March 1963	Withdrawn.

Two attempts were made in the 1960s to provide a bus service to the Aldwickbury Estates on the south eastern perimeter of Harpenden, some considerable distance from the nearest London Transport services.

ROUTE PROFILE

Harpenden – Aldwickbury Estates	
Winter 1960/1	Introduced. Operated by W and E F Kershaw Ltd trading as **County Coaches** of Batford. Weekdays = 1 hour.
1963	Saturday service withdrawn.
Winter 1967/8	Abandoned.
4 Nov 1968	Re-introduced. Operated by Harpenden Motor Coaches Ltd. Weekdays.
Jan 1969	Abandoned.

Major General Sir H A Wernher Bart, GCVO

Luton Hoo, Luton, Bedfordshire

Introduced in 1951 the Wernher Collection Service conveyed passengers from Luton's Midland Road Station and Park Square to and from Luton Hoo, which housed a collection of fine art. The service operated five days a week (with no service on Tuesdays or Fridays) from Easter (including Good Friday) until the last Sunday in September. The number of journeys per day of operation ranged from five to eight.

1s 0d Luton Hoo Bus ticket in 'Amusement Arcade' style produced by an unknown printer. D Seddon Collection

LUTON HOO BUS
1/-
03028

From inception in 1951 the Wernher Collection Service used a succession of second-hand coaches – the first, a 1935 Bedford WLB, was succeeded in 1955 by a Guy Vixen which, in turn, was replaced by a Bedford OB in 1957. The first new vehicle purchased for the service, in 1961, was reg. no. 323 DBM, an 11-seat Martin Walter bodied Bedford CALV. This vehicle is seen in Luton's Park Square in May 1970 with passengers disembarking through the minibus's rear exit. By the date of this photograph London Transport's Country Area and Green Line operations had passed to London Country Bus Services Ltd, which latter's fleet now included RF 567 seen behind the Bedford. P R Wallis

Eastern National's Midland Section services shared considerable interface with London Transport services in an arc swinging eastwards from Aylesbury through Tring, Dunstable and Luton to Hitchin. Seen in Hitchin on 5 April 1952 are no. 3822, a 1940 ECW-bodied Bristol K5G working Route 52B from Luton to Stofold, being duplicated by no. 3652 a 1936 Brush bodied Leyland Titan TD4. They were amongst the 245 vehicles transferred to United Counties with the Midland Section on 1 May 1952. A B Cross

Group Companies

Eastern National Omnibus Co Ltd

New Writtle Street, Chelmsford, Essex

Midland Section

ROUTE PROFILE

Route 164	**Bishop's Stortford – Royston** via Standon, Braughing, Buntingford.
Note:	This was the first post war company route to link Eastern National's Eastern and Midland Sections.
At 8 May 1945	Wednesdays only. Worked by Eastern National's Eastern Section depot at Bishop's Stortford. 1 journey Standon – Royston 1 journey Buntingford – Royston 2 journeys Royston – Chipping
12 March 1950	Extended to operate Bishop's Stortford – Royston. Daily = 1 journey Bishop's Stortford – Royston, 2/5 journeys Buntingford – Royston.
1 May 1952	With absorption of Eastern National's Midland Section into United Counties the latter company now worked certain Buntingford – Royston journeys. Eastern National continued to work the Bishop's Stortford – Royston journey.
6 May 1953	Withdrawn. United Counties Route 188 (Biggleswade – Royston) extended to Buntingford as partial replacement.

United Counties Omnibus Co Ltd

Houghton Road, Northampton

ROUTE PROFILE

	London (King's Cross) – Rushden via Highgate, Barnet, M1 Motorway, Ampthill, Bedford.
14 Nov 1969	Acquired from Birch Bros Ltd. Numbered 203M
25 April 1971	Re-numbered 200.
12 July 1985	Extant. By this date London terminal had changed to Marylebone (Great Central Street).

Crossley chassis were a popular choice with municipal operators in the immediate post-war years. Between 1946 and 1949 Luton Corporation Transport took delivery of 29 Crossley DD42 chassis, all of which were fitted with Crossley bodywork too. Less successful were the Brockhouse Turbo-transmitters fitted to many of Luton's Crossleys. These were removed in 1953, due to heavy fuel consumption, and replaced by constant mesh gearboxes. 53 seat low-bridge bodied no. 104 (FNM 104), dating from 1948, is seen on 27 April 1963 at the Cutenhoe Road terminus of Luton and District Transport routes 1/1A. P R Wallis

Municipal

Luton Corporation Transport

85 George Street, Luton, Bedfordshire
By 1950: 41 Bute Street, Luton, Bedfordshire

Luton had started operations in 1908 as a tramway undertaking, replacing trams with motor-buses in 1932. This latter year had also seen the introduction of a co-ordination agreement with Eastern National. A further co-ordination agreement with Eastern National was implemented on 2 January 1949, services thereafter being jointly operated and referred to as Luton and District Transport.

United Counties operational fleet virtually doubled in size to around 500 vehicles following the transfer of Eastern National's Midland Section in 1952. Bristol FLF6B no.623 is seen bound for Luton's Park Square in August 1966 on peak hour Route 32 from Luton Airport. London Transport RF 42 working Route 364A to Hitchin heads up Lea Road which at this point formed the LPTA boundary. LT routes 364/364A worked across Luton but were restricted from carrying local passengers within the borough under the terms of the 1933 Act. G Smith

The Luton & District Transport Agreement led to Luton Corporation buses appearing well outside the borough boundary. 1965 Neepsend bodied Dennis Loline III no. 186 is seen on the bleak Dunstable Downs. Luton's association with United Counties led to the adoption of Tilling like features on many of the undertaking's buses. The front upper deck window push out ventilators are typically Tilling. Almost so is the 3-piece destination display – except that Tilling buses showed the route number on the near side.
M J Dryhurst

Absolutely Tilling-like in appearance and specification were 30 Eastern Coach Works bodied Bristol RELL6Ls purchased by Luton Corporation Transport in 1967 and 1968. By this time the undertaking was incurring financial deficits and the Bristols were purchased in a hurried attempt to reduce costs by the introduction of one-man operation. In the event their entry into service was delayed by deteriorating industrial relations and, in one instance, sabotage. By the time no. 115 (PXE 115G) was photographed in the centre of Luton during the summer of 1969 the undertaking had entered into negotiations with United Counties which culminated in the sale of the Corporation's transport undertaking to United Counties on 4 January 1970.
C Essex

ROUTE PROFILE

Route 5	Luton – Studham via Dunstable, Kensworth.
Note:	This route, introduced under the authority of a wartime Defence Permit, was of particular interest in that it penetrated significantly into the LPTA. From 2 January 1949 Route 5 remained the only route licensed to Luton Corporation Transport, all other routes becoming licensed to Luton and District Transport.
Early 1944	Introduced. Mondays – Fridays = 2 journeys, Saturdays = 3 journeys.
31 July 1950	Withdrawn. Replaced by London Transport Route 376A.

The Chiltern Hills

Independents

W M Oborne, trading as:
Queen's Park Coaches
146 High Street, Aylesbury, Buckinghamshire

Queen's Park Coaches 2½d geographical stage Bell Punch ticket. D Seddon Collection

Seen in Aylesbury's Kingsbury Square awaiting departure time for Halton Camp is Queen's Park Coaches 1942-built 35-seat Willowbrook-bodied Dennis Lancet 2 reg.no. GPP 473. Eastern National acquired this bus along with the Queen's Park Coaches business in 1951, giving it fleet no. L126. As part of Eastern National's Midland Section the bus passed into United Counties ownership on 1 May 1952 and is recorded by The PSV Circle as being withdrawn that same year.
R M Warwick Collection

This operator had started a daily service in 1931 between Aylesbury and Halton RAF Camp via Weston Turville. On weekdays a 30 minute frequency was maintained, lengthened to hourly on Sundays. Following the death of Mr Oborne the operation and vehicles were sold to Eastern National in 1951, becoming integrated into the latter's Route 107.

R R Coaches, trading as:
Red Rose
Aylesbury Road, Wendover, Buckinghamshire

This concern also maintained a daily service between Aylesbury and Halton Camp but routed via Wendover. Eastern National Route 106 covered the same road. The two operators co-ordinated their timetables to provided two departures per hour, increased to four on Wednesdays and Saturdays. Red Rose's workings were acquired by Eastern National in 1950 although no vehicles were transferred.

Red Rover 4½d
geographical stage
Bell Punch ticket.
J M Aldridge Collection

Red Rover Omnibus Ltd

20 Kingsbury Square, Aylesbury, Buckinghamshire

Red Rover's origins were as a former London independent operator compulsorily acquired by London Transport under the terms of the 1933 Act. An earlier express coach operation between London and Aylesbury had been sold to Green Line in 1932. This sale helped to finance the acquisition of bus services from Aylesbury to Buckingham, Edgcott and Westcott, which remained the backbone of the company's operations for many years. Traffic increased during the war due to the establishment of new military camps and aerodromes in the area. In the post war years housing development, both on the outskirts of Aylesbury and in surrounding villages, helped to maintain passenger loadings as well as creating new service opportunity. In 1955 Red Rover was acquired from the founding Cain family by Keith Coaches (Mills and Adams), a substantial local coach operator. The Red Rover trading name was retained.

Red Rover was one of the few operators to stick with Dennis double-deck chassis in the 1930s. 1937 Dennis Lance II reg.no. DPP 199 fitted with Strachan highbridge bodywork is seen in Aylesbury (Kingsbury Square) in 1950.

Behind is LT RT 601 working trunk Route 301 to Watford Junction. Red Rover retained its loyalty to Dennis into post war days purchasing a Strachan-bodied Lance III double-decker reg. no. OPP 857 in 1951.
W J Wyse / courtesy G W Morant

B & B Services

(Proprietors J W Barnard late-1920s – 1961, P J W Reid from 1961)

Water End Road, Potten End, Hertfordshire

This operator was established in the late 1920s acquiring another local operator, Village Services Bus of Potten End, in 1933. Interestingly Mr P J W Reid was the nephew of Mr J R G Dell, proprietor of the neighbouring Rover Bus Services.

ROUTE PROFILE

	Potten End – Albury via Berkhamsted, Northchurch
At 8 May 1945	Main service operated: Potten End – Berkhamsted. Daily = 6–14 journeys. Extended to Northchurch Mondays–Fridays, 1 journey and to Albury on Saturdays, 4 journeys and Sundays, 3 journeys.
30 Sept 1964	Sunday service withdrawn.
31 Dec 1969	Extant.

ROUTE PROFILE

	Berkhamsted – Ashridge Hospital
At 8 May 1945	Daily = 2–11 journeys.
c1950	Withdrawn.

ROUTE PROFILE

	Berkhamsted – Apsley Mills via Boxmoor Station, Two Waters.
At 8 May 1945	Mondays–Fridays = 1 journey.
31 Dec 1969	Extant.

ROUTE PROFILE

	Potten End – Hemel Hempstead via Frithesden, Water End.
At 8 May 1945	Thursdays only = 1 return journey.
31 Dec 1969	Extant.

B & B Services reg.no. FNY 170 was a 1943-built Bedford OWB, rebodied in 1952 by Thurgood, which rather gave this 29-seat coach the appearance of a post-war Bedford OB model. It was photographed in service at Potten End on 18 April 1964.
Photobus / R Marshall

ROUTE PROFILE

	Potten End – Apsley Mills via Water End, Hemel Hempstead.
At 8 May 1945	Mondays – Fridays = 3 journeys.
31 Dec 1969	Extant.

C H Knight, trading as:

Bream Coach Service

74 Bury Road, Hemel Hempstead, Hertfordshire

ROUTE PROFILE

	Long Chaulden – Apsley Mills via Hemel Hempstead, Two Waters.
At 8 May 1945	Operated Hemel Hempstead – Apsley Mills. Weekday peak hours only = 13-21 journeys.
17 July 1955	Extended to operate Long Chaulden – Apsley Mills. Weekdays= 30/60minutes.

Bream Coach Service started business in the late 1920s. The original bus operation provided a works service between Hemel Hempstead and the factory of well known paper manufacturers John Dickinson and Co. at Apsley Mills. Reg.no. YNK 607, seen on layover in Hemel Hempstead Bus Station on 18 April 1964, was a 40-seat Thurgood-bodied Bedford SBG coach.
Photobus / R Marshall

Bream was an interesting example of a small operator co-existing with the mighty London Transport. As Hemel Hempstead developed it would have been expected that London Transport would seek to provide town bus services, as indeed it mostly did. Due to Bream's presence on the Apsley Mills route and a shortage of crews at its Two Waters Garage, LT did not contest Bream's application for the first bus service along Warners End Road.
Seen in Hemel Hempstead is reg.no. TXT 958, a 1958 Owen bus bodied Bedford SBG on the Long Chaulden route. R Marshall

4 Jan 1956	Timetable co-ordinated with London Transport Route 314A which had been extended to operate to Warners End from Hemel Hempstead.
17 Oct 1956	Sunday service introduced: Long Chaulden – Hemel Hempstead = 1 hr.
1960	Peak hour projections to/from Boxmoor Station Mondays–Fridays introduced.
29 Dec 1967	Withdrawn. Service incorporated into London Transport Route 314. Bream's Monday – Friday works service from Long Chaulden – Maylords Avenue (Rotax Factory) became LT Route 314C.

J R G Dell, trading as:

Rover Bus Services

The White House, Lye Green, Chesham, Buckinghamshire

ROUTE PROFILE

	Chesham – Hemel Hempstead via Lye Green or Latimer, Bovingdon, Boxmoor.
5 Aug 1944	Joint operation introduced with London Transport Route 316 on workings via Lye Green. Rover remained sole operator on workings via Latimer. London Transport 316 journeys departed Chesham via Codmore Cross whilst Rover journeys travelled via Nashleigh Hill. London Transport 316 journeys entered Hemel Hempstead via Fishery Road and St John's Road whilst Rover journeys travelled via Station Road. Daily = 30/45 minutes. 1 Monday–Friday journey extended from Chesham to Amersham. Works journeys to Apsley Mills on weekdays.
5 May 1964	Joint operation ceased. All journeys became operated by Rover Bus Services. Former London Transport routings via Codmore Cross and into Hemel Hempstead abandoned.
31 Dec 1969	Extant.

Lee & District Coach Services

326 Waterside, Chesham, Buckinghamshire

ROUTE PROFILE

	King's Ash – Chesham. Swan Bottom – Chesham via Chartridge.
At 8 May 1945	Wednesdays, Fridays, Saturdays, Sundays = Irregular.
3 Jan 1956	Bus service acquired by London Transport. Numbered 394D. Lee and District continued as a coach operator.

E 1935

D 2220

THE ROVER BUS SERVICES.

SCHOLAR'S TICKET

4D

OMNIBUS TICKET

1 2 3 4 5 6 7 8 9 10 11 12 13 14 15

27 28 29 30

This Ticket must be punched in the section in which the Passenger is entitled to travel, and must be shown, if demanded.

Bell Punch Co., Ltd., London.

This ticket is issued subject to the Conditions set forth on the Application for Scholar's Ticket Form.

NOT TRANSFERABLE

Available only on Rover Buses

Bell Punch Co., Ltd., London

1/3d 'Stock' Bell Punch ticket recorded by John Cunningham as having been issued on Rover Bus Services on 21 September 1954.
Rover Bus Services 4d Scholar's ticket printed by Bell Punch.
D Seddon Collection

From 1944 until 1951 London Transport used STL and later RT double-deckers on Route 316 providing a contrast in style and capacity to Rover's small Bedfords. Subsequently LT used single-deckers, latterly 26-seat GS class. Rover's 30-seat Duple bodied Bedford OB reg.no. NBH 941 is seen at the 316 stop in Chesham Broadway on 7 November 1953. The period of joint operation did not extend to Rover's acceptance of LT Rover tickets leading to the apparently contradictory note in LT timetables 'Rover tickets are not available on Rover Bus Services'.
J C Gillham

Whilst London Transport reduced the size of buses used on its workings of the Chesham – Hemel Hempstead route, Rover Bus Services increased the size of its contribution when 39-seat Duple Midland bus-bodied Bedford SBG reg.no. UBH 697 entered service in 1954. It is seen on layover in Chesham Broadway on 18 April 1964, less than a month before London Transport surrendered its share of the jointly operated service to Rover Bus Services.
Photobus / R Marshall

Lee & District Bedford OB reg.no. SMY 547 is seen in Chesham Broadway on 7 November 1953 loading at the LT stop for Route 394 which paralleled much of Lee & District's route. The crowded passenger load perhaps encouraged LT to acquire Lee & District in January 1956. J C Gillham

Land and Estates Ltd
Loudwater Estate, Rickmansworth, Hertfordshire

The Land and Estates' route provided a link between the exclusive Loudwater Estate and Rickmansworth LT Station. Originating before World War II, operation was re-instated by January 1947. Worked by Dennis Ace reg.no. BBP 339 eleven journeys ran on Mondays–Fridays and six on Saturdays, mostly at peak hours. After operation on 5 June 1950 London Transport took over the service as Route 336A.
The Omnibus Society

Knightswood Coaches Ltd
Bucks Garage, High Street, Watford, Hertfordshire

ROUTE PROFILE

	Elstree Aerodrome (Hog Lane) – Watford (Estcourt Road)
17 Sept 1963	Introduced. Tuesdays, Fridays, Saturdays, Sundays = 3 journeys.
Nov 1963	Reduced to 2 journeys.
c 1972	Sunday service withdrawn. Reduced to 1 journey.
c July 1976	Acquired by Campbell Consultants Ltd. Watford terminal now Exchange Road / Beechen Grove.
2 March 1984	Acquired by J P Mullany (t/a Mullany's Coaches). Re-routed via Bushey Arches.
27 May 1984 to 27 Aug 1984	Summer Sunday service introduced from Watford Junction to Aldenham Country Park. 4 journeys.
12 July 1985	Extant.

Campbell Consultants Ltd
Elton Way, Watford By Pass, Watford, Hertfordshire

Knightswood Coaches' route from Elstree Aerodrome linked a number of small settlements such as Patchetts Green, previously without a bus service, to Watford. Introduced on 17 September 1963 with three journeys on Tuesdays, Fridays, Saturdays and Sundays operation had been reduced to one journey on those weekdays by 1972. The route passed to Campbell Consultants in November 1975 and to Mullany's Coaches on 2 March 1984. Seen with original operator Knightswood Coaches at the Hog Lane Terminus at Elstree Aerodrome on 17 October 1964 is reg.no. MXX 375 easily recognised as former London Transport GS 75.
D M Persson

ROUTE PROFILE

	Patchett's Green – Borehamwood.
7 Nov 1977	Introduced. Mondays, Wednesdays, Thursdays, Saturdays = 1 journey.
8 May 1978	Withdrawn.

Latterly Knightswood Coaches habitually used one of their coaches for bus route duties. 1969-built Bedford VAS 5 reg.no. HRO 331G carried a diminutive 2½ bay 24-seat version of the then popular Plaxton Panorama coach body. Without any display of route details or destination, few but regular passengers would have known that this coach departing Watford (Estcourt Road) in September 1970 was working the bus service to Elstree Aerodrome.
G W Morant

H E Farmer, trading as:

The Gem

Monks Risborough, Buckinghamshire

ROUTE PROFILE

	High Wycombe – Princes Risborough via Lacey Green.
At 8 May 1945	Extant. Mondays, Tuesdays, Thursday, Fridays = 5 journeys, Saturdays = 6 journeys, Sundays = 3 journeys.
By August 1946	2 journeys introduced on Wednesdays. Sunday service increased to 4 journeys.
26 March 1949	Acquired by Thames Valley Traction Co. Ltd.

Surman's Coaches Ltd

Oakley Road Garage, Chinnor, Oxfordshire

ROUTE PROFILE

	Sydenham – High Wycombe via Chinnor, Radnage and Chinnor – High Wycombe via Princes Risborough.
by March 1957	Fridays only = 1 return journey on each route.
by 31 Dec 1969	Only Sydenham – High Wycombe route extant.

This view of The Gem's Dodge bus reg.no. ADF 797, fitted with headlight masks and with white paint applied to bumper and fenders, clearly dates from the Second World War period. The bus is seen loading in Queen Victoria Road, High Wycombe on the operator's route thence to Princes Risborough which reverted to daily operation once wartime restrictions eased. The shot recalls that host of small, family owned, sometimes carrier based, operators which emerged in the 1920s. Many later succumbed, sometimes tempted by overtures made by group operators as happened with The Gem who sold out to Thames Valley on 26 March 1949.
The Omnibus Society / J F Parke Collection

Group Companies

Eastern National Omnibus Co Ltd
New Writtle Street, Chelmsford, Essex

Midland Section
From Aylesbury long distance services worked to Luton (Route 16) and Bedford (Route 17). Eastern National also maintained town service 109 in Aylesbury between Haydon Hill and Southcourt.

United Counties Omnibus Co Ltd
Houghton Road, Northampton

ROUTE PROFILE

	Route 359 Aylesbury (Kingsbury Square) – Amersham Station via Great Missenden.
29 Sept 1942	Existing Eastern National Route 107 (Aylesbury – Great Missenden) extended to Amersham. Daily = 1 hour. Jointly operated with London Transport.
1 May 1952	United Counties assumed Eastern National's share of the route.
5 May 1964	Last day of joint operation. United Counties workings replaced by London Transport.

Eastern National Route 359 was a rarity in being one of only two joint operations between London Transport and a Tilling company in the immediate post war period. Joint working began on 29 September 1942 when existing Eastern National Route 107 (Aylesbury – Great Missenden) was extended to Amersham, partially to compensate for the withdrawal of Green Line Route 35 (Aylesbury – London) due to wartime exigencies. Eastern National no. 3996, a 1948 ECW-bodied Bristol K5G, is seen at Amersham station in 1950. P Picken

In the immediate post war years the only United Counties route to Aylesbury was lengthy 46 from Buckingham and Northampton. This all changed following the transfer of Eastern National's Midland Section to United Counties on 1 May 1952. United Counties became the joint operator with London Transport on Route 359 to Amersham. Photographed on that route in May 1962 at Aylesbury (Kingsbury Square) is United Counties number 109, a 1955 ECW-bodied Bristol LS5G. Joint operation of the 359 ceased after 5 May 1964 when London Transport replaced United Counties workings. P R Wallis

City of Oxford Motor Services Ltd

Cowley Road, Oxford

BET Group member City of Oxford worked a number of bus routes westwards from Aylesbury. As well as trunk routes 81 to Thame and 82 to Oxford, these also included several rural village routes which only operated on Wednesdays and Saturdays – Market Days in Aylesbury – as well as, in some cases, on Fridays.

Thames Valley Traction Co Ltd

83 Lower Thorn Street, Reading, Berkshire

Thames Valley had a substantial presence in High Wycombe dating back to the company's earliest days, a garage having been opened at Wycombe Marsh in 1924. From High Wycombe Thames Valley operated trunk routes to Aylesbury, Maidenhead, Reading and Windsor. A significant number of more local services ran too. As expansion of the Wycombe Marsh Garage was not possible a second garage was opened in High Wycombe at Desborough Road in 1946. The combined allocation approached 70 vehicles.

ROUTE PROFILE

Post World War II Profile High Wycombe Town Services jointly operated by Thames Valley and London Transport

Thames Valley 26	Mill End Road – Wycombe Marsh
Thames Valley 26A	Mill End Road – New Bowerdean Road
London Transport 326	Mill End Road – Wycombe March – Micklefield Estate
London Transport 326A	Mill End Road – New Bowerdean Road

These oldest established surviving joint workings between London Transport and a neighbouring operator dated back to 1 March 1929 when Amersham and District (controlled by London Transport's predecessor, London General) commenced joint working with Thames Valley on the latter's High Wycombe Town Service, originally introduced on 1 July 1927. Amersham & District operations were replaced by London Transport in July 1933 whilst the routes were re-numbered into the above series in October 1934.

This photograph, taken in High Wycombe on 29 June 1968, captures a then fading London Transport practice. The LT bus stop is festooned with plates for eleven Thames Valley and one City of Oxford routes – as well as solitary LT Route 305. The road from High Wycombe to West Wycombe upon which Thames Valley Bristol LL6B no. 568 is about to depart was more than adequately covered by the various Thames Valley and Oxford routes. None-the-less LT ran 2/3 weekday journeys on a West Wycombe spur of Route 305 to maintain their running rights over the road as enshrined in the 1933 Act. These 305 journeys were withdrawn from 23 November 1968. Thames Valley then had to replace LT flags with their own on bus stops along the road. G Smith

at 8 May 1945	Operation pattern established as in heading. Daily. Each route = 1 hour giving 15 minute combined frequency over common section through High Wycombe. Weekday peak hour projections from Mill End Road to/from Sands.
14 Dec 1954	London Transport 326A withdrawn. London Transport journeys to New Bowerdean Road now numbered 326.
1 July 1963	Circular terminal working introduced at Mill End Road via Dashwood Avenue.
31 Dec 1969	Extant.

Reconstruction work in the centre of High Wycombe in 1968/9 necessitated diversions. Thames Valley's 1952 ECW-bodied Bristol KSW6B no. 652 is seen in Denmark Street on 28 August 1969 on the joint 26A beside an LT 'dolly stop'. Following a practice adopted by most Tilling companies in the 1960s the bus has had its intermediate display blanked off. Ostensibly this was to save the cost of blind linen but it also revealed a generally defeatist management attitude to passenger erosion. G Smith

CHAPTER 4

The Thames Valley

Independents

The Royal Borough of Windsor, situated just outside the London Passenger Transport Area, was served by five independent bus operators in the immediate post war years, two of whom provided Windsor town services.

A V Cole, trading as:
Blue Bus Services
York Road, Windsor, Berkshire

By September 1957:
Blue Bus Services Ltd
273 Bath Road, Slough, Buckinghamshire

Blue Bus Services
1933-built 20-seat Duple-bodied Bedford WTB reg.no.
JG 4103 is seen loading in River Street, Windsor.
Behind stands a utility bodied Bedford OWB of Borough Bus Service on that operator's Clewer Green service.
The Omnibus Society / J F Parke Collection

ROUTE PROFILE

	Windsor – Maidenhead via Eton Wick, Dorney, Taplow.
at 8 May 1945	Operated Windsor – Taplow. Weekdays = 4 journeys, Sundays = 1 journey. Windsor – Dorney Reach. Daily = 2 hours. Windsor – Eton Wick. Daily = 30 minutes.
July 1955	Extended from Taplow to Maidenhead (Coach Station). Frequency: Windsor – Maidenhead. Weekdays only = 1/2 hours. Windsor – Dorney Reach. Daily = 1 hour. Windsor – Eton Wick. Daily = 30 minutes.
3 June 1966	Route acquired by Thames Valley Traction Co. Ltd. Numbered 22.
Note:	Blue Bus Services Ltd acquired another route in the South Eastern Traffic Area, between Maidenhead and Paley Street, on 2 March 1966 from Bray Transport Ltd. This route was subsequently disposed of to Thames Valley on 3 October 1969 becoming their route number 14.

Blue Bus Services dated back to 1923. In the late 1950s vehicle policy changed from using lightweight chassis, mostly Bedford, to choosing heavyweight makes. First vehicle into stock following this decision was reg.no. GOW 111 a 1950 Albion CX39 with dual purpose Reading bodywork. Sporting a mainly cream livery it is seen at Eton Wick. V C Jones courtesy Ian Allan Publishing Ltd

The last bus to be purchased by Blue Bus Services was 1957 Burlingham bodied Dennis Lancet UF reg.no. 239 DPC acquired in 1965. It is seen in January 1966 crossing Windsor Bridge followed by a London Transport RF saloon and passing LT RT 4553 heading into Windsor on Route 335 from Watford. The 3-mile road from Windsor to Slough via Eton had one of the most intensive service levels worked by LT's Country Bus Department – 13 bus plus two Green Line routes gave 294 departures in each direction over an 18 hour day on Mondays to Fridays. This level of service far exceeded traffic requirements and arose because most routes from Slough were scheduled to terminate at LT's Windsor Garage. P R Wallis

Frowen & Hill Ltd, trading as:

Borough Bus Services

64 Arthur Road, Windsor, Berkshire

Borough operated a daily 30-minute frequency town service to in Windsor to Clewer Green. Well loaded 1947 Bedford OB reg.no. DRX 296 is seen on 23 February 1952. Borough's reluctance to invest in larger capacity buses needed to meet increasing traffic demand caused by post war housing development resulted in its sale to Thames Valley on 12 May 1955. Thames Valley formed three new double-deck operated routes, numbered 51/51A/51B, by extending the Borough route to Foster Avenue, combining existing short workings on their Route 20 and introducing circular working. A B Cross

Imperial 3½d numerical-stage Bell Punch and 'Stock' Ultimate ticket headed 'Transport Services'. J M Aldridge and D Seddon Collections

A Moore & Sons (Windsor) Ltd, trading as:

Imperial

First Avenue, Clewer Hill Road, Windsor, Berkshire

ROUTE PROFILE

Route 1	Windsor (Thames Street) – Dedworth (Foster Avenue). Originally established 1926 between Windsor and Clewer.	
	1947	Diverted to Dedworth. Daily = 30 minutes.
31 Dec 1969	Extant.	

Imperial's Duple Midland bodied Bedford SBG reg.no. PNX 257, seen in River Street, Windsor, illustrates the diverse business activities characteristic of many early independents. Founder A Moore was a former London General bus driver who bought a 5-acre farm in 1917. He continued to farm it while part of the site was used to develop a carrier's business from which both bus and taxi cab operations developed. The fleet name – Imperial – was singularly appropriate for operations in Windsor, a principal residence of the British Monarch. P R Wallis

In the late 1950s several Tilling Group companies rebuilt early post-war half-cab saloons to suit one-man operation. Reg.no. DMO 668 was originally a 27ft 6in long coach bodied Bristol L6B delivered new to Thames Valley in 1948. In 1957 the chassis was extended to 30ft length, the original Bristol engine replaced by a Gardner 5LW unit and a new Eastern Coach Works full fronted body fitted. After sale by Thames Valley DMO 668 passed to Imperial with whom it is seen in June 1969. C Essex

ROUTE PROFILE

Route 2	**Windsor (High Street) – Dedworth (Martins Estate)** via Clewer Village and Dedworth Manor Estate. Originally established in 1936 as Windsor – Maidenhead Road
1947	Extended to Clewer (Vale Road). Daily = 30 minutes.
12 Aug 1950	Extended to Dedworth (Tudor Way). On Saturdays additional 30 minute service operated Windsor – Vale Road, buses marked 'Extra'.
1 Jan 1960	Entire service now operated Windsor – Martins Estate (Galleys Road). Frequency: Weekdays = 20 minutes, Sundays = 30 minutes.
31 Dec 1969	Extant.

ROUTE PROFILE

Route 3	**Windsor (River Street) – Dedworth (Martins Estate)** via Clewer Village and Dedworth Manor Estate.
1 Dec 1965	Introduced. Monday–Friday peak hours only = 4/5 journeys.
31 Dec 1969	Extant.

James Alfred Perry

The Cottage, Elm Road, Windsor, Berkshire

Acquired summer 1950 by: R E Jackson, trading as:

Crescent Coaches

Slough, Buckinghamshire

J A Perry was the sole survivor from several independents who once ran services to the Slough Trading Estate, all the others having sold out to London Transport in 1934.

ROUTE PROFILE

	Windsor (Thames Street) – Slough Trading Estate via Slough or Chalvey. Also **Slough station – Trading Estate.**
At 8 May 1945	Weekdays = 5–12 journeys.
Summer 1950	Acquired by R E Jackson (t/a Crescent Coaches).
1 July 1951	Acquired by Thames Valley Traction Co Ltd.
7 July 1951	Transferred to London Transport. Routes numbered 407/407A.

Crescent Coaches five small Bedfords were acquired by Thames Valley but not operated. Seen on Thames Valley premises awaiting subsequent sale are 1945 Duple utility bodied Bedford OWB reg.no. CRX 333 and 1947 Mulliner bodied Bedford OB reg.no. EBL 967. The latter is still displaying a route blind for the Slough Trading Estate to Windsor route. To the right is withdrawn Thames Valley 1929 Leyland Titan TD1 no. 181.
J F Higham / courtesy J C Gillham

ROUTE PROFILE

Slough (Station) – Cippenham (Eddie's Café)	
Jan 1948	Introduced. Daily = 30 minutes.
Summer 1950	Acquired by R E Jackson (t/a Crescent Coaches).
1 July 1951	Acquired by Thames Valley Traction Co Ltd.

Originating in the 1920s White Bus Service's principal route worked daily from Windsor to Bagshot where 1939-built Dennis Falcon reg.no. BRX 865 is seen on 14 August 1949. At the date of writing this book White Bus Service, still owned by the Jeatt family, remains in business. A weekdays bus service from Windsor continues to serve Windsor Great Park en route to a revised terminal at Ascot.
J C Gillham

C E Jeatt, trading as:

White Bus Service

North Street Garage, Winkfield, Berkshire

ROUTE PROFILE

Windsor (Central Station) – Crispin Hotel	
	via Copper Horse, Royal Lodge and Cumberland Lodge, serving private roads in Windsor Great Park for the benefit of estate workers.
At 8 May 1945	Tuesdays, Fridays and Saturdays = 2 journeys.
28 Oct 1962	Withdrawn. Workings incorporated into main Windsor – Sunninghill route.

ROUTE PROFILE

Windsor (Central Station) – Bagshot (The Square),	
	via Crispin Hotel, Blacknest, Sunninghill.
At 8 May 1945	Daily = 5/8 journeys.
28 Oct 1962	Section from Sunninghill to Bagshot withdrawn. Journeys via Estate roads in Windsor Great Park incorporated. Now operated: Windsor – Sunninghill (Schools). Weekdays = 4/7 journeys.
31 Dec 1969	Extant.

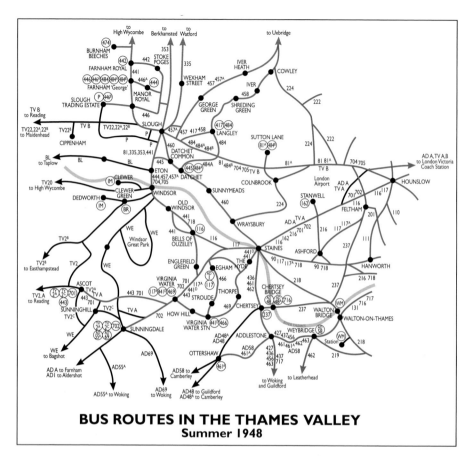

BUS ROUTES IN THE THAMES VALLEY
Summer 1948

Codes used on map

AD – Aldershot & District
TV – Thames Valley
BL – Blue Bus Services
BR – Borough Bus Service
IM – Imperial
P – J.A. Perry
WE – White Bus Service
WM – Walton-on-Thames
      Motor Co Ltd

Group Companies

Aldershot & District Traction Co Ltd

Halimote Road, Aldershot, Hampshire

Thames Valley Traction Co Ltd

83 Lower Thorn Street, Reading, Berkshire

Thames Valley and Aldershot Omnibus Co Ltd, trading as:

Alder Valley

Halimote Road, Aldershot, Hampshire

Aldershot and District and Thames Valley, both NBC companies since 1969, merged on 1 January 1972 to form Alder Valley. Alder Valley recognised Heathrow Airport as a useful traffic objective although projection of services to that point was fragmented. Express Service De-regulation Day, 6 October 1980, sounded the death knell for the long established limited-stop London bus services. Alder Valley introduced a raft of new London express services using the M3 and M4 motorways, these attracted through passengers, so causing the limited-stop workings to fade away.

ROUTE PROFILE

	Aldershot – Egham (Station) via Farnborough, Camberley, Bagshot, Sunningdale, Virginia Water.
Note:	Aldershot & District's original route between Aldershot and Farnborough, established in 1912, had been progressively extended to reach Egham in 1921.
At 8 May 1945	Daily = 1 hour. Numbered 1. (Weekdays only after 19 Dec 1965.)
1 Jan 1972	Operation assumed by Alder Valley.
14 May 1972	Altered to work Camberley – Egham only.
24 Feb 1974	Combined with former Route 52 to work Basingstoke – Egham via Camberley.
3 Nov 1975	Extended from Egham to Staines on withdrawal of Green Line 701.
4 Sept 1977	Extended from Staines to Heathrow Airport Central. Worked Basingstoke – Heathrow Airport via Camberley and Staines. Re-numbered 201.
30 April 1984	New routeing introduced. Worked Farnham – Heathrow Airport Central via Aldershot, Farnborough, Camberley, Bagshot, Egham, Staines. Numbered X18/X28. Weekdays = 2 hours.
12 July 1985	Extant.

For 34 years Aldershot & District maintained a single bus dormy shed at Egham, well within the London Transport Special Area. The basic, wooden constructed premises, situated in a lane off Hummer Road, just to the north of Egham's High Street, opened on 7 May 1923 coincident with the introduction of an improved frequency and reduced running time on Route 1. 1945-built utility Guy Arab II no. 893 (EOT 30), re-bodied with an East Lancs lowbridge body in 1954, reverses out of the shed prior to taking up duties. The last Aldershot & District bus worked out of Egham dormy shed on 2 June 1957 after which the premises closed. Regular frequency Aldershot & District express Route A from Farnham to London (Victoria Coach Station), which paralleled Route 1 between Aldershot and Egham High Street, had its final fare stage for London journeys at Egham Fire Station. J M Aldridge

Red London Transport RM 1177 on Route 117 stands alongside Aldershot & District's 1965 Weymann-bodied Dennis Loline III no. 524 at Egham station. Aldershot & District Route 1 formed the company's original route which had been extended to Egham in 1921, running rights for A&D between the LPTA boundary at Virginia Water and Egham being enshrined in the 1933 Act. This was the scene on 3 December 1971 within the last month of A&D's separate existence. Six months later over 50 years of through bus service between Aldershot and Egham would be severed. P R Wallis

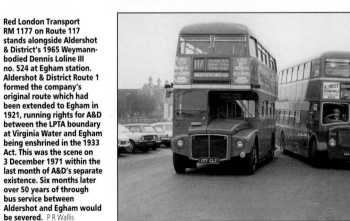

Captured in the sunshine of a balmy June evening in 1961 LT RF 421 on Central Area Route 237 from Hounslow passes Aldershot & District's East Lancs lowbridge bodied Dennis Lance III no. 138 at Chertsey Bridge. From this terminal A&D routes 48 and 48A worked to Guildford and Camberley respectively whilst local Route 48B to Longcross had been introduced on 9 May 1949. Workings on 48A to Weybridge which had been suspended at the beginning of World War II were replaced from 18 March 1946 by new Route 58 from Camberley via Ottershaw and Addlestone. This post-war incursion by A&D into the LPTA only lasted until 2 October 1950 when Route 58 was withdrawn.
M J Dryhurst

ROUTE PROFILE

	Reading – **London (Victoria Coach Station)** via Wokingham, Bracknell, Ascot, Sunningdale, Egham, Chiswick.
17 May 1947	Operation by Thames Valley resumed following wartime disruption. Route letter A. Daily = 7 journeys.
1 Jan 1972	Operation assumed by Alder Valley.
14 Oct 1975	Picking up restrictions between Sunningdale and Staines lifted following withdrawal of Green Line route 701.
28 July 1976	Diverted via Cargo Tunnel to Heathrow Central and thence via Bath Road to regain original line of route along Great West Road. Re-numbered 310. Frequency now: Daily = 2 hours.
23 July 1978	Diverted via Egham by pass and M4 motorway between Heathrow and Chiswick. No intermediate fares available between Heathrow and London (unlike route 300). Two evening journeys on which intermediate fares were available numbered 311.
13 April 1980	310/311 re-numbered X10/X11 respectively.
4 Oct 1980	X10/X11 withdrawn – superseded by new Londonlink express services X2/X3/X6.

Thames Valley introduced its Reading to London via Wokingham route on 21 May 1927. Initially licensed as an express service with advanced booking facility a restriction on carrying passengers wholly within the LPTA applied – the last inward boarding point being Sunningdale. From 1 March 1961 advanced booking was formally abolished although in practice insistence on its use had lapsed in earlier years. Thereafter Thames Valley referred to London routes A and B as 'Limited Stop Bus Services'. Seen at Reading Stations' terminus on 13 July 1963 is 1956-built Bristol Lodekka LD6G no. 751 (MBL 832) which, like all double-deckers bought for use on Thames Valley's London routes since 1951, was fitted with coach seats and platform doors. Alongside is 1951-built ECW lowbridge-bodied Bristol KSW6B no. 646 (GJB 284).
P R Wallis

The heyday for Thames Valley's London routes A and B was probably reached in the 1950s when many journeys needed duplication to meet passenger demand. On one such occasion Thames Valley had pressed an 'ordinary bus' no. 659 (HBL 61), a 1952-built ECW lowbridge-bodied Bristol KSW 6B, into service to work a Relief journey on Route B from Victoria Coach Station. Two buses were out-stationed at Victoria Coach station for use on Route B.
R H G Simpson

Below **Ledbury Transport, trading as Thackray's Way, introduced a Reading to London route following the A4 Bath Road in 1929, control passing to Thames Valley on 19 December 1935. The route was conductor operated and, since it had an LT 'consent', journeys were possible wholly within the LPTA. As an example the first fare stage outwards was from Victoria Coach Station to Kensington High Street. On August Bank Holiday 1960 (then the first Monday of the month) brand new Bristol Lodekka FLF6G no. 834, fitted with a sliding door on its ECW body, speeds westwards along King Street Hammersmith. Bringing up the rear is an LT N1 class trolleybus on Route 666.**
M J Dryhurst

ROUTE PROFILE

	Reading – London (Victoria Coach Station) via Maidenhead, Slough, Colnbrook, Chiswick.
17 May 1947	Operation by Thames Valley resumed following wartime disruption. Route letter B. Daily = 1 hour.
1 Jan 1972	Operation assumed by Alder Valley.
28 March 1976	Diverted to serve Heathrow Airport Central. Re-numbered 300. Frequency now: Daily Reading – Heathrow = 1 hour. Heathrow – Victoria = 2 hours.
23 July 1978	Speeded up using Twyford and Colnbrook By-passes and M4 Motorway between Heathrow and Chiswick. Frequency restored to: Daily = 1 hour.
13 April 1980	Re-numbered X12.
6 Oct 1980	Diverted to serve Woodley and direct via M4/A4 between Heathrow and Hammersmith. No longer served Chiswick.
3 July 1983	Diverted at Hyde Park Corner to terminate at Baker Street in lieu of Victoria Coach Station.
18 May 1984	Withdrawn.

Slough was a 'border' town between London Transport's and Thames Valley's territories, where some integration of services between these two operators was implemented from 1957 onwards. Slough Station forecourt remained the principal terminal for many routes as evidenced in this view taken on 22 March 1969. Thames Valley ECW lowbridge-bodied Bristol KSW 6B no. 733 (JRX 808) waits time in the company of London Transport Country Area green RT 3420 (LYR 839) and RF 631 (NLE631). London Transport Central Area Route 81 (from Hounslow) and Route 81C (from Heathrow Airport) also terminated at Slough Station at this time, bringing red RTs and RMs based at Hounslow to Slough. J M Aldridge

ROUTE PROFILE

Reading – Windsor (Riverside Station Coach Park)
via Henley, Marlow, Bourne End, Maidenhead.

On Easter Sunday 1957 Thames Valley introduced a seasonal summer service worked by open-top double-deck buses between Reading and Maidenhead. This initiative was the brainchild of the company's relatively new Managing Director, Mr Thomas G Pruett, who had previously been with Brighton, Hove & District. Four Bristol K5Gs were acquired from Mr Pruett's former company for use on this route and entered service in an all-over cream livery. At the time this operation was unique in being the only inland open-top bus service in the country.

1958 Summer Season	Extended to work Reading to Windsor = 2 hours.
1959 Summer Season	Re-introduced. Saturdays/Sundays = 4/5, 11/12 July then daily from 18 July to 31 August inclusive = 2 hours.
1960 Summer Season	Plans to re-introduce the service were frustrated by crew shortages. It never ran again.

ROUTE PROFILE

Route 64	Slough Station – Britwell via Salt Hill and Farnham Road. Co-ordinated timetable with London Transport services.
11 Dec 1957	Route 64 introduced by Thames Valley. Operated Slough Station – Britwell (Long Furlong Drive). Weekdays = 40 minutes. Co-ordinated timetable between Slough (High Street) and Britwell with existing London Transport routes 484 (Langley Village), 484A (Datchet) and 484B (Colnbrook) which on same date were extended from Farnham Road to new terminal at Britwell.

Right **Thames Valley's no. 771 (CAP 132) was one of four 1940-built ECW-bodied Bristol K5Gs acquired for the company's 'Riverside' service. Three of these four buses, including 771, were converted to open-top and painted in Thames Valley livery by Brighton, Hove and District before transfer, whilst Thames Valley itself converted the fourth bus. No. 771 was photographed in Henley during the inaugural year of the route's operation – 1957.**
R H G Simpson

LONDON TRANSPORT CONNECTIONS 1945–1985

13 Oct 1958	Thames Valley 64 and London Transport 484/484A/484B extended in Britwell to new terminal at Wentworth Avenue. In Britwell, Thames Valley route travelled via Long Furlong Drive, whilst London Transport routes travelled via Doddsfield Road.
17 May 1959	Sunday service introduced on Thames Valley Route 64 = 1 hour. On same date new London Transport Route 441A introduced [Windsor Castle–Slough–Britwell (Wentworth Avenue)] = 1 hour. Both routes co-ordinated to give a 30 minute headway between Slough and Britwell.
8 July 1959	Weekday London Transport workings on routes 484/484A/484B to Britwell replaced by new Slough area local Route 400.
19 Sept 1959	Thames Valley Route 64 extended in Britwell to Calbroke Road. Weekday frequency increased to 30 minutes. Continued to work to co-ordinated timetable with London Transport Route 400 (weekdays) or 441A (Sundays) to give a combined 15-minute headway on weekdays, 30 mins on Suns, between Slough and Britwell (Wentworth Avenue).
8 Nov 1964	Sunday workings to Britwell on London Transport Route 441A replaced by Route 400.
31 Dec 1969	Extant.

ROUTE PROFILE

Route 60   Maidenhead (Halifax Road) – Langley (the Harrow)
Route 69   Maidenhead (Sealeys Stores) – Langley (the Harrow)
Both routes via Maidenhead, Bath Road, Salt Hill, Slough.

| 23 Jan 1966 | Certain weekday journeys on existing Thames Valley routes 60/69 projected beyond Slough to new terminus at Langley. Weekdays = 1 hour. Worked to a co-ordinated timetable with new London Transport routes 407/407A (Cippenham – Langley) to give a combined 30-minute frequency over common section of route between Everitts Corner – Slough – Langley. London Transport routes 407/407A also co-ordinated with Thames Valley routes 61/61A (Cippenham (Mercian Way) – Slough Station) to give a combined 30-minute weekday frequency over common section of route between Cippenham (Mercian Way) and Slough High Street. |
| 31 Dec 1969 | Extant. |

ROUTE PROFILE

Reading – Heathrow Airport Central
via Wokingham, Bracknell, Windsor, Slough.

10 April 1983	Existing Alder Valley Route 191 (Reading – Windsor) extended to Heathrow Airport (Central Bus Station) via Slough and Colnbrook By-pass. Daily = 1 hour.
14 April 1984	Most evening and Sunday journeys replaced by route 198 (Reading – Heathrow Airport), = 1 hour.
12 July 1985	Extant.

Although both undertakings had been controlled by the BTC since 1948 it was not until 11 December 1957 that London Transport and Thames Valley, perhaps mindful of the Chambers report, introduced their first co-ordinated working in Slough. New Thames Valley Route 64 from Slough Station to the Britwell Housing Estate on the western edge of Slough worked to a co-ordinated timetable with LT routes 484, 484A and 484B (Later 400). Typical Tilling Group bus of its era 1952 ECW-bodied Bristol KSW6B no. 655 is seen laying over at Slough Station working Route 64 on 27 April 1963.
P R Wallis

Municipal

Reading Transport

Mill Lane, Reading, Berkshire

Reading Transport's predecessor, Reading Corporation Transport, was the very epitome of a medium-sized municipal transport undertaking. Tramways were operated from 1901 to 1939. Trolleybuses started to replace trams on key trunk routes from 1936 until they, in turn, were finally supplanted by buses in 1968.

Initially Reading Transport deployed ordinary buses to work its share of Route X1. 1981-built MCW Metrobus no. 180 (HCF 180W) is seen about to depart from Southend Central Bus Station on its epic 3¾ -hour long journey back to Reading. This view dates from 29 April 1982, shortly before joint operation with Southend Transport ceased.
P R Wallis

Until November 1957 no corporation route had ever worked beyond the borough boundary and, with the exception of routes to the Woodley area taken over from Alder Valley in the early 1970s, Reading's operations continued to be largely confined to its traditional town territory. That long established operating pattern changed dramatically from Express Service Deregulation Day on 6 October 1980. Reading Transport became partners with fellow municipal operator Southend Transport in ambitious Route X1 which linked Reading with Southend-on-Sea via Central London. Subsequent operational experience led to differences in approach emerging between the route's two partners. Reading Transport, with easy access to the

Following cessation of joint operation Reading Transport introduced a dedicated livery for double-deckers working its Reading – London X1 service. MCW Metrobus MK II no. 192 (LMO 192X), fitted with bus seats, displays its 'Goldline – London Express' livery whilst rounding Hyde Park Corner in July 1982. The crimson and cream livery had origins dating right back to Reading's municipal tramway. G Rixon

A higher standard of passenger comfort was introduced to route X1 in 1983 when Reading Transport put five Leyland Titans, fitted with high back coach seats and capable of a 70mph top speed, into service. No. 78 (RMO 78Y) is seen circumnavigating Hyde Park Corner in June 1983 whilst working a peak hour journey which projected to Tilehurst in Reading's suburbs. G Rixon

Reading Transport's 'Goldline' division also embraced private hire activity for which duties four 45-seat Plaxton Paramount bodied Leyland Tiger coaches were bought in 1983. This June 1983 shot of no. 203 (RMO 203Y), taken at Hyde Park Corner, shows that these coaches were sometimes to be found on Route X1. C Essex

M4 motorway at 'their' end, favoured a fast, very limited stop service whilst Southend Transport, with no motorway at 'its' end of the route, was much keener to develop intermediate traffic. The operating partnership was dissolved from 17 May 1982 when the route was split. Thereafter Reading Transport worked its section of the X1 to a newly adopted terminal in London at Aldgate Minories Bus Station.

ROUTE PROFILE

	Reading – Southend-on-Sea via Maidenhead, Slough, Heathrow Airport Central, Hammersmith, Hyde Park Corner, Trafalgar Square, Blackfriars, Aldgate, Canning Town, Dagenham, Basildon.
6 Oct 1980	Introduced. Express service operated jointly with Southend Transport. Numbered X1. Daily = 2 hours.
26 Feb 1981	Stage carriage licence granted.
28 Feb 1981	Revised timetable. Most journeys diverted at Maidenhead Thicket to travel via M4 motorway to Heathrow.
16 Jan 1982	London Bus Agreement obtained. Although still subject to some restrictions passengers could be carried for certain journeys wholly within the London Transport area.
16 May 1982	Joint operation with Southend Transport ceased.
17 May 1982	Re-branded as 'Goldline – London Express'. Numbered X1. Daily = 1 hour. Operated Reading – London (Aldgate). Additional peak hour journeys Mondays–Fridays projected in Reading to/from Caversham and Tilehurst.
12 July 1985	Extant.

Alder Valley introduced express Route X11 from Reading to London (Tower Hill) on 8 June 1981 in order to cream passengers from the municipally operated X1. Two weekday departures at 08.50 and 10.50 were timed ten minutes ahead of X1 journeys. X11 used the M4 motorway to reach London in just one hour. Alder Valley's ECW bodied Bristol VRT no. 933 loads at Reading Station at the stop also used by X1 in April 1982. X11 was withdrawn as part of a reorganisation of Alder Valley's London services on 22 January 1984. P R Wallis

CHAPTER 5

Surrey

Independents

M C Ash

101 Woodgate Avenue, Chessington, Surrey

From 16 August 1971 adopted trading name as:

Mole Valley Transport Services

From August 1973 office at: 30 Brighton Road, Surbiton, Surrey
From September 1975 office at: 10 Church Street, Esher, Surrey
From February 1980 office at:
Bridge Chambers, 37 Bridge Street, Leatherhead, Surrey

Michael Ash's Mole Valley operated in an affluent commuter belt area, home
to many wealthy families who lived in the area's exclusive housing set
amongst its leafy avenues. The level of car ownership was amongst the
highest in the country so the area was certainly not promising territory for

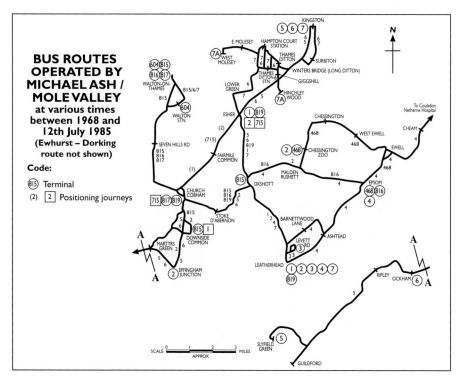

BUS ROUTES
OPERATED BY
MICHAEL ASH /
MOLE VALLEY
at various times
between 1968 and
12th July 1985
(Ewhurst – Dorking
route not shown)

Code:

(815) Terminal

(2) [2] Positioning journeys

Mole Valley's nearly new Strachans-bodied Ford Transit no. 2 (BTR 478K) is seen on layover at Chessington Zoo in June 1972. Mole Valley had introduced Route 468 on 29 August 1971 thereby restoring a Sunday service between Epsom and Chessington Zoo lost since London Transport's withdrawal of such Sunday operation after 28 September 1969. London Transport had continued with a weekday operation of Route 468 which subsequently passed to London Country Bus Services on its vesting date 1 January 1970. Mole Valley's Sunday operation of Route 468 ceased after 23 September 1973. T K Brookes

bus operators. Mole Valley's operations presented a complex and frequently changing network as Michael Ash, with a fleet never larger than three minibuses, attempted to plug gaps following retrenchment by both London Transport and London Country. Although a number of interesting new initiatives were introduced Mole Valley itself was forced to constantly review its own pattern of service and frequencies in the light of ever decreasing patronage and variable levels of County Council support. For ease of review Mole Valley's operations have been split into three phases.

Phase 1 – Occasional Operation 1968–1969

From 29 November 1975 Mole Valley recast its network in conjunction with the replacement of Monday – Friday London Country Route 416 journeys between Leatherhead and Esher. At the same time route numbering was simplified with this service starting a fresh sequence as Route 1. Commer KC6055 with 27-seat Rootes body reg.no. PKL 118R is seen in Claremont Lane, Esher working Route 1 on 9 August 1977. D M Persson

Michael Ash started as a 'Saturday only' operator using a Duple bodied Bedford SB3 coach reg. no. RCJ 808 with a service from Church Cobham to Epsom on 15 June 1968. The first replacement of part of a London Transport service followed on 19 October 1968 with Saturday journeys between Church Cobham and Downside, formerly part of London Transport Route 215. These first ventures, which also included a Saturday service introduced on 7 December 1968 from Church Cobham to Ockham, ceased after operation on 8 February 1969. Mr Ash briefly re-emerged as a bus operator with a service from Ewhurst to Dorking which ran for three Saturdays in December 1969. London Transport had abandoned Route 449 between these terminals in October 1958.

Mole Valley no. 1 (NRO 255V), a Dormobile bodied Ford Transit supplied new in 1980, is seen in May 1981 travelling along Esher Road, East Molesey working Route 7 to Hampton Court Station. Mole Valley's apt slogan 'Bus Services in Miniature' was displayed on the rear panels of some vehicles. G Rixon

Mole Valley 25p Setright Speed ticket. D Seddon Collection

Phase 2 – Into Full-time Operation 1970–1975

Full-time operation began on 18 May 1970 when a Church Cobham to Downside service was introduced on weekdays in replacement of a free service previously arranged by Esher Urban District Council. Expansion which followed was outside the reduced London Transport area. Epsom, Leatherhead and Walton-on-Thames were reached and Mole Valley's fleet grew to three vehicles. A brief tenure as the final operator of the long established Walton Station service lasted from 30 December 1974 to June 1975.

Phase 3 – Revised Network 1975–1985

Kingston was first reached on 31 March 1980 with a one day a week shopping service from Ockham. A more significant development occurred on 29 September 1980 when Mole Valley Route 7 was introduced between Esher and Surbiton. Mole Valley's original operations, centred on Church Cobham, were experiencing increasing difficulties, with the Leatherhead – Church Cobham – Downside Route 2 suffering drastic cutbacks during 1983 before withdrawal after running on 28 June 1984. This brought an end to Mole Valley operations in Church Cobham. Thus at the end of the period reviewed by this book (12 July 1985) despite valiant efforts made in adapting services in attempts to stimulate demand whilst retaining commercial viability, Mole Valley's sole remaining bus service was Route 7 (Leatherhead – Kingston).

ROUTE PROFILE

Route 7	**Leatherhead – Kingston** via Oxshott, Esher, Hampton Court, Thames Ditton, Surbiton.
29 Sept 1980	Introduced. Mondays–Fridays = 7 journeys. Operated Esher – Surbiton.
Note:	London Transport Route 201 (Kingston – Hampton Court) and section of Route 215 (Esher – Hampton Court) were withdrawn after 27 September 1980.
5 May 1981	Projected from Surbiton to Kingston.
2 Nov 1981	Projected from Esher to Leatherhead replacing Route 1. Operated Leatherhead – Kingston, Mondays–Fridays = 4/6 journeys.
31 Jan 1983	Part service diverted via Thames Ditton Station (numbered Route 6).
17 May 1983	Route 6 withdrawn.
12 July 1985	Route 7 extant.

Walton-on-Thames Motor Co Ltd

72 Bridge Street, Walton-on-Thames, Surrey

Walton-on-Thames Motor Co. 6d TIM ticket.
D Seddon Collection

Walton-on-Thames Motor Co's route originated in the 1920s acting as a feeder to the railway station 1½ miles from the town. Operating wholly within London Transport's 'Special Area' the route somehow escaped acquisition by LT following the 1933 Act. Seen in 1963 is 28-seat 1949 Mulliner-bodied Bedford OB reg.no. JDF 306, outside the operator's premises at the junction of Bridge Street and New Zealand Avenue.
M J Dryhurst

ROUTE PROFILE

Walton-on-Thames (Bridge) – Walton-on-Thames (Station) via Bridge Street, High Street, Hersham Road.

Note: Buses were authorised to depart station up to 10 minutes before scheduled departure time if connecting trains had arrived.

At 8 May 1945	Extant. Weekdays = 30 minutes with enhanced frequency up to every 7 minutes at Monday–Friday peak hours. Sundays = 60 minutes.
By June 1952	Sunday frequency increased to 30 minutes.
April 1962	Sunday service discontinued.
May 1970	Acquired by Walton Lodge Garage Ltd.
October 1970	Following issue of a Ministry of Transport Prohibition Notice against Walton Lodge Garage's remaining Bedford OB coach, service taken up by F.G. Wilder and Son Ltd, trading as Golden Miller Services, using Walton Lodge Garage's licence.
19 November 1970	Route formally acquired by F.G. Wilder & Son Ltd. Numbered 604. Truncated from Walton Bridge to new terminal at Walton (Bridge Street). Sat. p.m. service withdrawn.
7 December 1970	Mondays–Fridays service extended beyond Walton Station to Oatlands Village. (4 Sat. journeys similarly extended from 21.10.1972).
4 May 1973	Reduced to operate Monday–Friday peak hours only.
24 December 1974	Operation discontinued by F.G. Wilder & Son Ltd.
30 December 1974	Reintroduced by M.C. Ash, t/a Mole Valley Transport Services. Operated Walton (Bridge Street) – Walton Station Monday–Friday peak hours only. Numbered 604.
June 1975	Operation discontinued by M.C. Ash.

Ben Stanley Ltd,

32 Burwood Road, Hersham, Surrey

Guildford area

Guildford was a particularly interesting town for bus enthusiasts in that substantial independent operation was to be found intermixed with services provided by both BET-owned Aldershot & District as well as London Transport. This wealth of independent activity was partially attributable to the enlightened attitude of Guildford Corporation's Watch Committee in the 1920s. Before the advent of the Road Traffic Act 1930, which charged newly created Regional Traffic Commissioners with road service licensing, local council Watch Committees had been responsible for authorising bus services in their particular cities or towns. The Watch Committee in Guildford was keen to encourage competition and so granted licences to smaller operators even when these latter sought to cover roads already worked by larger undertakings.

The 1933 Act made Guildford a 'border' town between London Transport's territory to the east and that of Aldershot & District to the west. That Act caused a significant cross-town bus link to be broken when, in August 1933, the Guildford – Dorking section of Aldershot & District route 25 (Aldershot – Guildford – Dorking) passed to London Transport, being

Brand new Aldershot & District 68-seat Alexander-bodied Dennis Loline III no. 440 (132 DOR) had yet to have an advertisement display mounted onto its offside illuminated advertisement panel when photographed at Guildford's Farnham Road Bus Station in August 1962. The Loline was working 30-minute frequency town service 30 to Onslow Village which was one of the routes considered under the 1967 proposals to link Aldershot & District with London Transport services to form cross-Guildford bus links. P R Wallis

incorporated into the latter's Route 425. This left only one regular cross-town bus route remaining in Guildford – Aldershot & District Route 31A which operated just to the west of the LPTA boundary between Wood Street Green and Puttenham via Guildford Town Centre. Following World War II, in August 1945, the 31A was re-numbered 67 and foreshortened to work between Wood Street Green and Peasmarsh – still crossing Guildford Town Centre. The opening of Guildford's first bus stations – Onslow Street in 1949 followed by Farnham Road in 1950 – improved interchange arrangements in the town centre. The creation of these new facilities precipitated the withdrawal of Guildford's last cross-town bus route in October 1950 when Aldershot & District Route 67 was truncated to work between Guildford (Farnham Road Bus Station) and Wood Street Green.

It was not until 1967 that consideration was given to establishing fresh cross-town bus services. Proposals put forward at that time were based upon linking existing Aldershot & District and London Transport routes to form cross-town services.

PROPOSED GUILDFORD CROSS-TOWN BUS ROUTES 1967

Rydes Hill Estate	(A&D 26)	–	Town Centre –	Merrow (Bushy Hill)	(LT 408A)
Dennisvllle	(A&D 27)	–	Town Centre –	Merrow (Bushy Hill)	(LT 408A)
Stoughton	(A&D 28D)	–	Town Centre –	Merrow (Bushy Hill)	(LT 408A)
Onslow Village	(A&D 30)	–	Town Centre –	Burpham	(LT 415)
Wood Street Green	(A&D 67)	–	Town Centre –	Burpham	(LT415)
Wonersh	(A&D 23)	–	Town Centre –	Burpham	(LT 415)

Key: A&D – Aldershot & District LT – London Transport

Subsequently the local SURREY ADVERTISER newspaper carried a report that these proposed cross-town bus services 'were not necessary'. And at a council meeting a vote to endorse the proposals was lost. Thus Guildford was fated to remain very much a 'border' town.

Independents

A T Brady, trading as:

Brown Motor Services

Motena, Forest Green, Dorking, Surrey

Brown Motor Services was formed in 1924, routes between Forest Green and Guildford and Holmbury St Mary and Horsham being extant in 1945.

Brown Motor Services first reached Horsham in 1924, subsequently developing a route from Holmbury St Mary to Horsham via Forest Green and Ockley. For many years this route operated on six days of the week – there being no service on Thursdays which was early closing day in Horsham. Duple bodied utility Bedford OWB reg.no. JPL 582, new to Brown Motor Services in 1944, was photographed at Wallis Wood on 24 April 1949 whilst working the Horsham route. J C Gillham

Centre Brown Motor Services started its Forest Green – Guildford route in 1928. From 24 February 1930 London Transport's predecessors on the Guildford – Dorking corridor, Aldershot and District and East Surrey, implemented an agreement with Brown Motor Services as well as with Tillingbourne Valley Services which introduced a co-ordinated timetable over a lengthy common section of route between Guildford and Albury. Brown Motor Services daily 2-hour frequency route was subsequently referred to in LT District timetables as a 'service offering additional facilities over part of Route 425'. Willowbrook-bodied Albion Nimbus reg.no. 335 KPL, new to Brown Motor Services in 1959, is seen in Guildford's Farnham Road Bus Station in July 1969. C Essex

Bottom Since 1946 Brown Motor Services had shared traffic from Wallis Wood and Oakwood Hill into Horsham with Hants & Sussex, the purchasers of A. Lazzell's Ewhurst – Horsham bus route. Following the demise of Hants & Sussex bus operations in the Horsham area (detailed in Chapter 6) London Transport introduced Route 852 (Ewhurst – Horsham – Three Bridges) which absorbed former Hants & Sussex routes 33 (Horsham – Three Bridges) and 34 (Ewhurst – Horsham). London Transport's operation of the Ewhurst – Horsham section of Route 852 was short lived with Brown Motor Services taking up this service from 18 May 1955. This second route to Horsham, which had some journeys projected from Ewhurst to Forest Green, largely paralleled Brown Motor Services original Horsham route. As a consequence of falling traffic this original Horsham route was withdrawn on 18 March 1961. Brown Motor Services first diesel engined vehicle was this 1950 built Duple 32-seat Leyland Comet coach reg.no. OPB 536. It was photographed at Ewhurst (Bull's Head) in September 1964 when working the Horsham route. P R Wallis

P Crouch & Son Ltd, trading as:

Blue Bus

285 Stoughton Road, Guildford, Surrey

This old established operator's service from Guildford to Worplesden was acquired by Aldershot & District on 13 August 1945.

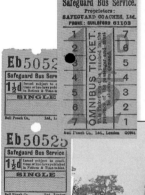

T W & G P Hammond, trading as:

B Hammond & Sons

Great Tangley, Wonersh, Guildford, Surrey

This concern used small capacity locally built Dennis Ace buses on its sole route from Wonersh to Guildford which was acquired by Aldershot & District on 14 September 1953.

Safeguard Coaches Ltd

83 Woodbridge Road, Guildford, Surrey

By 1958 office at: Sutton Building, Onslow Street, Guildford, Surrey

By 1965 office at: Friary Square, Guildford , Surrey

ROUTE PROFILE

Town Service	Guildford – Dennisville – Guildford Cathedral.
At 8 May 1945	Operated Guildford – Dennisville jointly with Aldershot & District Route 27. Combined frequency: Daily = 15 minutes.
27 May 1963	Extended Weekday morning peak hours and daily in afternoons and early evening to Guildford Cathedral.
31 Dec 1969	Extant.

Founded in 1926, Safeguard pioneered town services in Guildford. Initial competition with Aldershot & District led to an agreement in 1930 which avoided further rivalry. Safeguard benefited from post-war housing development on the north western perimeter of Guildford allowing progressive extension of services. The first 36ft-long saloon in the fleet was 53-seat Willowbrook bodied AEC Reliance reg.no. 1637 PF, new in 1963. It is seen on Safeguard's busiest route to Westborough Estate in September 1964. P R Wallis

For many years Safeguard's fleet included a large proportion of Bedford coaches as well as some buses. Willowbrook 45-seat bus bodied Bedford VAM 70 reg.no. UAA 752H, new in 1969, was photographed at Guildford's Onslow Street Bus Station. London Transport was responsible for administering Onslow Street Bus Station whilst the nearby Farnham Road Bus Station, most easily reached by pedestrians from Onslow Street by means of a footbridge over the River Wey, was an Aldershot and District responsibility.
Photobus / R Marshall

ROUTE PROFILE

Town Service	Guildford – Westborough Estate.
At 8 May 1945	Weekdays = 10 minutes, Sundays = 20 minutes.
By 1959	Frequency now: Weekdays = 12 minutes, Sundays = 20 minutes
31 Dec 1969	Extant.

ROUTE PROFILE

Town Service	Guildford – Northway.
Summer 1953	Introduced. Daily = 30 minutes.
31 Dec 1969	Extant.

Tillingbourne Valley Services and London Passenger Transport Board Exchange ticket.
D Seddon Collection

Tillingbourne Valley Services Ltd

New Road, Chilworth, Guildford, Surrey

Originating as a carrier's business in the early 1920s a bus service to Guildford was first introduced in 1924. Despite intense competition regular services developed from Farley Green to Guildford via Chilworth and between Peaslake and Guildford via Merrow. After early attempts by the London Passenger Transport Board to acquire the business, following the 1933 Act, were resisted many years of harmonious co-operation prevailed between the country's largest bus operator and one of the smallest, in the form of the six vehicle Tillingbourne Valley. From 24 April 1935 the Peaslake to Guildford route became jointly operated with London Transport with full inter-availability of return and season tickets.

Until early post war days Tillingbourne Valley standardised on Thornycroft chassis built at Basingstoke, Hampshire. Reg.no. HPL 265 was a 1939 Nippy with 20-seat Waveney body. It is seen at Guildford's Farnham Road Bus Station on 8 September 1954 by which date Thornycroft psvs had become quite rare. The bus is working the Guildford Town Service to Warren Road. J C Gillham

Following the demise of Thornycrofts from its fleet from the mid 1950s Tillingbourne Valley bus routes were maintained by lightweight Austin and Bedford coaches. Reg.no. OEV 889 was a 1949-built Duple Vista bodied Bedford OB acquired by Tillingbourne in 1959. The coach was photographed in August 1962 in Guildford's Onslow Street Bus Station, terminus for the Peaslake route jointly operated with London Transport. P R Wallis

Tillingbourne Valley's 26-seat Eastern Coach Works bodied Guy Vixen reg.no. MXX 303, formerly London Transport GS3, was photographed at Farley Green's Kingsfield terminus on 30 March 1963 during the bus's first month in service with Tillingbourne. Tillingbourne quickly moved to standardise on ex LT GS class saloons over the next seven years. Altogether the firm operated no less than 13 examples of the 1953-built 84-strong GS class. P R Wallis

In a similar manner to Brown Motor Service's route, the Farley Green route became co-ordinated with London Transport Route 425 over a common section between Albury and Guildford.

ROUTE PROFILE

	Guildford – Farley Green via Shalford, Chilworth, Albury.
At 8 May 1945	Daily = 1 hour
28 Nov 1965	Frequency reduced to: Daily = 2 hours
31 Dec 1969	Extant.

ROUTE PROFILE

	Guildford – Peaslake – Ewhurst via Merrow, Shere, Gomshall.
At 8 May 1945	Operated Guildford – Peaslake. Joint with London Transport Route 448 which had occasional journeys projected beyond Peaslake to/from Ewhurst. Combined frequency: Daily = 30 minutes. 1 vehicle provided by Tillingbourne Valley, 2 vehicles provided by London Transport. Tillingbourne Valley did not use route number.
12 Aug 1964	London Transport withdraw from route 448. Entire service became operated by Tillingbourne Valley. Frequency: Daily = 30 minutes Guildford – Peaslake. Occasional weekday journeys projected beyond Peaslake to/from Ewhurst.
28 Nov 1965	Projections to Ewhurst withdrawn. Now operated Guildford – Peaslake. Frequency: Weekdays = 45 minutes, Sundays = 90 minutes.
31 Dec 1969	Extant.

This September 1964 shot shows Tillingbourne Valley's reg.no. MXX 304, former London Transport GS4, powering uphill passed St Lukes Hospital in Warren Road on the 15-minute journey time Guildford town service. P R Wallis

ROUTE PROFILE

Town Service	Guildford – Warren Road.
At 8 May 1945	Daily = 1 hour
28 Nov 1965	Frequency reduced to 2 hours.
31 Dec 1969	Extant.

ROUTE PROFILE

Town Service	Guildford – Pewley Hill.
12 Aug 1964	Introduced. Replaced London Transport Route 448A which covered this route from introduction on 9 August 1950 until withdrawal after operation on 11 August 1964. London Transport referred to the outer terminal as Pewley Way. Weekdays = 4/8 journeys.
26 Nov 1965	Withdrawn.

Tillingbourne Valley Coaches

New Road, Chilworth, Guildford, Surrey

This was a separate business from Tillingbourne Valley Services Ltd formed circa 1931 when the coaching and bus interests of Tillingbourne Valley were separated. It was owned by Lionel Rhees, the son-in-law of Tillingbourne Valley's founder George Trice.

ROUTE PROFILE

Blackheath – Guildford via Barnett Hill, Wonersh	
Oct 1947	Introduced. Tuesdays, Thursdays, Fridays and Saturdays only. 1 return journey limited-stop. Only return fares to Guildford available.
May 1953	Licence transferred to Mrs H Rhees.
1954	Acquired by H D Rackcliffe of 4 Mangles Road, Guildford, Surrey. Reduced to operate Fridays only.
Feb 1955	Acquired by Cookes Coaches (Stoughton) Ltd., 260 Worplesdon Road, Guildford, Surrey.
By 1956	Withdrawn.

Yellow Bus Services loyally supported Guildford based chassis manufacturer Dennis. Reg.no. PPC105 was a 1951 front-engined Dennis Lancet III whose coachwork by Gurney-Nutting incorporated a full front in an attempt to give a modern appearance at a time when volume under floor engined chassis were emerging. The bus is seen at Guildford's Onslow Street Bus Station on 6 September 1956 working a town service with the rear of an Aldershot & District Dennis Lance III similarly employed visible in the background.
R L Wilson

S Hayter, trading as:

Yellow Bus Services

Woodlands, Worplesdon Road, Stoughton, Guildford, Surrey

From November 1951 proprietor became Mrs S Hayter.
Licences held by E Glew, Executor and Manager.

From 5 November 1953, title became:

Yellow Bus Services Ltd

Originating in 1921 Yellow Bus Services established a considerable presence in Guildford operating three town services as well as country routes to Camberley and Farnham, the latter serving villages to the south of the Hog's Back. Mr Hayter enjoyed a reputation as an employer who paid considerable attention to staff welfare during a period when not all employers shared such enlightened attitudes.

Yellow Bus Services multi-fare Single / Return Bell Punch ticket.
J M Aldridge Collection

ROUTE PROFILE

Town Service	Guildford – Stoughton (Royal Hotel) via Manor Road.
At 26 March 1945	Daily. Operated jointly with Aldershot & District Route 28A to give combined 15 minute frequency.
15 June 1958	Acquired by Aldershot & District. Numbered 28A.

ROUTE PROFILE

Town Service	Guildford – Rydes Hill Estate via Worplesdon Road.
At 26 March 1945	Daily. Operated jointly with Aldershot & District Route 26 to give combined 15 minute frequency.
15 June 1958	Acquired by Aldershot & District. Numbered 26.

ROUTE PROFILE

Town Service	Guildford – Bellfields Estate via Weyside Road.
At 8 May 1945	Weekdays = 15 minutes, Sunday = 30 minutes.
15 June 1958	Acquired by Aldershot & District. Numbered 29C.
Note:	Operated to Paynters Close until Bellfields Estate built by 1948.

ROUTE PROFILE

	Guildford – Camberley via Normandy, Ash Vale, Frimley.
At 8 May 1945	Daily = 1 hour.
21 March 1954	Withdrawn.

ROUTE PROFILE

	Guildford – Farnham via Puttenham, Seale or Cutmill, Runfold.
At 8 May 1945	Daily = 1 hour.
15 June 1958	Acquired by A&D. Numbered 65 (via Seale), 66 (via Cutmill).

Group Companies

Alone amongst post-war BET companies Aldershot & District stayed loyal to Dennis, its local buider of double-deck chassis. A&D was the sole recipient of 32 'tin-fronted' Dennis Lance K4s built in 1954. No.233, fitted with Weymann lowbridge bodywork, is seen at Guildford's Farnham Road Bus Station in August 1962 appropriately working Route 27 to Dennisville which was operated jointly with Safeguard. Cross-town working in Guildford was inhibited by the LPTA boundary so all routes were short, lending themselves to set piece blind displays. P R Wallis

Aldershot & District Traction Co Ltd

Halimote Road, Aldershot, Hampshire

Both Guildford and Woking were 'border' towns between London Transport country services running broadly to the east and Aldershot & District to the west.

Thames Valley Traction Co Ltd

83 Lower Thorn Street, Reading, Berkshire

On 5 April 1954 Thames Valley buses reached Guildford for the first time by their lengthy new Route 75 from Reading via Bracknell, operated jointly with Aldershot & District.

Dorking & Redhill Areas

Independents

A J Charlwood, trading as:

Surrey & Sussex Coachways

66/70 South Street, Dorking, Surrey

Right and below
Ahead of its time John Charlwood's first initiative was what in later years would have been termed a 'Heritage' or 'Leisure Bus' service with a prospect of attracting local authority sponsorship. But back in 1967 the concept of offering visitors to beauty spots in the Surrey Hills a bus service giving connectional facilities with Southern Region trains at Ockley Station as well as with London Transport trunk Route 414 at Capel did not attract such support – so the service soon folded. A much reduced operation followed. Surrey and Sussex Coachways 1949-built Duple Vista bodied Bedford OB reg.no. GDL 75 was photographed at Dorking Bus Station.
Both J M Aldridge Collection

ROUTE PROFILE

	Capel – Abinger Common (Parkhurst Corner) via Ockley, Coldharbour, Leith Hill.
3 June 1967	Introduced. Daily = 8 journeys.
By Aug 1967	Abandoned.

ROUTE PROFILE

	Capel – **Dorking** via Ockley, Leith Hill, Coldharbour.
5 Aug 1967	Introduced. Saturdays and Sundays = 4 journeys.
4 Nov 1967	Sunday service withdrawn.
14 April 1968	Sunday service re-introduced. Frequency now = 2/3 journeys.
7 Oct 1968	Daily service introduced = 2/3 journeys.
Note:	London Transport Route 433 (Dorking – Coldharbour) withdrawn after 4 October 1968.
1 Nov 1968	Reduced to operate Fridays only = 1 journey.
31 Dec 1969	Extant.

John Wylde of North Downs Rural Transport (detailed in Chapters 6 and 8) printed tickets for Surrey and Sussex Coachways, including this 2s 6d return, with a home-use Adana printing machine.
D Seddon Collection

P F Browne & J Brown, trading as:

Browne's Transport (Redhill)

Woodlands, Chapel Road, Smallfield, Horley, Surrey

By 1965 title became:

Browne's Luxury Coaches (Redhill) Ltd.

The withdrawal by London Transport on 19 October 1958 of occasional spur workings off Route 424 from Horley to Outwood and Horne led Mr P F Browne of Streatham, London to seek the first post-Chambers Report London Transport 'Consent' to operate a bus service in the Country Area. Mr Browne proposed to trade as Surrey County Transport. Subsequently he formed a partnership with Mr J Brown. Operations started on 7 March 1959 with a Redhill to Horley route which not only covered the withdrawn sections of London Transport Route 424 but also provided the first ever bus service to South Nutfield. The initial high frequency of the route proved over optimistic. In June 1959 the timetable was drastically pruned and at this juncture Mr P F Browne left the partnership.

Browne's first vehicles were two Bedford CAVs reg.nos. NDO 502/503. Both are seen at the Clarendon Road North Terminus in Redhill about to work the 4pm departure on 26 September 1959. NDO 502, driven by Mr J Brown, is on the service journey to Horley whilst NDO 503, driven by his wife Mrs P J Brown, is duplicating to Outwood. Beside the bus stop fixed to a convenient tree passengers may be seen crammed into the 11-seat Martin Walter body. Access was by rear doors necessitating the driver getting out at each stop to open and close them. J C Gillham

By June 1965 a hiatus had been reached with Mr J Brown wishing to withdraw the bus service. At the time he was quoted in the EVENING STANDARD as saying 'The number of passengers now using the bus is negligible. The service is completely uneconomical to run. I have to employ two drivers and it just doesn't work out. I have a coach hire business with six vehicles and any week that I make a profit on the coach hiring it all goes on subsidising the bus service'. A further complication was that Mr Brown has been provided with a council house by Godstone Rural District Council conditional upon him providing a local bus service. The Council threatened eviction if the bus service ceased.

In passing it is interesting to note that at this time John Wylde, then Honorary Manager of the Orpington Rural Transport Association, made an application in a personal capacity to take over the Redhill to Horley route using a proposed trading name of Redhill Rural Transport. In the event Mr Brown decided to re-organise a much reduced operation so Mr Wylde's proposal was not pursued.

ROUTE PROFILE

	Redhill – Horley via South Nutfield, Outwood Common, Horne or Rookery Farm, Smallfield.
7 March 1959	Introduced. Daily. Redhill – Horley: = 2/5 journeys. Outwood Common – Horley: weekdays = 16/17 journeys (approx 1 hour), Sundays = 4 journeys.
June 1959	Routeing via Horne abandoned. Sunday service withdrawn. Now operated: Weekdays Redhill – Horley = 5/6 journeys. Outwood Common – Horley = 6/8 journeys.
28 June 1965	Withdrawn.

ROUTE PROFILE

	Outwood – Horley via Smallfield.
5 Nov 1965	Introduced. Fridays only = 1 journey.
31 Dec 1969	Extant.

ROUTE PROFILE

	Outwood – Redhill via South Nutfield.
21 Dec1965	Introduced. Operated South Nutfield – Redhill Tuesdays and Fridays = 1 journey.
19 April 1966	Tuesday journeys projected from South Nutfield to/from Outwood.
31 Dec 1969	Extant.

Trojan Ltd of Croydon was a producer of small capacity psv's in the 1950s, long before the term 'minibus' had entered into popular parlance. Browne's Transport operated forward control Trojan reg no. SAP 238, photographed at Outwood Mill, between 1961 and 1963. The 13-seat Trojan built body achieved an internal height of 6ft 0in which was superior to contemporary specifications offered by the Austin / Morris J2 or Commer 1500.
J M Aldridge

CHAPTER 6

North Sussex and Kent

North Sussex

Independents

F H Kilner (Transport) Ltd, trading as:

Hants and Sussex

Part of Hants and Sussex Motor Services Ltd Group

Registered Office: South Leigh Road, Emsworth, Hampshire

From origins in 1937 the Hants and Sussex Group had developed rapidly, led by the entrepreneurial flair and tenacity of founder Basil Williams. A foothold had been gained in the Horsham area with the acquisition of F H Kilner's route from Plaistow to Horsham in February 1945 shortly thereafter being consolidated with the purchase of both Comfy Bus Service and Ewhurst & District. The Group's rapid expansion – over 130 new vehicles were delivered between 1947 and 1951 – had been financed on borrowings rather than by the introduction of fresh capital. Bank indebtedness increased alarmingly as revenues, frustrated by delays in obtaining approval for fare increases and hit by falling traffic, decreased. By 1954 the resultant cash flow crisis manifested itself with increasing service disruption and unreliability. The crunch came on 9 December 1954 when the Bank appointed a Receiver to the business which led to the cessation of the Horsham area operations after service on 21 December 1954.

Basil Williams pursued the commercial opportunity of town service operation in expanding Crawley New Town. The Hants & Sussex established presence on the Ifield Road with Route 33 led to a successful application resulting in weekday hourly frequency Route 33A from Crawley to Langley Green being introduced on 25 May 1954. Peak hour journeys were projected to Three Bridges and Manor Royal Industrial Estate. 1949 Duple bodied Bedford OB no. 148 (GOU 721) is seen at Langley Green in the summer of 1954. Following cessation of Hants & Sussex operations in the Horsham area Route 33A was partially absorbed by London Transport Route 476. A B Cross

ROUTE PROFILE

	Plaistow – Horsham via Loxwood, Alfold, Broadbridge Heath.
Feb 1945	Acquired from F H Kilner (t/a Sunbeam Bus Service), Loxwood, Sussex. Daily = 1 hour.
April 1947	Numbered 31.
21 Dec 1954	Withdrawn. Replaced by Aldershot & District route 50A.

ROUTE PROFILE

Town Service	**Horsham – Roffey Corner** (direct or via Littlehaven).
3 Oct 1946	Acquired from W F Alexander (t/a Comfy Bus Service). Daily. Co-ordinated timetable with London Transport Route 434. Combined frequency = 20 minutes.
April 1947	Following consent from LT to use double deck buses on journeys to Roffey Corner, journeys via Littlehaven truncated to terminate there. Numbered: 32 Horsham – Roffey Corner; 32A Horsham – Littlehaven.
25 Feb 1948	Route 32A journeys extended to terminate at Roffey Corner.
21 Dec 1954	Withdrawn. Route 32 absorbed into London Transport Route 434.

ROUTE PROFILE

	Horsham – Three Bridges via Roffey Cnr, Faygate, Ifield, Crawley.
3 Oct 1946	Acquired from W F Alexander (t/a Comfy Bus Service). Weekdays = 3/6 journeys.
April 1947	Numbered 33.
27 May 1954	Frequency became: Weekdays, approx = 2 hours, Suns = 2 journeys. Most journeys operated Horsham to Crawley.
21 Dec 1954	Withdrawn. Replaced by London Transport Route 852.

ROUTE PROFILE

	Ewhurst – Horsham via Oakwood Hill, Broadbridge Heath.
Nov1946	Acquired from A Lazzell (t/a Ewhurst & District Bus Service, Ewhurst Garage, Guildford, Surrey). Weekdays = 1/5 journeys. Sundays = 4 journeys.
April 1947	Numbered 34.
21 Dec 1954	Withdrawn. Replaced by London Transport Route 852.

From 1949 and until cessation of the business operation of the Hants & Sussex Horsham area bus routes was largely entrusted to five Duple bodied Bedford OB buses as well as double-deck Leyland Titan PD1 no. L054 illustrated on page 9. One of these Bedfords, no. 151 (HAA 564), is seen during layover at Ewhurst Bull's Head before returning to Horsham Carfax on Route 34. No. 151 was one of a number of Hants & Sussex Bedford OB buses converted from petrol to Perkins P6 diesel engine power in 1951/1952 in pursuit of operating cost economies. Hants & Sussex use of bold painted fleet names along with high ranking fleet numbers followed the style of contemporary, larger group owned bus operators.
D A Jones / London Trolleybus Preservation Society

James Mitchell multi-value and 'Stock' Bell Punch ticket. The latter was recorded by John Cunningham as issued by Mitchell on 13 September 1952.
D Seddon Collection

James Mitchell ran the first independent bus route to reach Horsham in 1921 subsequently developing three rural routes to the town. After the early post war passenger boom had passed Mitchell faced the common problem of decreasing traffic combined with increasing costs. Duple bodied Bedford OB reg.no. GBP 555 is seen at the Carfax terminal in Horsham in June 1961 around the time Sunday operation was withdrawn. London Transport declined an approach from Mitchell to take over the routes so Mrs Mabel Mitchell, then the principal, decided to withdraw from bus operation at Easter 1969.
M J Dryhurst

J Mitchell

Station Road, Warnham, Horsham, Sussex

In 1954 title became: J & M A Mitchell, trading as:

J Mitchell

ROUTE PROFILE

	Horsham Circular via Roffey Corner, Colgate, Faygate, Rusper.
At 8 May 1945	Daily = Irregular.
Autumn 1954	Part service diverted to Pease Pottage.
Autumn 1967	Part service diverted via Lamb's Green (to replace part London Transport Route 852 withdrawn after 2 October 1965).
5 April 1969	Withdrawn.

ROUTE PROFILE

	Ockley – Horsham via Warnham, Broadbridge Heath.
At 8 May 1945	Weekdays. 2 journeys (except Thursday) Ockley – Horsham. 2/8 short workings Warnham – Horsham.
5 April 1969	Withdrawn.

ROUTE PROFILE

	Horsham – Rusper via Holbrook Corner.
At 8 May 1945	Daily = Irregular.
5 April 1969	Withdrawn.

North Sussex Rural Transport

(Principal J D Wylde)

1 Tower Road, Orpington, Kent

Horsham Rural District Council, together with Rusper Parish Council, became concerned at the loss of transport facilities which would follow the withdrawal of London Transport Route 852 (Crawley – Horsham via Ifield) after 2 October 1965. These bodies established contact with John Wylde, then honorary manager of the Orpington Rural Transport Association, to investigate whether a similar organisation could be set up. Trial operation was agreed on Saturdays starting 30 October 1965 using a hired Orpington Rural Transport vehicle. The trial service ran for five consecutive Saturdays with John Wylde driving. He concluded that the response was 'encouraging' but the initiative was not pursued further.

J D Wylde, Mrs M F Wylde and R H Edwards, trading as:

North Downs Rural Transport

1 Tower Road, Orpington, Kent

Subsequently:

North Downs Rural Transport Ltd (for dates see text)

The Garage, Forest Green, Dorking, Surrey

From April 1972: Oasthouse Way, Cray Avenue, Orpington, Kent

Note: Although Horsham ceased to be in the London Transport area, following the transfer of Country Area operations to London Country Bus Services Ltd from 1 January 1970, the fortunes of North Downs operations in that area are followed until their demise in April 1972. Thus full details of John Wylde's involvement in bus operations in the South of England are recorded in this volume.

North Downs Rural Transport
1s 0d ticket printed by John
Wylde on a home-use Adana
printing machine.
D Seddon Collection

Three and a half years after his first, brief foray into bus operation in the Horsham area John Wylde reappeared on the scene as the principal of the North Downs Rural Transport partnership which assumed operation of most of J and M A Mitchell's Horsham area rural bus routes from 8 April 1969. On the same date North Downs introduced a new bus route from Orpington to Croydon, the subsequent development of which is detailed in Chapter 8.

An extensive service revision introduced on 9 October 1969 extended Horsham area operations to reach Crawley. On the same date route numbers, in an 8xx series, were introduced reflecting previous London Transport practice in the area. Horsham area operations doubled in scale from 2 November 1970 when the old-established routes of Brown Motor Services (see Chapter 5) were acquired upon the retirement of that concern's proprietor, Mr A T Brady. Included in the deal was Brady's garage at Forest Green. At this time a new company, North Downs Rural Transport Ltd, was formed to acquire the Brady business. The licences for the other North Downs Horsham area routes were subsequently transferred from the original partnership to the limited company on 14 April 1971.

Evidence of financial problems with North Downs operations became manifest when Route 850 (Horsham – Crawley) was withdrawn after 3 July 1971, compensatory adjustments being made at that time to Route 852 in order to continue services to the village of Warnham. Despite the difficulties, exacerbated by a shortage of drivers, A J Charlwood's Fridays only route from Capel to Dorking (see Chapter 5) was acquired from 9 July 1971, the route being modified to terminate at North Downs' garage at Forest Green instead of Capel.

Further expansion took place in February 1972 when a new Tuesdays only route from Forest Green to Crawley revived route number 850. An attractive timetable produced at this time included details of a newly introduced 'Independent Rover Ticket' (priced at 30p, 25p for children) available for a day's unlimited travel on all North Downs Rural Transport and Tillingbourne Valley bus services.

These initiatives were not sufficient to beat the downward spiral of North Downs operations in the Horsham area. Service unreliability increased as the company's efforts to prioritise available serviceable vehicles for school contract runs led to significant lost-mileage being incurred, particularly on

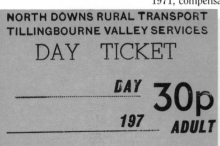

Unissued 'Independent Rover
Ticket'. North Downs Collection

North Downs no. 17 (WKG34) was one of three 1961-built Willowbrook dual purpose bodied Albion Nimbus acquired from Western Welsh in 1971. Brown Motor Services chocolate and cream livery was perpetuated by Forest Green based North Downs vehicles as evidenced by no. 17 seen at Colgate. A G Whitlam

routes 845 and 852. North Downs' Horsham area operations ceased after service on 15 April 1972.

In many respect North Downs' demise mirrored the decline over 17 years earlier of Hants & Sussex bus routes in the Horsham area. Both failures illustrated the great difficulties of providing rural bus services in an area of relative affluence, and hence increasing car ownership, at times before Council subsidy for such bus services had become common place.

Note: Readers seeking details of post-North Downs operation of the various routes are recommended to Lawrence James' excellent book INDEPENDENT BUS OPERATORS INTO HORSHAM.

ROUTE PROFILE

Route 850	Horsham – Crawley
	via Warnham, Ockley, Capel, Rusper, Lambs Green, Ifield.
8 April 1969	Acquired from J & M A Mitchell.
	Operated Horsham – Ockley only. Weekdays = Irregular.
9 Oct 1969	Extended to operate Horsham – Crawley.
	Route number introduced. Weekdays = 2 hours.
3 July 1971	Withdrawn.

1963 built 29-seat Marshall Cambrette-bodied Bedford VAS1 reg.no. 3255 PJ was the last new bus to be purchased by Brown Motor Services, passing to North Downs with the sale of the business. Numbered 15 in the North Downs fleet it was photographed at The Parrot, Forest Green in 1971. A G Whitlam

ROUTE PROFILE

Route 851	Horsham Circular
	via Roffey Corner, Colgate, Faygate, Lambs Green, Rusper.
8 April 1969	Acquired from J & M A Mitchell. Weekdays = 2 hours.
9 Oct 1969	Route number introduced.
3 July 1971	Some journeys diverted via North Heath Lane.
15 April 1972	Withdrawn. (Tillingbourne Valley Services assumed operation from 17 April 1972, West Sussex County Council having agreed to subsidise the operation).

ROUTE PROFILE

Route 852	Crawley – Horsham via Ifield, Lambs Green, Faygate, Colgate, Roffey Corner.
9 Oct 1969	Introduced. Weekdays = 1 journey.
By 2 Nov 1970	Amalgamated with Routes 850/851.

ROUTE PROFILE

Route 845	Forest Green – Guildford via Holmbury St Mary, Abinger Hammer, Gomshall, Shere, Albury, Chilworth, Shalford.
2 Nov 1970	Acquired from A T Brady (t/a Brown Motor Services). Weekdays = 2 hours.
15 April 1972	Withdrawn. (D A McCann, t/a Brown Motors Services, assumed operation from 24 April 1972).

ROUTE PROFILE

Route 852	Forest Green – Horsham via Ewhurst, Wallis Wood, Oakwood Hill, Rowhook, Broadbridge Heath.
2 Nov 1970	Acquired from A T Brady (t/a Brown Motor Services). Weekdays = 6 journeys.
14 April 1971	Some journeys operated direct between Forest Green and Wallis Wood.
5 July 1971	Some journeys diverted at Rowhook via Warnham to compensate for withdrawal of Route 850.
Feb 1972	All journeys diverted via Warnham. Peak hour journeys extended to Horsham Station.
By 1 April 1972	Reduced to operate Tuesdays, Wednesdays, Fridays and Saturdays only.
15 April 1972	Withdrawn. (D A McCann, t/a Brown Motor Services assumed operation from 25 April 1972).

ROUTE PROFILE

Route 844	Forest Green – Dorking, via Wallis Wood, Oakwood Hill, Ockley, Leith Hill, Coldharbour.
9 July 1971	Acquired from A J Charlwood (t/a Surrey and Sussex Coachways). Fridays only = 1 journey.
14 April 1972	Withdrawn. (D A McCann, t/a Brown Motor Services assumed operation from 25 April 1972).

ROUTE PROFILE

Route 850	Forest Green – Crawley via Wallis Wood, Oakwood Hill, Ockley, Capel, Rusper, Lambs Green.
Feb 1972	Introduced. Tuesdays only = 1 journey.
By 1 April 1972	Abandoned.

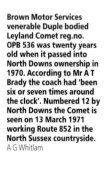

Brown Motor Services venerable Duple bodied Leyland Comet reg.no. OPB 536 was twenty years old when it passed into North Downs ownership in 1970. According to Mr A T Brady the coach had 'been six or seven times around the clock'. Numbered 12 by North Downs the Comet is seen on 13 March 1971 working Route 852 in the North Sussex countryside.
A G Whitlam

Mrs J Sargent

32 Cantelupe Road, East Grinstead, Sussex

In 1948 title became:

Sargents of East Grinstead Ltd

This small operator provided bus services in the rural hinterland between the territories of London Transport, Maidstone & District and Southdown. In 1948 the service was reorganised to provide a neat three-way connectional facility at Cowden Crossroads between buses from East Grinstead and those on the Edenbridge – Crowborough route.

ROUTE PROFILE

	East Grinstead – **Edenbridge** via Cowden Crossroads.
At 8 May 1945	Numbered 3. Daily.
1948	Curtailed to operate East Grinstead – Cowden Crossroads. Connections at Cowden Crossroads with Route 3 to/from Edenbridge and Crowborough. Daily = 7/10 journeys.
25 March 1951	Acquired by Southdown. Operated without route number.
30 Sept 1951	Transferred to Maidstone & District. Numbered 135.

ROUTE PROFILE

	East Grinstead – **Ashurst Wood**.
c 1946	Introduced. Daily. Numbered 3A. 7/10 journeys.
25 March 1951	Acquired by Southdown. Operated without route number.
30 Sept 1951	Transferred to Maidstone & District. Numbered 136.

ROUTE PROFILE

	Edenbridge – Crowborough via Cowden Crossroads.
1948	Introduced. Numbered 3. Daily = 3/5 journeys. Connections at Cowden Crossroads with Route 3 to/from East Grinstead.
25 March 1951	Acquired by Southdown. Operated without route number.
30 Sept 1951	Transferred to Maidstone & District.

ROUTE PROFILE

	East Grinstead – **Crawley (Tushmore Lane)**, via Felbridge, Tinsley Green, Gatwick.
24 Feb 1948	Introduced. Workmen's service. Mondays–Fridays = 2 return journeys.
25 March 1951	Acquired by Southdown. Operated without route number.
30 April 1951	Transferred to London Transport. Numbered 438/438A.

Major Operators

Aldershot & District Traction Co Ltd

Halimote Road, Aldershot, Hampshire

Much rivalry had existed between Aldershot & District and Hants & Sussex. The former had introduced Route 50 (Haslemere – Horsham) in January 1948 which paralleled Hants & Sussex Route 31 between Plaistow and Horsham. With the demise of Hants & Sussex, Route 31 passed to Aldershot & District on 22 December 1954 being re-numbered 50A. 1950 Strachan-bodied Dennis Lancet 3 no. 178 is seen on the outskirts of Horsham in September 1964. P R Wallis

Southdown Motor Services Ltd

5 Steine Street, Brighton, Sussex

The third largest BET Group company, with a fleet of around 750 buses and coaches, shared much interface with London Transport in North Sussex. Lengthy trunk routes, often offering intermediate connectional facilities

This particularly interesting photograph of Southdown's no. 1500 (LUF 500), numerically that company's first under-floor engined Leyland Royal Tiger bus, could well date from 1952 – the year that no. 1500 along with nine similar sister vehicles nos. 1501–1509 entered service. The year 1952 represented something of a watershed for the industry in that it saw the first volume quantities of under-floor engined single-deck buses enter service – other leading contemporary chassis makes included the AEC Regal IV (many of which went to London Transport's Green Line as the RF Class) and the Bristol LS (which went to BTC controlled companies). As may be seen Southdown, like a minority of other operators, chose to specify rear entrances for its build of East Lancs bodies – the batch 1500–1509 were later re-built to the more usual front entrance

configuration in 1958/1959. No. 1500, working lengthy 2 hour 6 minute journey time Route 36 to Brighton, is seen in East Grinstead approaching a London

Transport bus stop which did not cater for any LT routes – those detailed on the flag are either Southdown or Maidstone & District. This ably illustrates

London Transport's policy of providing all bus stops in any district touched by its own services.
The Omnibus Society / J F Parke Collection

At Crawley some post-war housing development was beyond the boundary of the LPTA defined back in 1933. A 'mileage operated' trade off accommodation was reached between London Transport and Southdown which resulted in certain LT routes being projected south of the LPTA boundary in return for which Southdown was able to operate into north Crawley. Southdown's Northern Counties-bodied Leyland Titan PD3 no. 832 is seen at Gossops Green working town service 79 on a busy pre-Christmas Saturday in December 1961 duplicated by a lightweight Beadle semi-chassis-less re-build of 1953. M J Dryhurst

with other routes, were characteristic of Southdown. Horsham was served by a number of such routes from Worthing (Route 2) Brighton (Route 17) Petersfield (Route 61) Chichester (routes 63 and 63A) and Bognor Regis (Route 69). Further east the small village of Turners Hill enjoyed advertised timetable connections between Southdown routes 86/88 from Haywards Heath and London Transport Route 434 from Crawley and East Grinstead. Both the latter towns were also served by other Southdown routes.

Salient developments of town bus services in Crawley New Town: 1953–1959

Operator and route		Terminals	Date	Notes
LT	483	Town Centre – Northgate	06.05.53	Introduced. First town service.
LT	476	Town Centre – Langley Green	19.05.54	Introduced.
HS	33A	Town Centre – Langley Green	25.05.54	Introduced. Withdrawn as a consequence of failure of operator on 21.12.54. Absorbed into LT Route 476.
LT	426A	Ifield – Three Bridges	11.08.54	Introduced.
LT	405	Three Bridges – Tilgate	17.10.56	Peak hour journeys off 405 (West Croydon – Horsham), projected to Tilgate.
LT	476	Ifield – Tilgate	17.10.56	Peak hour journeys projected to Tilgate.
SD	23	Brighton – Manor Royal	17.10.56	Peak hour journeys projected from Town Centre to Manor Royal Industrial Area.
LT	476	Ifield – Tilgate	01.05.57	Regular daily service introduced to Tilgate.
SD	23 23A	Brighton – Northgate Pease Pottage – Northgate	19.01.58	All journeys on Route 23 extended from Town Centre to Northgate with peak hour extensions to Manor Royal. Route 23A introduced. As a consequence LT Route 483 withdrawn.
SD	76	Gossops Green – Manor Royal	31.08.59	Introduced. Peak hours only.
SD	79	Town Centre – Gossops Green	10.12.59	Introduced.
	Key:	HS – Hants & Sussex	LT – London Transport	SD – Southdown

Kent

Independents

Ashby Commercial Vehicles Ltd, trading as:
Ashline Coaches
Quarry Hill Garage, Tonbridge, Kent

Ashline Coaches operated three long established, weekdays only, rural bus routes from Tonbridge to Lower Hayesden, Underriver and Weald. These services were acquired by Maidstone and District on 8 September 1948. Ashline Coaches Leyland Cub reg. no. DRR 793 is seen at the Tonbridge Station terminal shared with London Transport buses on routes 402 to Bromley, 403 to Wallington and 454 to Chipstead via Sevenoaks. *The Omnibus Society / J F Parke Collection*

London Transport enjoyed running rights to the spa town of Tunbridge Wells, located well beyond the boundary of the London Passenger Transport Area, under the terms of the 1933 Act. London Transport maintained a small garage in Tunbridge Wells for coaches used to work Green Line Route 704, which took almost 3½ hours to travel from Tunbridge Wells to Windsor via London. This Green Line route was not allowed to carry local passengers between Tunbridge Wells and Tonbridge in order to afford protection to the bus routes of the dominant local operator, BET group member Maidstone & District. Fellow BET group company Southdown also reached Tunbridge Wells with routes from the south. From 6 June 1948 Southdown's Route 122 from Brighton was extended beyond Tunbridge Wells to Gravesend, working to a daily hourly frequency and becoming jointly-operated with Maidstone & District. Although buses worked right through, Southdown crews did not work north of Tunbridge Wells, as Maidstone & District crews manned the vehicles on the section thence to Gravesend.

Tunbridge Wells was also served by two independent operators in the post-war period. L.B. Atkins (trading as Beacon Motor Services) of The Broadway, Croft Road, Crowborough, Sussex operated several routes based on the operator's home town, one of which reached Tunbridge Wells on Fridays only. Atkins' operations were acquired on 26 November 1949 by Southdown, who formed a separate company – Beacon Motor Services (Crowborough) Ltd. to control the operation. In 1954 all licences were transferred to Southdown.

P G Warren of Ticehurst, Sussex worked into Tunbridge Wells from Burwash, with another Fridays-only service. The operator's name subsequently changed to Warrens Coaches Ltd. in 1949 and later to Warrens Coaches (Kent and Sussex) Ltd. in 1959, the Burwash – Tunbridge Wells continuing unchanged until withdrawn in the summer of 1965.

G L French, trading as:

Pilgrim Coaches

Hodsell Street, Wrotham, Kent

ROUTE PROFILE

Wrotham – Fairseat (Daffodil Cafe).	
Feb 1955	Introduced. Operated Tuesdays and Fridays only.
Summer 1955	Withdrawn.

Dr H N Heffernan, trading as:

Thames Weald

West Kingsdown, Sevenoaks, Kent

From 23 May 1963 title changed to:

Thames Weald Ltd

What was to prove to be one of the most durable, but at times ethereal, independent operators in the London Transport area began in August 1961 as the Thames Weald Travel Society. Led by Dr Nesbitt Heffernan, a consultant psychiatrist, the Society introduced a limited private bus service in replacement of London Transport Route 492 (West Kingsdown – Gravesend) which had been withdrawn in October 1958. Following the successful application by Dr Heffernan for a stage carriage licence the service became available for public use from 5 October 1961. For the next eighteen months Thames Weald, initially using a Commer minibus reg.no. 509 TKO, continued to operate on a voluntary staff basis using part-time drivers supplemented by Dr Heffernan and his wife. Operations assumed a more formal footing from 23 May 1963 when the limited liability company was formed

Thames Weald was hiring Orpington Rural Transport Association's Austin J2 Omnicoach reg.no. NPV 828 when this photograph was taken at Fawkham Green on 18 May 1964. From May 1963 Fawkham Green enjoyed 3/5 Monday to Friday journeys on Sevenoaks – Gravesend Route A. On Saturdays just one through journey operated but five short workings form Sevenoaks connected at West Kingsdown with Saturday only LT Route 452 onward to Fawkham Green and Dartford. G R Croughton / courtesy North Downs Collection

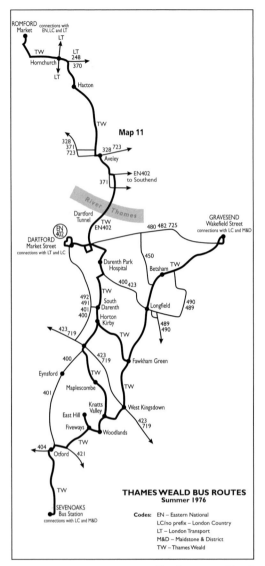

ROMFORD Market — connections with EN, LC and LT

LT

TW Hornchurch

LT 248
370

LT

Hacton

TW

Map 11

328
371
723

328 723
723

Aveley

371

EN402
to Southend

River Thames

Dartford Tunnel

TW
EN402

EN
402

DARTFORD
Market Street
connections with LT and LC

480 482 725

GRAVESEND
Wakefield Street
connections with LC and M&D

450

Darenth Park
Hospital

Betsham

TW

400 423

492
491
401
400

TW
South
Darenth

Longfield

490
489

Horton
Kirby

489
490

423
719

TW

400

423
719

Fawkham Green

Eynsford

TW

401

Maplescombe

TW

East Hill

Knatts
Valley

West Kingsdown

Fiveways

423
719

Woodlands

404

TW

Otford

421

TW

SEVENOAKS
Bus Station
connections with LC and M&D

THAMES WEALD BUS ROUTES
Summer 1976

Codes: EN – Eastern National
LC/no prefix – London Country
LT – London Transport
M&D – Maidstone & District
TW – Thames Weald

and the first full-time driver employed. Dr Heffernan explained that the name Thames Weald was 'coined to designate the high woodland of the North Downs beyond the valley of the River Darent. You will not find it on your maps but it has a population of some thousands spread over a score of hamlets, its settlements go back to Roman times and its churches are 10th century'. He continued by stating that Thames Weald 'aims to perpetuate the fading image of the village bus proprietor, his fleet in his back yard ready to turn out for any need'.

London Transport's withdrawal from bus operation through the Dartford Tunnel in 1967 led to Thames Weald's transformation from the idyll of a village bus proprietor to inter-urban operator. The Tunnel, which had opened to traffic on 18 November 1963, had initially attracted intensive coverage by London Transport. High frequency Route 300 worked from Grays whilst Green Line Route 722 had been extended to form an Aldgate – Dartford link. Expectations of passenger traffic did not materialise for within a year the Green Line extension had been withdrawn whilst Route 300 suffered progressive frequency reductions. In an effort to stem continuing losses double deck RT-class operated Route 300 was replaced on 2 June 1965 by Route 399 worked by 26-seat GS class buses. The 399 proved unviable too and was withdrawn from operation on 12 May 1967, leaving the Tunnel link between Essex and Kent without a bus service.

On 19 August 1967 Thames Weald introduced a new lengthy route from Romford through the Dartford Tunnel to Sevenoaks. Dubbed 'Tunnel Express' two buses were needed on weekdays to maintain the service. This new initiative eclipsed the original Gravesend route which thereafter went into a rapid decline. The 'Tunnel Express' was further expanded from 10 July 1971 when the southern section was projected from Sevenoaks to Crawley thereby giving a through Romford – Crawley route with a journey time of 2 hours 55 minutes. Interestingly this lengthened 'Tunnel Express' connected with Green Line routes 724 (Romford – Watford – High Wycombe) and 727 (Crawley – Watford – Luton Airport), so making it possible for any person so inclined to complete a circuit of the outer perimeter of London – approximating to a circuit of the present-day M25 motorway – using just three routes.

The early 1970s marked the zenith of Thames Weald's operation. For on 7 January 1974 the Crawley extension ran for the last time, the 'Tunnel Express' thereafter reverting to its original operation between Romford and Sevenoaks. The latter half of the decade saw further declines in frequency coincident with the emergence of an air of secrecy by Thames Weald about its operations. Timetables were not issued or displayed on the roadside and it would seem that at times road service licences were allowed to lapse – all these factors making it difficult to be absolutely certain of routes followed or frequencies. Thames Weald suffered from vehicle maintenance problems too. By 1978, being reduced to one roadworthy vehicle, it became necessary to hire another coach on Saturdays to maintain the service. This coach was hired from October 1978 from Mr G L S Digby (trading as Mildmay Motors). Initial co-operation led to conflict in 1979 when Mr Digby applied in his own right for a licence to operate most of the Thames Weald route. At about the same time London Country, at the behest of both Essex and Kent County Councils, concerned about the unreliability of the Thames Weald service, sought a licence to operate from Dartford to Romford.

A hearing before the Metropolitan Traffic Commissioners to consider the rival applications was held in September 1979. Important evidence in support of Thames Weald's application to retain its licence was provided by J T King, vice-chairman of The Omnibus Society. Mr King demonstrated that Thames Weald used its profitable operation on the Essex side of the Thames to cross-subsidise its uneconomic but socially desirable service on the Kent bank. The commissioners decided in favour of Thames Weald, the established operator, who were now able to provide two vehicles for the route and so dispense with the hired coach. Thames Weald recovered from this nadir in its existence, in 1982 increasing the frequency of the 'Tunnel Express'.

On 3 July 1984 Thames Weald began a further metamorphosis into long-distance operator with the introduction of a Saturday service from Romford to Maidstone. This was the precursor of other lengthy routes, introduction of which falls without the timescale of this volume.

ROUTE PROFILE

Sevenoaks – Gravesend via Otford, Knatts Valley or East Hill, West Kingsdown, Fawkham Green, Betsham.	
5 Oct 1961	Introduced. Thursdays only.
7 Dec 1961	Revised to operate: Mondays–Fridays = 1/3 journeys.
By May 1963	Revised to operate: Weekdays = 1/5 journeys.
19 Aug 1967	Truncated to operate Knatts Valley – Gravesend only. Mondays–Fridays = 4 journeys.
By Oct 1969	Reduced to 2 journeys.
By Nov 1970	Reduced to 1 journey
By 1976	Revised to operate: Tuesdays and Saturdays only = 1 journey.
By 1978	Revised to operate 1 return journey Sevenoaks – Gravesend Tuesdays only.
3 June 1982	Withdrawn.

ROUTE PROFILE

Southfleet – Meopham (Hook Green) via Longfield.	
31 May 1964	Introduced. Sundays only, approx = 2 hours. Replaced section of Sunday service London Transport Route 489A (Gravesend – Meopham) withdrawn after 25 October 1962. Connected at Southfleet with London Transport Route 489 to/from Gravesend.
May 1967	Withdrawn.

Ā 8393

OMNIBUS TICKET.

Thames Weald

TUNNEL EXPRESS

from the Weald of Essex
to the Weald of Kent

Thames Weald's 1964-built
29-seat Plaxton-bodied
Bedford VAS 1 reg.no. HMK
140B is seen in Market
Street, Dartford working a
Tunnel Express journey in
1971. To its nearside stands
London Transport's
Bexleyheath Garage-based
RT 2659 (LYR 643) waiting
departure time for a
Route 96 journey to
Woolwich. A G Whitlam

ROUTE PROFILE

Tunnel Express. Romford – Sevenoaks – Crawley
via Hornchurch, Aveley, Dartford Tunnel, Dartford, Horton Kirby,
Farningham, Knatts Valley, Otford, Edenbrige, Horley, Gatwick Airport.

19 Aug 1967	Introduced. Operated Romford – Sevenoaks. Weekdays = 5 journeys, Sundays = 2 journeys. Route letter D.
10 July 1971	Projected from Sevenoaks to/from Crawley. Now operated Romford – Crawley. Weekdays = 2/3 through journeys, Sevenoaks – Romford section = 2 hours. Sundays = 1 through journey.
7 Jan 1974	Section Sevenoaks – Crawley withdrawn. Now operated Romford – Sevenoaks
By 1976	Reduced to operate Wednesdays, Fridays and Saturdays only: Sevenoaks – Romford = 1 return journey. Dartford – Romford = 2/3 journeys.
3 June 1982	Sevenoaks – Romford section increased to operate weekdays. Loop working introduced at Hornchurch. Additional journeys West Kingsdown – Sevenoaks on Mondays–Fridays at peak hours.
14 Dec 1982	Sevenoaks – Romford section reduced to operate Wednesdays–Saturdays only.
24 Sept 1983	Two Saturday journeys into Romford diverted via Gidea Park.
3 July 1984	Saturday journey introduced. Romford – Maidstone.
12 July 1985	Extant.

This notice unequivocally expresses Dr Heffernan's strongly held views concerning the problems of litter and smoking on his vehicles. J M Aldridge

IMPORTANT NOTICE FROM THE DIRECTOR

The losses on this service are so great that it is out of the question to employ a staff of cleaners. I am no longer prepared to spend my evenings & week-ends on my hands & knees clearing out litter. Neither am I prepared to run dirty buses.

Therefore the service will be WITHDRAWN at the end of the year unless there is clear evidence before that date that SMOKING & the depositing of LITTER have entirely CEASED.

The articles which give rise to the most serious hygiene problems are :-

cigarette ash	half-eaten toffees
chewing gum	iced lollies
apple cores	soiled paper tissues

Kindly bring this notice to the attention of any fellow passenger whose co-operation appears to be needed

SMOKING PROHIBITED

NO SMOKING

During the 1966 LT work-to-rule Thames Weald operated two substitute bus routes. The only such operator to letter their routes, proprietor Dr Heffernan explained 'with Bexley, Blackfen, Blendon, Brook Hospital and Blackheath on the timetable it was inevitable that we should call it Route B rather than Route 89'. 20-seat Plaxton-bodied Bedford J2 reg.no. EMH 822B is seen at Bexley Station on the last day of Thames Weald service 26 February 1966 after which operation reverted to London Transport.
J G S Smith / courtesy J C Gillham

Despite its Manchester registration OVR 798H this Williams Deansgate-bodied Mercedes-Benz was supplied new to Thames Weald in 1970. It was photographed outside Dr Heffernan's house in West Kingsdown on a Tunnel Express working.
A G Whitlam

With clear route branding for the Tunnel Express, Thames Weald's 1981-built former demonstrator Dodge S66C reg.no. PKR 399W fitted with a 27-seat Rootes body was photographed whilst on layover in Romford in January 1985. M J Dryhurst

H T Horlock & Son

Granby Garage, 29 The Hill, Northfleet, Gravesend, Kent

ROUTE PROFILE

	Stansted – Gravesend.
1962	Introduced. Saturdays only.
31 Dec 1969	Extant.

G L S Digby, trading as:

Mildmay Motors

10 Mildmay Place, Shoreham, Sevenoaks, Kent.

ROUTE PROFILE

	Shoreham – Farnborough Hospital via Otford, Kemsing, Knockholt Pound, Green Street Green, Orpington.
26 Dec 1977	Introduced. Sundays / Bank holidays = 1 journey.
19 March 1978	Withdrawn. This service is known to have been very erratic in operation. Whilst 19 March 1978 was the expiry date of the licence it was observed operating on 23 April 1978.

Eastern National's Leyland National 2 no. 1938 (STW 19W) was photographed at Southend's Central Bus Station on 29 April 1982 about to depart on a Route 402 journey to Victoria via the Dartford Tunnel. P R Wallis

Major Operators

Eastern National Omnibus Co Ltd

New Writtle Street, Chelmsford, Essex

The extension of occasional journeys on Eastern National Route 2 from Grays to Dartford from 23 July 1967 represented the first bus service to travel through the Dartford Tunnel following London Transport's withdrawal of Route 399 after operation on 12 May 1967.

ROUTE PROFILE

	Southend – Dartford – London (Victoria) via Basildon, Grays, Dartford Tunnel.
23 July 1967	3 Weekday, 2 Sunday journeys on existing Route 2 (Southend – Grays) projected beyond Grays via Dartford Tunnel to Dartford. 1s minimum fare in Kent.
2 Oct 1968	Route 2 extension to Dartford replaced by new Limited Stop Route 402. Operated Southend – Dartford. Daily = 2 journeys.
23 Nov 1980	Projected from Dartford to London (Victoria). Daily = 4 journeys. Restriction on carriage of local traffic between Dartford Tunnel Approach and Victoria.
15 Jan 1983	Weekday frequency increased to 2 hours.
12 July 1985	Extant.

Maidstone & District Motor Services Ltd

Knightrider House, Knightrider Street, Maidstone, Kent

One of the larger BET Group companies Maidstone & District shared considerable interface with London Transport bus services in an arc swinging north eastwards from East Grinstead through Edenbridge and Sevenoaks up to Gravesend. The company had been by far the most severely affected of the 'provincial operating companies' by the implementation of the 1933 Act. Fifty-five vehicles, depots at Dartford and Gravesend, all Gravesend town bus services as well as those sections of company routes between Dartford and both Gravesend and Meopham had been surrendered to London Transport

One Maidstone & District bus route still worked from Dartford. Originating in 1930, summer only Route 40 to Sheerness was resumed in 1946 following wartime suspension. Intended mainly for day trippers a restriction applied on local passengers between Dartford and Denton. Seen in the early post-war travel boom when 3/4 daily journeys operated, is 1947 Beadle-bodied AEC Regal II no. SO20 at Gravesend (Overcliffe). By the 1960s operation had reduced to one Saturday and Sunday journey. This route was subsequently projected to start at Thamesmead and later Woolwich, and renumbered 300 in 1974 and 700 in 1983.
R Bristow / courtesy The M&D and East Kent Bus Club

It seems incredible to recall that the small Kent village of Wrotham once enjoyed daily hourly frequency routes to places as distant and disparate as Brighton and Welwyn Garden City. In this 1965 view Maidstone & District no. DH434, a 1953 Weymann Orion-bodied Leyland Titan PD2/12, passes Green Line RMC 1483 outside St George's Church. The 68-mile long Route 122 between Brighton and Gravesend was operated jointly by Maidstone & District and Southdown. Although M&D had been an early convert to rear engined double-deckers, Southdown's aversion to this concept compelled M&D to use front engined buses on this route due to inter-working arrangements which involved crews of either company driving the other's buses.
V C Jones / courtesy Ian Allan Publishing Ltd

on 1 July 1933. London Transport was afforded further protection by the Act in becoming the only bus operator allowed to carry local traffic within the borough of Gravesend.

Being part of the BET Group, a rival in many respects to the state owned BTC, spurred Maidstone & District into restoring some presence on Gravesend town services by opening up routes to developing areas on the eastern side of the town beyond the LPTA boundary. The first of these, Route 46 to Valley Drive, was introduced on 22 September 1948 although the protection afforded to London Transport prevented Maidstone & District from carrying local passengers between Gravesend and Denton. By the time London Transport's Country Bus Department passed to the NBC on 1 January 1970, as well as Route 26, Maidstone & District had started Route 21, also to Valley Drive as well as routes 27 and 56 to River View Park.

CHAPTER 7

Central Area Independents 1955–1969

Independents

West London Coachways Ltd

594-6 London Road, Ashford, Middlesex

ROUTE PROFILE

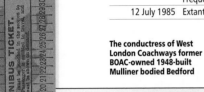

West London Coachways 1½d 'stock' Bell Punch ticket recorded by John Cunningham as issued on the Feltham – Bedfont route on 14 October 1956. D Seddon Collection

	Feltham Station – Bedfont (Northumberland Crescent).
1 Sept 1955	Introduced. Weekdays = 15 minutes. Sundays = 30/60 minutes.
4 May 1958	Sunday service withdrawn.
1 Jan 1962	Acquired by Tourist Coachways Ltd, 54A Lampton Road, Hounslow, Middlesex.
20 Jan 1967	Acquired by F G Wilder & Son Ltd, (t/a Golden Miller Services).
1 Feb 1968	Numbered 601.
13 Jan 1969	Circular terminal working introduced at Bedfont Green. Frequency now Weekdays = 20/30 minutes.
12 July 1985	Extant.

The conductress of West London Coachways former BOAC-owned 1948-built Mulliner bodied Bedford OB reg.no. JXH 634 takes a break at the Northumberland Crescent, Bedfont terminus located just to the north of the main Hounslow – Staines A315 road. J M Aldridge

George Mash, the principal of Tourist Coachways, was a former manager of major London coach operator Samuelson New Transport which was owned jointly by the BET and Tilling Groups. During Tourist Coachways tenure on the Feltham Station – Bedfont bus route coaches were habitually deployed such as reg.no. OUO 587, a 1953-built Duple bodied Bedford SB acquired from Ansell & Co. of Camberwell, another company controlled by Mr Mash. This shot, taken at Feltham terminus, dates from 18 April 1964.
Photobus / R Marshall

Thomas E Berry, trading as:

Falcon Coaches

163 Broad Lane, Hampton , Middlesex

ROUTE PROFILE

	Hampton (Station)–Hampton (Station). Circular service via Oak Avenue, Swan Road, Hanworth Road.
19 January 1957	Introduced on weekdays. Operated hourly in both clockwise and anticlockwise directions.
17 March 1958	Circular loop on all journeys bar one extended at Hanworth to travel via Bear Road and Twickenham Road rather than Swan Road – thereby offering connections with London Transport Routes 90 and 111. Also revised routeing near Hanworth station.
September 1958	Remaining journey via Swan Road withdrawn.
By January 1960	Saturday service withdrawn in late morning and early afternoon.
By July 1960	Saturday service discontinued.
12 June 1963	Withdrawn.

Falcon Coaches started the second post-Chambers Report independent service within London Transport's Special Area. The route's introduction on 19 January 1957 resulted from a petition signed by over 2,000 Hampton area residents seeking a local bus service. Falcon Coaches Thurgood-bodied Bedford OB reg.no. HRO 281 is seen outside Hampton Station on 22 November 1957 with exemplary route information displayed on its painted boards. Unfortunately the investment by proprietor Thomas Berry into the bus service failed to produce a profit. Mr Berry stated that the route was losing £6 per week just before its withdrawal after operation on 12 June 1963.
J C Gillham

Emergency Bus Services during the 1958 London Transport Strike

On Monday 5 May 1958 all London Transport road passenger services were suspended as a result of a strike by crews. The dispute centred on the refusal of London Transport to award an 8s 6d a week pay increase already agreed for Central Area staff to their colleagues in the Country Bus and Coach Department. Support for the strike amongst crews was total and no London Transport bus ran in service until a return to work was agreed for 21 June 1958. Eastern National crews showed support for the striking London Transport staff by refusing to work bus services across the LPTA boundary from June 3. London Transport Underground as well as British Railways train services continued to operate normally during the strike.

The People's League for the Defence of Freedom

The People's League bought and hired about twenty buses which it operated from a base at Kendall's Car Park on Wandsworth Common. Dealer Cyril Green Enterprises sourced many of these vehicles. Former Lytham St Annes Corporation 1944-built Duple utility-bodied Daimler CWA6 reg.no. FTD 618 is seen at Grosvenor Gardens, Victoria working the League's Route 1.
J M Aldridge

175 High Holborn, London WC1

Chairman Edward Martell, Secretary Brian Goddard

This right wing organisation introduced buses on certain routes in London from Saturday 31 May 1958 at first offering passengers 'A Free Ride At Your Own Risk'. Short term licences were obtained from 13 June after which date the 'Freedom Buses' charged a flat fare of 6d for any distance. Services ran from 5am until early evening.

A leaflet issued by the League planned to run 22 bus routes 'as the service develops' but only the seven routes listed were authorised before the strike ended.

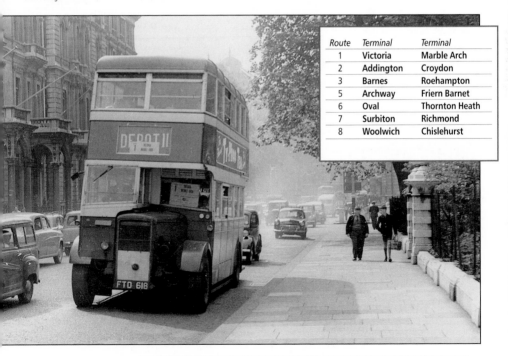

Route	Terminal	Terminal
1	Victoria	Marble Arch
2	Addington	Croydon
3	Barnes	Roehampton
5	Archway	Friern Barnet
6	Oval	Thornton Heath
7	Surbiton	Richmond
8	Woolwich	Chislehurst

Former Lytham St Annes Corporation reg.no. BTF 28 was a 1937-built torque | converter transmission Leyland Titan TD4c. Fitted with distinctive full-fronted | Leyland bodywork the bus was photographed in Brixton Road at The Oval | working The People's League Route 6 thence to Thornton Heath. J M Aldridge

People's League
FREEDOM BUS SERVICE
###

The People's League, having applied for and received licences to ply for hire in the London areas, is reorganising its Bus Service (which began giving free lifts on May 31st, 1958) as follows:—

FARES.—As from Friday, June 13th, 1958, a flat rate charge of 6d. is made for any journey anywhere on a route.

TICKETS.—A numbered ticket is issued.

RUNNING CONDITIONS.—Buses are run in full conformity with the Regulations governing Public Service Vehicles.
Only experienced drivers are used. Drivers and conductors are registered and paid.

ROUTES.—The following is the list of routes it is planned to run as the service develops:—

Route 1. Victoria to Marble Arch

Route 2. Addington to Croydon

Route 3. Barnes to Roehampton

Route 4. Boreham Wood to Colindale

Route 5. Archway to Friern Barnet

Route 6. Oval to Thornton Heath

Route 7. Surbiton to Richmond

Route 8. Woolwich to Chislehurst

Route 9. Barking to Becontree

Route 10. Waterloo to Russell Square

Route 11. Elephant and Castle to New Cross

Route 12. Victoria to Oxford Circus

Route 13. Clapham Common to Streatham Common

Route 14. Victoria to Peckham

Route 15. Harold Hill to Romford

Route 16. Putney to Brixton

Route 19. Clapham Junction to Streatham

Route 17. South Mimms to Cockfosters

Route 18. Victoria Station to London Bridge

Route 20. Golders Green to Kilburn

Route 21. Hayes to Northolt

Route 22. Clapham Junction to Tooting

HOURS.—Services will vary according to the requirements of each route. Earliest buses, 5 a.m. Last buses, early evening.

PRIVATE PARTIES.--Buses can be hired for private parties by arrangement

LOST PROPERTY.—Lost property left on buses should be claimed at 175 High Holborn, London, W.C.1.

ENQUIRIES.—Telephone COV 1051 and ask for Bus Control Room. Office open 8 a.m. to 9 p.m.

###

THE PEOPLE'S LEAGUE FOR THE DEFENCE OF FREEDOM
Chairman: Edward Martell.   Secretary - General Brian Goddard

175 High Holborn, London, W.C.1
Telephone: COV 1051 (4 lines)

###

FOR DETAILS OF MEMBERSHIP OF THE PEOPLE'S LEAGUE APPLY TO THE SECRETARY, 175 HIGH HOLBORN, W.C.1

Printed by C.P.U. Ltd., 175 High Holborn, London, W.C.1

Above **Another former Lytham St Annes Corporation bus hired by The People's League was 1937-built all Leyland LT7c single-decker formerly no. 41 (BTF 21) in that Lancashire fleet. When photographed at The Oval on League Route 6 the bus was carrying incorrect registration no. BTC 624 which had somehow become transposed with the registration from sister vehicle no. 40.** J M Aldridge

Right **Seen in Brixton Road at The Oval was reg.no. ABE 335, a former Lincolnshire Road Car Co. Harrington bodied Leyland Tiger TS8 coach, also on People's League Route 6.** J M Aldridge

The most modern vehicles hired by The People's League were a pair of former Lancaster Corporation 1947-built all Crossley SD42/3s. Reg.no. HTC 614 was seen outside East Croydon station whilst deployed on League Route 2. J M Aldridge

Independent Operators

A number of independent operators obtained short term licences during the strike.

Exact periods of operation remain uncertain.

The most unusual bus to take to the streets of London during the LT strike was former Aldershot & District 1947 Dennis Lancet 3 reg.no. EOU 441. Sold to motor dealers M P H W Sales it had been converted into a bubble car transporter but was rapidly re-adapted as well as was possible to carry passengers. Seen in Northumberland Avenue the bus operated a free circular service around the West **End.** V C Jones courtesy Ian Allan Publishing Ltd

Above right **After the 1958 strike certain Liberal Party Associations became critical of London Transport's performance and monopoly status in the Special Area. Finchley Liberals introduced a free bus service between Finchley and Golders Green which shadowed LT Route 102. Finchley Coaches Burlingham-bodied Dennis Falcon reg.no. RPG 491 is seen on hire for this route in October 1958 emerging from The Bishop's Avenue into Lyttleton Road. Effectively a private hire, no fares could be charged but there was probably a provision to make 'donations' to the local Liberal party.** D W K Jones courtesy J C Gillham

Operator	Terminals
Camden Coaches, Sevenoaks, Kent	Tatsfield – Sevenoaks (schools)
Chiltern Queens Ltd, Woodcote, Oxon.	Chiswick – Hyde Park Corner
Paynes Coaches (Croydon) Ltd.	Shirley – East Croydon Station
Edward Thomas, Ewell, Surrey	Chessington – Richmond Station
Whitefriars Coaches, Wembley, Middlesex	Harrow-on-the-Hill Station – London Airport (Heathrow)
Wright Bros, Harlow, Essex	Potter Street – Harlow Station Hare Street – Harlow Station Cannons Gate – Harlow Station

Banstead Coaches Ltd

1 Shrubland Road, Banstead, Surrey

Banstead Coaches Bus
Routes at 8 June 1964.

Banstead Coaches 'stock'
Ultimate ticket recorded by John
Cunningham as issued on the
Chipstead Valley route in 1960.
D Seddon Collection

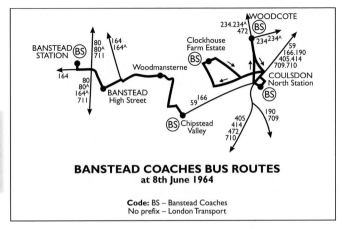

BANSTEAD COACHES BUS ROUTES
at 8th June 1964

Code: BS – Banstead Coaches
No prefix – London Transport

Woodmansterne residents,
faced with a walk of up to
one mile to their nearest LT
bus route, had long agitated
for their own service. These
aspirations were fulfilled
from 2 March 1959 when
Banstead Coaches bus route
between Chipstead Valley
and Banstead started. The
first bus used was 1949-
built Mulliner bodied
Bedford OB reg.no. HCG 581.
Sporting a shocking pink
livery, which quickly gained
the vehicle the sobriquet of
the 'Candy Floss Bus', the
Bedford takes aboard an
encouraging number of
passengers at The Mid-day
Sun terminal, Chipstead
Valley. J M Aldridge

ROUTE PROFILE

Chipstead Valley – Banstead via Woodmansterne Lane.	
2 March 1959	Introduced. Daily = 30/40 minutes to Banstead (Victoria). Extended peak hours and Sundays to Banstead Station.
1 Nov 1959	Sunday service discontinued for Winter. Re-introduced summer seasons 1960/1961/1962 only.
Oct 1973	Extension to Banstead Station withdrawn. Now operated Chipstead Valley – Banstead (Victoria).
12 July 1985	Extant.

ROUTE PROFILE

Coulsdon North Station – Woodcote (Foxley Lane) Circular.	
8 June 1964	Introduced. Weekdays = 1 hour.
13 Jan 1967	Withdrawn.

Banstead Coaches Bedford OB reg.no. HCG 581 was replaced in 1960 by 1953-built Duple Midland 40-seat Bedford SBO reg.no. LCJ 929 acquired from Yeomans of Canon Pyon, Shropshire. This bus is seen at The Mid-day Sun, Chipstead Valley on 18 July 1964. R Marshall

Banstead Coaches second Duple Midland-bodied Bedford SB service bus, reg.no. SNT 602, also originated with a Shropshire operator, having been supplied new in 1959 to Jones Coachways of Market Drayton. It passed into Banstead Coaches ownership in 1964 to augment the fleet coincident with the introduction of the two new bus routes at Coulsdon. This bus is seen pulling into Brighton Road, Coulsdon. J M Aldridge

The same bus loading at Coulsdon terminal. J M Aldridge

Banstead Coaches 1972-built 47-seat Willowbrook-bodied Bedford YRQ reg.no. DAR 527K is seen in Banstead High Street in March 1978. C Essex

ROUTE PROFILE

Coulsdon North Station
- Clockhouse Farm Estate (The Mount) Circular.

Note: London Transport had introduced Saturdays-only Route 263 between Coulsdon North Station and Clockhouse Farm Estate on 26 January 1957. After repeated representations from the Estate's residents for a full weekday bus service, London Transport granted Banstead Coaches a 'consent' to operate such a service. The Saturdays-only London Transport Route 263 operated for the last time on 6 June 1964.

8 June 1964	Introduced. Weekdays = 20/40 minutes.
31 March 1980	Withdrawn. Subsequently replaced by Tandridge Taxis Ltd, from 22 July 1980. (see Chapter 9).

Cemetery Bus Service
Automatickets.
D Seddon Collection

Metropolitan Borough of St Pancras

From 1 April 1965 responsibility transferred to London Borough of Camden.

ROUTE PROFILE

St Pancras & Islington Cemetery – Internal Service.

6 Sept 1959	Experimental service operated each Sunday in September 1959 using an Austin 12-seat minibus borrowed from the Public Health Department.
March 1962	Regular operation began with the purchase by the Cemeteries Department of reg. no. 760 DXY, a Ford Transit/Strachan minibus. Operated Sundays, Bank Holidays and Christmas Day. Proper bus stops and timetables were provided.
1971	At decimalisation the fare was 1p. Ultimate tickets issued
12 July 1985	Extant.

The most bizarre bus route described in this book was that provided for visitors to the St Pancras and Islington Cemetery. Established in the 1850s when burial places were being developed in what was then countryside around London the Cemetery, which featured an extensive internal road network, was located between the villages of Finchley, Friern Barnet and Fortis Green. The original Ford Transit used on the service was replaced by another Transit with Strachans bodywork no. 835 (HLD 529N) which is seen in the Cemetery on 8 April 1977. D M Persson

K R's Car Hire and Photographic Service Ltd

Willowgrove, Chislehurst, Kent

The idea of this route was to link London Transport bus stops at Frognal Corner and Cray Road with St Mary's Hospital. There is considerable doubt as to whether the authorised frequency of 7 minutes was maintained by this minibus operator.

ROUTE PROFILE

	Sidcup (Frognal Corner) – Foot's Cray Road via Watery Lane, Queen Mary's Hospital.
24 May 1960	Introduced. Daily = 7 minutes. Break in service between 12.30 and 1.30pm.
June 1961	Abandoned.

T T French, trading as:

French Car Service

37 Swaffield Road, London SW18

The Danebury Avenue circular was introduced to link a newly constructed housing estate at Alton West with Roehampton before London Transport got around to providing a bus service. As far as is known French's fleet comprised just one Duple bodied Bedford OB, reg. no. HFJ 152, which would have been insufficient to maintain the licensed peak hour frequency.

ROUTE PROFILE

	Alton West Estate – Roehampton Circular via Danebury Avenue.
1 June 1961	Introduced. Weekdays. Licensed to operate every 15 minutes in each direction, increased to 7½ minutes at peak hours.
10 Oct 1961	Believed withdrawn.
Note:	London Transport Route 85A was introduced to Alton West Estate from 11 October 1961.

Samuelson New Transport Co Ltd

(owned jointly by BET and THC groups)

3 Eccleston Place, London SW1

ROUTE PROFILE

	Blackfriars Station – Orpington Station via Elephant & Castle, Herne Hill, West Dulwich, Penge, Beckenham, Bromley, Bickley, Petts Wood.
17 June 1963	Introduced. Night service. Daily (except Saturday / Sunday night).
11 Aug 1963	Short period licence expired.

R W Bird

263 Chipperfield, St Paul's Cray, Kent

ROUTE PROFILE

	Holborn Viaduct Station – Orpington Station. Route as per Samuelson New Transport from Blackfriars Station.
23 Sept 1963	Introduced. Daily. 2 journeys in outward direction only at 01.20am and 01.51am.
Unknown date	Withdrawn. Road service licence surrendered November 1966.

Samuelson New Transport and subsequently R W Bird's services replaced a night train service to Orpington withdrawn by British Railways. Although passengers would mostly have been newspaper workers from the Fleet Street area returning home, the services were available to the general public.

E Clarke & Son (Coaches) Ltd

55 Blenheim Road, Penge, Kent

Clarke's short one mile long route between Elmers End (Green) and Shirley (Orchard Avenue) has the distinction of being the shortest lived bus service operated with a London Transport 'consent' – being abandoned after it is first day of operation! Introduced – and withdrawn – on 13 December 1965 the weekday 30-minute frequency route was intended to provide residents of the The Glade and Orchard Avenue with links to London Transport bus stops at both Elmers End and Wickham Road in Shirley. Apparently the plug was pulled on the route due to difficulties caused by road works.

Substitute Bus Services 1966

As a result of their opposition to cuts in Central Area bus mileage introduced on Sunday 23 January 1966, Central Area crews imposed a ban on the working of voluntary overtime and rest days. London Transport decided to counter the effects of this action by withdrawing operations from sections of routes which were lightly used or covered by other bus routes with the aim of consolidating service on main routes. London Transport's announcement of its intentions sparked much public protest which prompted London Transport to announce, on Thursday 27 January 1966, that it would 'give consent to other operators to run services covering sections of road from which London Transport bus services will be withdrawn completely because of the overtime ban'. Such operators would have to charge standard LT fares.

The first of the 'substitute services' commenced on Monday 31 January 1966. Subsequently agreement was reached on 24 February 1966 between London Transport and Unions representing the crews to end the ban. Although many of the substitute services operated for the last time on Saturday 26 February 1966 London Transport continued to suffer from a shortage of crews which had been exacerbated by staff leaving during the dispute. This meant that some substitute services continued until 19 March 1966. In the case of two routes, 98B and 235, London Transport never did restore a service and these remained in independent hands.

Most substitute services covered only part of the London Transport route for which they substituted. Four London Transport routes, 52, 52A, 151 and 261, had different sections covered by different operators. Only five London Transport routes were worked from terminal to terminal by a substitute service – 160, 234, 235, 261 and 265. All the substitute services ran in the suburbs, the nearest approach to Central London being Pulleine Coaches on the 52, 52A at Notting Hill Gate and Seth Coaches on the 187A at St John's Wood. Contemporary reports suggest that the services were in general well received by the public, the use of luxury coaches in many cases being complemented by courtesy and helpfulness shown by the operating staff. John Page, MP for Harrow West and a critic of London Transport's monopoly status, had introduced a Private Member's Bill in Parliament seeking to break London Transport's monopoly which, by a singular

A VARIETY OF OPERATORS WORKING 'SUBSTITUTE SERVICES'

Substitute services were introduced at very short notice, most operators using coaches. Route information displayed on the vehicles ranged form non-existent to elaborate. Ticket systems varied too. Some operators did not bother with tickets at all, others issued cloakroom tickets. A number including Conway Hunt, Hall's Coaches and Pulleine Coaches used traditional Bell Punch tickets. Valliant issued Ultimate tickets from hastily acquired brand new ticket machines.

Hall's Coaches brand new Plaxton Panorama bodied Bedford VAL14 reg.no. LHM 24D is seen in Staines Road Feltham on 18 February 1966 covering Route 116. 'Minimax' referred to on the destination display was a factory not a fare system! T Wright

Leesway Coaches used Plaxton bodied Bedford SBO reg.no. NWW 514 still bearing the livery and sporting the fleetname of its previous owner Ryland Coaches. It is seen at South Harrow Station with an exemplary route information display which included showing the route number 187 three times. T Wright

coincidence, came before the House of Commons on 8 February 1966 during the dispute. Although his Bill was defeated Mr Page described the substitute services as 'the biggest break in the London Transport bus monopoly for 40 years'.

Southgate Coaches acquired Burlingham bodied Ford 'Thames' 570E reg. no. TKY 688 from Valliant Direct Coaches in January 1966 pressing it straight into service on substitute Route 125. Lacking any route information display the coach is seen at Hampden Square, Oridge on 5 February 1966.
J G S Smith / courtesy J C Gillham

SUBSTITUTE BUS SERVICES 1966

Operator	LT route number	Terminals	Days of operation	Period of operation	Frequency in minutes
Capital Coaches Ltd	234A	Purley – Old Lodge Lane	Sat Sun	5 Feb – 19 Mar	10/40
Carshalton Belle	151	St Helier Ave – Hackbridge	Daily	31 Jan – 26 Feb	15/30
Coachmaster Tours	234	Wallington – Selsdon	Sat	5 Feb – 26 Feb	30
Conway Hunt Ltd	9	Hammersmith Broadway – Mortlake	Weekdays	§	
	27	Twickenham Station–Teddington Station	Sat Sun	§	
	285	Kingston – London Airport Central	Daily	12 Feb – 26 Feb	30
Lewis Cronshaw Ltd	52/52A	Burnt Oak – Neasden	Daily	31 Jan – 26 Feb	15
	240	Mill Hill Broadway – Golders Green	Weekdays	31 Jan – 19 Feb	20
	245A	Golders Green – Cricklewood	Sat	5 Feb – 19 Mar	15
Finsbury Coaches Ltd	261	Arnos Grove – Barnet (Chesterfield Rd)	Weekdays	11 Feb – 19 Mar	90
Fountain Coaches Ltd	90	Staines Bridge – Hanworth	Daily	31 Jan – 19 Feb	15/60
Hall's Coaches Ltd	116	Staines Bridge – Feltham	Daily	31 Jan – 19 Feb	20
Happy Wanderer Coaches	265	Kingston – Copt Gilders Estate	Weekdays	12 Feb – 26 Feb	30/60
Leesway Coaches	187	Alperton Station – South Harrow Station	Sat Sun	5 Feb – 19 Mar	30
Leighton Coach Co Ltd	162/162A	Barking – Mayesbrook Park	Weekdays	17 Feb – 26 Feb	30
Linkline Coaches	187	Kensal Rise Station – Harlesden	Sat Sun	5 Feb – 19 Mar	¶
Modern Travel	162	Wanstead Station – Forest Gate Station	Mon–Fri	21 Feb – 25 Feb	¶
Paynes Coaches (Croydon) Ltd	151	Belmont – Carshalton	Weekdays	7 Feb – 26 Feb	15/30
Popular Coaches Ltd	56	Poplar – Cubitt Town	Mon–Fri	8 Feb – 18 Mar	15/20
Pulleine Coaches	52/A	Notting Hill Gate – Harrow Road	Daily	14 Feb – 26 Feb	10
	160/160A	Catford – Welling	Sat Sun	12 Feb – 13 Mar	40/80
Charles Rickard (Tours) Ltd	97	Brentford – Northfields Station	Daily	§	
Seth Coaches Ltd	187/187A	Hampstead Heath – Maida Vale	Daily	2 Feb – 18 Mar	15/30
Southgate Coaches	125	Whetstone – Southgate Station (extended Sundays to Winchmore Hill)	Daily	31 Jan – 26 Feb	15/30
Super Coaches (Upminster) Ltd	169B	Barkingside – Hainhault Industrial Estate	M–F peaks	31 Jan – 25 Feb	30
Thames Weald Ltd	89	Bexley Station – Blackfen	Weekdays	3 Feb – 26 Feb	40/80
	89	Welling Corner – Blackheath Station	Weekdays	3 Feb – 26 Feb	40/80
Twentieth Century Coaches	261	Barnet (Church) – Barnet (Chesterfield Rd)	M–F peaks	3 Feb – 19 Mar	20
Valliant Direct Coaches Ltd	79/79A	Wembley – Queensbury	Weekdays	31 Jan – 26 Feb	15
	79/79A	Perivale – Alperton	Weekdays	4 Feb – 26 Feb	15/30
	97	Ealing Broadway – Greenford	Daily	18 Feb – 26 Feb	¶
	230	Rayners Lane Station – Kenton	M–F peaks	31 Jan – 18 Mar	15
Wimbledon Coaches	189	Clapham South Station – South Wimbledon	Mon–Fri	7 Feb – 18 Mar	15/30

Key:	
Mon–Fri	Mondays to Fridays
M–F peaks	Monday to Friday peak hours
Sat	Saturdays
Sun	Sundays
Weekdays	Mondays to Saturdays
§	Authorised but no evidence of operation
¶	Not known

CAPITAL COACHES LTD.

FARE **4ᴰ** SINGLE

ROUTE 234a

To hire this Coach telephone :
REGent 4987.

252

Hall's Coaches 1965 built
Plaxton bodied Bedford SB5
reg no. FGF 472C discharges
passengers in Clarence
Street, Staines whilst
working Route 116.
J M Aldridge

Capital Coaches locally printed ticket for Route 234A.
J M Aldridge collection

Routes 98B and 235

These two routes, which remained in independent hands after the London
Transport dispute was settled, experienced mixed fortunes. Short Richmond

Continental Pioneer's
reg.no. FMO 946 was a
former Thames Valley
1951-built ECW-bodied
Bristol LL6B. In a practice

adopted by various group
operators the bus was
subsequently rebuilt for one
man operation. This
involved moving the

entrance from rear to front
along with the instalment
of a hatch for fare collection
– a rather awkward
arrangement for the driver

who had to twist sideways
on his seat. The bus is seen
at Friar's Stile Road
terminus, Richmond Hill.
M J Dryhurst

Hill Route 235 continued substantially unchanged in independent hands for over 14 years. In contrast Route 98B experienced a much more chequered history. London Transport routes 98 (Saturdays) and 98B (Mondays–Fridays and Sundays) were lengthy operations fringing the western extremities of the Central Area working from Hounslow (98) or Feltham (98B) to Rayners Lane Station, both being withdrawn at the beginning of the 1966 dispute. The Harrow Public Transport Users Association played a pivotal role in encouraging independent operation to cover the section northwards from Ruislip. Progress faltered frequently – in the first five years of independent operation no fewer than six different undertakings attempted to run the 98B – with significant periods when no service at all operated. Finally, from May 1971, stability was achieved after Elmtree Transport took up the route.

When it acquired 1949 built Leyland Titan RTL 633 from London Transport in October 1965, Isleworth Coaches would have had no expectation of becoming the operator of London Transport Route 235 just three months later. As a consequence of the shake-up following London Transport crews' overtime ban in early 1966 operation of Route 235 passed to Isleworth Coaches from 31 January 1966. Still displaying its LT fleet number but with London Transport fleet name painted over, RTL 633 was photographed working route 235 on 14 July 1966. G Mead

ROUTE PROFILE

Route 235	Richmond Station – Richmond Hill (Friar's Stile Road).
31 Jan 1966	Introduced. Operated by D C Blackford (trading as Isleworth Coaches) Lower Square, Isleworth, Middlesex. Weekdays = 20/30 minutes.
8 May 1968	Acquired by Continental Pioneer Holidays Ltd (trading as Pioneer Coaches) 4 Church Court, George Street, Richmond, Surrey. Frequency now: Weekdays = 30 minutes (Monday–Friday peaks = 22 minutes).
April 1974	Title changed to Continental Pioneer Ltd, Cedar Terrace, Richmond.
31 Aug 1976	Circular terminal working introduced at Richmond Hill.
27 Sept 1980	Withdrawn.
Notes:	1. London Transport Route 235 was withdrawn after operation on 29 January 1966.
	2. London Transport Route 71 was diverted to absorb this service from 29 September 1980.

Continental Pioneer habitually used former London Transport RF class vehicles on Route 235. Reg.no. LYF 394 started life in 1951 as Green Line coach RF 43 passing to London Country in 1970. The bus is seen in Sheen Road, Richmond on 2 April 1977.

Map of Elmtree Transport operated Route 98B with connecting London Transport Services – Summer 1976.

This vehicle was subsequently owned by a series of preservationists after sale by Continental Pioneer in 1978. Following serious fire damage the remains passed to Metrobus Ltd in 1994 as a source of spares. D M Persson

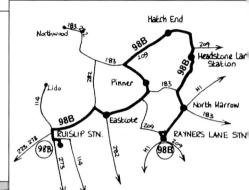

Willowbrook dual-purpose bodied Ford R192 reg.no. PGX 235L was bought new by Continental Pioneer in 1973 for use as the '235 Hill Bus'. J M Aldridge

Confused passenger? The potential passenger reading the timetable display at North Harrow Station might well have been bemused by the stop/go antics on Route 98B and not realised that a coach had replaced the expected red London Transport RT class double decker. Duple Britannia-bodied AEC Reliance reg.no. YVD 656 is seen in May 1966 during Valliant Direct Coaches brief four week tenure on Route 98B.
M J Dryhurst

Elm's Coaches assumption of operation of Route 98B heralded a period of relative stability. Amongst the variety of interesting vehicles used by Elm's Coaches on the route were two very rare 1955-built Harrington Contender chassisless buses originally supplied new to Maidstone & District. Powered by a distinctive sounding Rootes TS3 2-stroke diesel engine reg. no. UKN 209 was photographed in Ruislip in May 1967. C Essex

Former Yorkshire Woollen District Park Royal-bodied AEC Reliance reg.no. DHD 193 was caught by the camera at Ruislip Station during Atlas Coaches two month stint in 1970 on the 98B. Behind stands London Transport's Uxbridge Garage based RT 2299 (KGU 328).
Photobus / R Marshall

ROUTE PROFILE

Route 98B	**Ruislip (Station) – Rayners Lane (Station)** via Eastcote, Pinner, Hatch End, Headstone Lane, North Harrow.
15 Feb 1966	Introduced. Operated Ruislip – Pinner. Weekdays = 30 minutes. Operator: World Wide Coaches Ltd 90/110 Camberwell Road, London SE 5.
24 Feb 1966	Withdrawn.
25 Feb 1966	Re-introduced. Operated Ruislip – Pinner. Weekdays = 30 minutes. Operator: Hall's Coaches Ltd, Hounslow, Middlesex.
1 March 1966	Withdrawn.
2 May 1966	Re-introduced. Operated Ruislip – North Harrow. Weekdays =60 minutes. Operator: Valliant Direct Coaches Ltd, 77 New Broadway, Ealing, London W5.
28 May 1966	Withdrawn.
1 Aug 1966	Re-introduced. Operated Ruislip – North Harrow. Weekdays = 30 minutes. Operator: H F Cheek & Sons (t/a Elm's Coaches), 384 Kenton Road, Kenton, Middlesex.
28 Nov 1966	Extended to Rayners Lane Station. Service now Ruislip – Rayners Lane Station. Weekdays = 30 minutes.
26 March 1970	Withdrawn.
31 March 1970	Re-introduced. Weekdays = 30 minutes. Operator: A H Plaskow and M Margo (t/a Atlas Coaches) 44 The Highlands, Edgware, Middlesex.
23 May 1970	Withdrawn.
23 Oct 1970	Re-introduced. Weekdays = 80 minutes. Operator: A G Bassom and M Thornton (t/a Thamesmead Motor Services), London SE 21.
21 Nov 1970	Saturday service discontinued.
14 Dec 1970	Operation of Monday–Friday service became erratic.
7 Jan 1971	Withdrawn.
24 May 1971	Re-introduced. Mondays–Fridays = 45 minutes. Operator: B J P Cheek (t/a Elmtree Transport), Canning Road, Wealdstone, Middlesex.
12 July 1985	Extant.

98B

**RUISLIP STATION — PINNER
HATCH END — NORTH HARROW
RAYNERS LANE STATION**

DAILY EXCEPT SUNDAYS

	a.m.	a.m.	a.m.	p.m.	p.m.	p.m.	p.m.	p.m.
Ruislip Stn.	8.15	9.35	10.55	12.15	1.35	2.55	4.15	5.35
Eastcote Village	8.22	9.42	11.2	12.22	1.42	3.2	4.22	5.42
Pinner Red Lion	8.29	9.49	11.9	12.29	1.49	3.9	4.29	5.49
Hatch End Stn.	8.37	9.57	11.17	12.37	1.57	3.17	4.37	5.57
Headstone Lane Stn.	8.41	10.1	11.21	12.41	2.1	3.21	4.41	6.1
North Harrow Stn.	8.47	10.7	11.27	12.47	2.7	3.27	4.47	6.7
Rayners Lane Stn.	8.50	10.10	11.30	12.50	2.10	3.30	4.50	6.10

	a.m.	a.m.	a.m.	p.m.	p.m.	p.m.	p.m.	p.m.
Rayners Lane Stn.	8.55	10.15	11.35	12.55	2.15	3.35	4.55	6.15
North Harrow Stn.	8.58	10.18	11.38	12.58	2.18	3.38	4.58	6.18
Headstone Lane Stn.	9.4	10.24	11.44	1.4	2.24	3.44	5.4	6.24
Hatch End Stn.	9.8	10.28	11.48	1.8	2.28	3.48	5.8	6.28
Pinner Red Lion	9.16	10.36	11.56	1.16	2.36	3.56	5.16	6.36
Eastcote Village	9.23	10.43	12.3	1.23	2.43	4.3	5.23	6.43
Ruislip Stn.	9.30	10.50	12.10	1.30	2.50	4.10	5.30	6.50

BUSES STOP AT ALL THE USUAL INTERMEDIATE STOPS

Please tender the correct fare as buses may be one man operated

THAMESMEAD MOTOR SERVICES

Proprietors: A. Bassom   M. Thornton

Ia COURT LANE, DULWICH, LONDON, S.E.21

Telephone: ERITH 31011

T/T No. 1

October 1970

Still sporting an NBC motif former Eastern Counties 1961-built ECW-bodied Bristol MW5G reg.no. 8008 VF of Elmtree Transport was photographed on the 98B in February 1977. It looks like a tight squeeze for the Mini! G W Morant

A dedicated 'Omnibus Terminal' off Bedfont Lane to the north of Feltham Station dated back to West London Coachways introduction of the Bedfont route on 1 September 1955. Former East Midland Leyland Tiger Cub reg.no. ORR 345 is seen at the terminal on 8 April 1967 some three months after Golden Miller's acquisition of the route. Within a further three years the terminal had been moved to the opposite side of Bedfont Lane. J C Gillham

F G Wilder & Son Ltd, trading as:

Golden Miller Services

Fern Grove, Feltham, Middlesex

From January 1985 associated with Telling's Coaches of Weybridge Ltd, 20A Wintersells Road, Byfleet, Surrey

Coach operator Golden Miller diversified into bus operation on 20 January 1967 with the acquisition from Tourist Coachways of the first post-Chambers Report independently operated London bus service from Feltham Station to Bedfont. This route was numbered 601 on 1 February 1968. That same date saw Golden Miller introduce two further routes from Feltham to Shepperton (602) and Hanworth (603). In October 1970 Golden Miller became involved with the operation of the long established Walton Station bus

Golden Miller Bus Routes – Summer 1976.

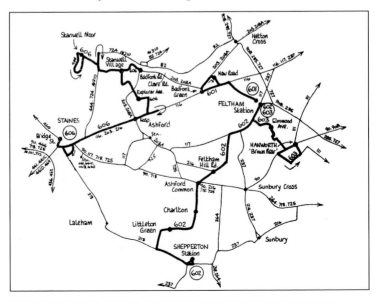

Golden Miller bought this 1967 Strachans-bodied Ford R192 bus reg.no. TUR 347E from Bream Coach Services of Hemel Hempstead following acquisition of that operator's Long Chaulden route by London Transport. The bus is seen on 22 June 1970 on the southern forecourt at Feltham station used as a terminal point for routes 602 and 603. The destination blind is set for a short working to Charlton Village as Route 602A.
P R Wallis

Golden Miller's reg.no. FMO 24 was supplied new to Thames Valley in 1950 as a half cab Windover-bodied Bristol L6B coach. In 1958 Thames Valley scrapped the original body, rebuilt the chassis to 30ft length and installed a Gardner 5LW engine. Eastern Coach Works then fitted a brand new 39-seat full fronted body suitable for one-man operation. The re-designated Bristol LL5G bus was photographed on Feltham station's southern forecourt in September 1970. T K Brookes

Golden Miller's Plaxton-bodied Bedford YRQ reg.no. SYO 602N is seen in July 1975 setting off down Feltham High Street bound for Shepperton on Route 602. Capital Transport

Rear-engined Leyland Panther Cub saloons did not always prove popular with their original operators so creating good bargains on the second hand market. Former Park Royal-bodied models supplied new in 1965 to Manchester City Transport passed to SELNEC Passenger Executive on its formation on 1 November 1969. The latter quickly withdrew them in 1970/71. Reg.nos. BND 868C and BND 876C both passed to Golden Miller being seen together at Feltham Station terminus in July 1972.
T Wright

A pair of 1961-built AEC Reliances fitted with 45-seat Roe bodies built to Park Royal design and originally supplied new to Doncaster Corporation Transport were acquired by Golden Miller via dealer North of Sherburn-in-Elmet in November 1970. Reg.no. 8629 DT was photographed in September 1971.
G W Morant

service as described in Chapter 5. Golden Miller introduced a further bus route on 1 November 1971 when Route 606 started working between Staines and Stanwell Moor. The pattern for many future years operation was thus established needing four buses, one each on routes 601, 602, 603, and 606. Fare boxes were fitted to speed up operations.

ROUTE PROFILE

Route 602	Feltham Station – Shepperton Station via Ashford Common, Charlton.
1 Feb 1968	Introduced. Weekdays = 1 hour.
13 May 1968	Short workings introduced Feltham – Charlton Village numbered 602A.
c 1971	602A short workings discontinued.
30 March 1985	Saturday service discontinued.
8 April 1985	Frequency reduced to Mondays–Fridays = 4 journeys
12 July 1985	Extant.

ROUTE PROFILE

Route 603	Feltham Station – Hanworth via Elmwood Avenue.
1 Feb 1968	Introduced. Weekdays = 1 hour.
9 June 1969	Frequency increased to 30 minutes (20mins morning peak).
6 April 1985	Frequency altered to 25/35 minutes.
12 July 1985	Extant.

Route 605	Stanwell Moor – Stanwell Schools
Sept 1976	Introduced.Schooldays only, two return journeys
4 April 1985	Withdrawn

ROUTE PROFILE

Route 606	Staines – Stanwell Moor via Stanwell Village.
1 Nov 1971	Introduced. Weekdays = 1 hour. Operated Staines (Station) – Stanwell Village. Extended irregularly to Stanwell Moor.
15 July 1972	Projected in Staines to terminate Moor Lane.
By Aug 1981	Staines terminal now Bus Station.
12 July 1985	Extant.

P C Sampson, trading as:

Sampson Coaches

53 Chandos Road, Cheshunt, Hertfordshire

From 10 January 1972:

Sampson Coaches and Travel Ltd

250 Turners Hill, Cheshunt, Hertfordshire

ROUTE PROFILE

	Hammond Street – Chase Farm Hospital via Cheshunt, Waltham Cross, Forty Hill.
7 Jan 1968	Introduced. Operated Cheshunt – Chase Farm Hospital. Sundays and Bank Holidays. 1 journey.
15 Dec 1969	Extended to commence from Hammond Street.
26 Dec 1969	Bank Holiday operation ceased.
21 June 1970	Abandoned.
Feb 1975	Re-introduced. Now operated via Enfield in lieu of Forty Hill.
March 1975	Abandoned.

L G Orpwood, trading as:

C & O Motors

246 Brook Street, Northumberland Heath, Erith, Kent

This short lived operation offered a Sunday service over the Bexleyheath – Slade Green section of London Transport Route 122 (Crystal Palace – Slade Green Station) which latter operator did not cover that portion of the route on Sundays.

The route proved to be a precursor for the larger scale operations of Thamesmead Motor Services, detailed in Chapter 9. Andrew Bassom, who was regularly the conductor on one of the Duple-bodied Ford Thames Trader coaches often used by C & O Motors, subsequently became co-founder of Thamesmead Motor Services.

ROUTE PROFILE

	Bexleyheath – Slade Green Station via Barnehurst, Northumberland Heath.
6 Oct 1968	Introduced. Sundays only = 60 minutes. No local passengers conveyed Bexleyheath – top of Colyers Lane, Northumberland Heath.
22 Dec 1968	Frequency became irregular – total 16 journeys.
11 May 1969	Abandoned.

Principals of Orpington area
Independent bus operators
1963–1981.

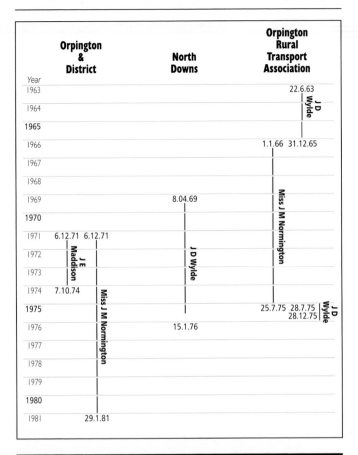

CHAPTER 8

Orpington Area 1963–1985

This area became a focus for intensive independent bus activity. Although wholly within London Transport's Central Area, and subsequently the revised London Transport/Greater London Council Area, London Transport appeared unable or unwilling to plug a significant operational gap with its own bus service provision. For just over four years, from December 1971, three independent operators, North Downs, Orpington Rural Transport Association and Orpington & District existed somewhat uneasily side by side. The situation was further complicated by dual appointments held by certain of the principals of these businesses. A study of the Route Profiles will reveal the mixed fortunes of the various routes. Over the period reviewed the original Orpington Rural Transport Association route from Orpington to Biggin Hill was covered, at various times, by four different operators whilst the East Croydon – Orpington road was served by no less than six different undertakings.

Orpington Rural Transport Association

4 Tower Road, Orpington, Kent
By 1972 office at: 7 Moyser Drive, Orpington, Kent

Orpington achieved national prominence in 1962 when a stunning by-election victory was won by Liberal MP Eric Lubbock. Local Liberal Councillors were active on constituency affairs, too. One initiative led to he formation of the Orpington Rural Transport Association with the aim of promoting a bus service between Biggin Hill and Orpington via Berry's Green and Downe. John Wylde, a schoolteacher who had also gained previous experience working with London Transport, principally as a scheduler, was appointed Honorary Operating Manager.

The Association's initial application for London Transport's 'consent' goaded a reluctant London Transport into introducing its own experimental Route 479 between the terminals. In their wisdom London Transport refused to route the 479 via Berry's Green and Downe, where the Association felt that most demand existed. London Transport quickly justified its own scepticism – according to John Wylde 'London Transport regarded routes operated with GS class vehicles as non viable *ipso facto*' – and declared the 479 trial a failure thereafter granting the Association a 'consent'. Operation by Orpington Rural Transport started on 22 June 1963, initially using a Bedford CA minibus hired from Westerham Coaches. The route was operated for over one year using volunteer drivers but an increase in the level of service, from 1 September 1964, justified the employment of the first full time driver. The service continued to grow apace. A regular headway weekday timetable was implemented form 22 March 1965 whilst on 1 January 1966 Miss Joan M Normington, a former Women's Royal Army Corps vehicle maintenance instructor, was appointed Operating Manager.

Orpington Rural Transport Association 2s 3d single/return ticket and 1s 9d geographical stage tickets. Both were printed for ORTA by John Russell, a friend of John Wylde, using a home use Adana printing machine.
North Downs Collection

Orpington Rural Transport Association's 12-seat Austin J2 Omnicoach reg.no. NPV 828 was photographed on 18 July 1964 at the then terminal for inward bound journeys to Orpington in Sevenoaks Road – designated War Memorial. On 1 September 1964, coincident with an upgrading of the Orpington – Biggin Hill route from two days per week to four days per week operation, the service was projected to terminate at Orpington Station. Photobus / R Marshall

In 1965 the ORTA purchased two new 12-seat Commer 2500 series minibuses. Coach builders Harrington converted the bodies to include a raised roof over the gangway to meet then current headroom requirements for PSV minibuses. A roller blind destination display was incorporated whilst the sides of the roofs, as well as the rear doors, were used for advertising displays. Reg.no. FPM 282C is seen on lay-over at Biggin Hill Post Office. C F Klapper

ORPINGTON RURAL TRANSPORT

CROWN TICKET

AVAILABLE FOR
UNLIMITED TRAVEL
ON DAY OF ISSUE
BETWEEN 09.00 & 17.00

5/

Orpington Rural Transport
Association home printed 5s
Crown Ticket.
North Downs Collection

On 28 March 1967 the Orpington Rural Transport route expanded considerably with projections beyond Biggin Hill to both New Addington and Tatsfield – although service to the latter was frustrated by inadequate road surfaces and was soon suspended. The other extension proved much more successful, affording connectional facilities at New Addington with London Transport bus routes into Croydon – a principal shopping centre as well as railhead for the district.

Orpington Rural Transport's operations broadly continued to this now established pattern for several more years, although the Saturday service was curtailed to work from Orpington to Biggin Hill only from 23 March 1970. The early 1970s saw Orpington Rural Transport experience increasing financial difficulties. Saturday operation was axed after 30 June 1973. Although a modest route extension was implemented in September 1974, to serve the new Hillingdale Estate at Biggin Hill Valley, operational difficulties persisted. Miss Normington, who since December 1971 had combined the dual responsibilities of being Operating Manager of the Orpington Rural Transport Association with that as a principal of Orpington & District, resigned from the former post on 25 July 1975. By this juncture the partners of the Association had made contact with John Wylde – Orpington Rural Transport Association's original Operating Manager, by now the principal of North Downs. An accommodation was reached whereby John Wylde was re-appointed as the Association's Operating Manager from 28 July 1975. Effectively North Downs all but took over the Association's route, giving it route number 858 in the North Downs 'series', although the route remained licensed to the Orpington Rural Transport Association with North Downs' vehicles operating legally 'on hire' to the Association.

The declining fortunes of North Downs itself soon impacted this arrangement with John Wylde resigning as the Association's Operating Manager on 12 December 1975. To avoid any further deterioration in its by-now perilous financial position the Association's partners immediately disbanded the Orpington Rural Transport Association. As will be seen from the Route Profile subsequent operation over the Orpington – Biggin Hill Valley road was assumed by Miss Normington's Orpington & District concern.

J. D. Wylde, Mrs M F Wylde and R H Edwards trading as:

North Downs Rural Transport

1 Tower Road, Orpington, Kent

On 2 November 1970 North Downs Transport Services Limited, with registered office at Oast House Way, Orpington, Kent was formed. It was the intention that this new company should acquire the assets and take control of the Orpington based operations of the North Downs Rural Transport partnership. The timing was coincident with the formation of North Downs Rural Transport Limited which absorbed the partnership's interests in the Horsham area (see Chapter 6). In the event North Downs Transport Services Limited remained dormant and the partnership of J D Wylde, Mrs M F Wylde and R H Edwards continued to trade in respect of Orpington based activities, although adopting a revised trading title of:

North Downs

North Downs 3d numerical stage ticket produced by Glasgow Numerical Printing Co. Ltd. and overwritten by hand to increase fare value to 6d. North Downs Collection

Subsequent changes of office:

    c April 1971: The Garage, Forest Green, Dorking, Surrey
      April 1972: Oast House Way, Cray Avenue, Orpington, Kent
    September 1972: 4 Tower Road, Orpington, Kent

NORTH
DOWNS
TRANSPORT

ADULT

36p

RETURN

North Downs 36p Adult Return ticket printed by John Wylde using a home use Adana printing machine. North Downs Collection

With no direct London Transport bus service between Croydon and Orpington, passengers contemplating such a journey mostly chose to travel by London Transport Route 119 to Bromley, once there changing to Route 61 for Orpington – an indirect and time consuming journey. In 1968 the Orpington Rural Transport Association partnership considered the prospects of an application to London Transport for a 'consent' to run a through bus route from Croydon to Orpington. They did not proceed with such application partly because a £500 loan, obtained from the London Borough of Bromley in connection with the extension of their existing route from Biggin Hill to New Addington, prevented them from undertaking further expansion until that loan was repaid. It was not – in any case they thought London Transport would refuse 'consent'.

John Wylde, former Operating Manager of the Orpington Rural Transport Association, formed a partnership with his wife Mary and Roy Edwards. The trading name North Downs Rural Transport was adopted to signify a kindred spirit with the Orpington Rural Transport Association. London Transport's 'consent' for an East Croydon – Orpington bus route was obtained remarkably quickly but the applicants were most surprised to receive an objection to their road service licence application from the Orpington Rural Transport Association. On enquiry John Wylde discovered that the objection had been lodged by Miss Normington, as Operating Manager of the Orpington Rural Transport Association without reference to its partners – although the latter took no subsequent action to have the objection withdrawn. John Wylde felt saddened that 'the intention of amicability and co-operation between the two Rural Transport undertakings was thus sadly frustrated'.

In the meantime, as detailed in Chapter 6, North Downs became involved in Horsham area operations which began on 8 April 1969 – the same day as the delayed East Croydon – Orpington service started. Route numbers in an 85x series, reminiscent of previous London Transport Country Bus practice in the areas, were introduced later in 1969. From 23 August 1970 there was substantial expansion of North Downs outer London operations.

North Downs first Ford Transit 1969 built Williams Deansgate-bodied no. 2 (APX 928G) is dwarfed by London Transport's Sidcup Garage based RT 3301 (LYR 520) in this shot taken at Orpington station on 21 February 1971. The North Downs minibus was working a Sunday service on Route 854 to Ramsden Estate – a route covered on weekdays by London Country Route 493. Behind stands a Maidstone & District Daimler Fleetline working rail replacement duties on contract to British Railways. This view dates from a very significant time in British history – On 15 February 1971 the country formally adopted the use of decimal currency. Most bus operators changed to decimal currency one week later on 21 February 1971. A G Whitlam

---

NORTH DOWNS

Season Ticket no. _0 0 5_

From   3 0 OCT 1972

Until   2 9 ~~OCT~~ NOV 1972

BETWEEN ORPINGTON
AND EAST CROYDON

This ticket is NOT TRANSFERABLE and must be given up on expiry.

Signed _M. Gregory_ (Holder)

Issued by _C Slater_

Rate £ 7.50

North Downs home produced monthly season ticket, in this case with manual correction. North Downs Collection

---

New Route 855 (Croydon to Forestdale) was introduced, Route 853 (Orpington – Croydon) was doubled in frequency and Sunday Route 854 (Orpington – Ramsden Estate) started. The peak vehicle requirement ran to six buses at Orpington as well as a further two at Horsham.

The Horsham area operations further expanded with the acquisition of A T Brady's Brown Motor Services on 2 November 1970. However severe problems began to be experienced, leading to reductions in frequency and, finally, abandonment of the Horsham operations after 15 April 1972. Thereafter North Downs operation was concentrated on Route 853 between East Croydon and Orpington. Problems still beset the partnership, a particular difficulty emerging in 1974 was the expiry, at short notice, of the lease on the Old Fordyce Yard at Orpington, which could accommodate full size buses. North Downs reverted to the use of Ford Transit minibuses which could, if necessary, be parked overnight in the street. By this time John Wylde had obtained employment as Transport Co-ordinator with Leicestershire County Council and was necessarily absent from the Orpington area much of the time. His subsequent appointment to a post with Northumberland County Council in November 1975 heralded the end of the late, brief accord between Orpington Rural Transport Association and North Downs, with the demise of the former. North Downs operations lingered on fitfully over the New Year before Route 853 was abandoned on 15 January 1976. John Wylde explained that 'The Certificates of Fitness for the minibuses were due to expire and it was felt that it was not justifiable to seek a renewal'.

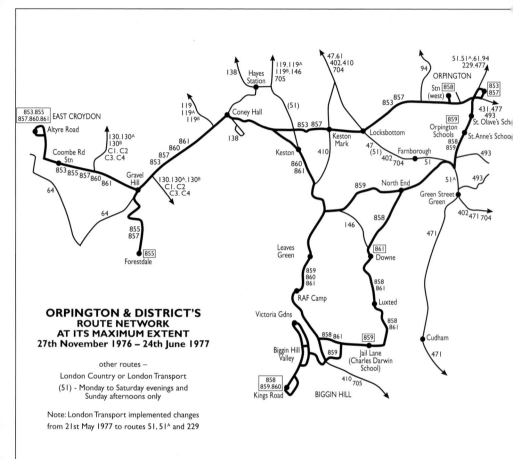

ORPINGTON & DISTRICT'S
ROUTE NETWORK
AT ITS MAXIMUM EXTENT
27th November 1976 – 24th June 1977

other routes –
London Country or London Transport
(51) - Monday to Saturday evenings and
Sunday afternoons only

Note: London Transport implemented changes
from 21st May 1977 to routes 51, 51^ and 229

J E Maddison and Miss J M Normington, trading as:

Orpington & District Omnibuses

1 Tower Road, Orpington, Kent

On 7 October 1974 J E Maddison left the partnership. Miss J M Normington continued as Principal.

Office now at: 7 Moyser Drive, Orpington, Kent

The decision by North Downs to withdraw from the Forestdale route in 1971 opened a window of opportunity that led to the formation of Orpington & District. John Maddison, a foreman driver with North Downs, joined in partnership with Miss Normington. Whilst Maddison left North Downs employment, Miss Normington retained her post as Operating Manager of the Orpington Rural Transport Association successfully juggling both commitments for a further four years. Operation of the Forestdale route started on 6 December 1971 using full size saloons, better able to cope with the high peak demands than North Downs minibuses. An ambitious leap into Sunday

Orpington & District reg.no. MKG 479 was a former Western Welsh 1956-built Willowbrook bodied Leyland Tiger Cub. This bus is seen turning from Addiscombe Road into Park Hill Road at East Croydon working the Forestdale route in March 1973. G W Morant

operations followed in June 1972. As well as the Forestdale route workings were extended on this day to cover withdrawn North Downs facilities on the East Croydon – Orpington and Orpington – Ramsden Estate routes. These operations did not prove lucrative and were withdrawn in February 1973.

The difficulties being experienced by both North Downs and the Orpington Rural Transport Association towards the end of 1975 resulted in a quantum leap in the scale of Orpington & District's operation. On 15 December 1975 Orpington & District assumed operation of the Orpington Rural Transport Association's Orpington – Biggin Hill route. On 24 January 1976 Orpington & District, by then the sole surviving independent bus operator in the Orpington area, took up the East Croydon – Orpington route following the collapse of North Downs earlier that month. The introduction of new Route 860 from Biggin Hill to East Croydon on 5 January 1976 was intended to partially compensate for the abandonment of the section of the former Orpington Rural Transport Association route from Biggin Hill to New Addington from which point many passengers had transferred to London Transport's Croydon-bound buses.

Orpington & District combined much school contract work with its stage carriage services leading to a high double-deck content of its fleet. Eight second-hand Leyland Atlanteans were operated including no. 3 (NRN 563) which was a 1960-built Metro-Cammell bodied PDR 1/1 model originally new to Ribble Motor Services. This bus is seen in November 1977 travelling along Coombe Road in New Addington. C Essex

With additional commitments, demands on the Orpington & District fleet increased. Before too long strains were felt and the need to release vehicles for school duties led to the demise of the recently introduced 860 in June 1977. Despite having secured a sound operating base at Oak Farm, Farnborough Hill, Orpington & District started to enter that downward spiral experienced by its immediate independent predecessors in the area. Service reliability began to decline whilst vehicle maintenance problems increased. John Winter, employed by Orpington & District at this time, observed in WYLDE'S REFLECTIONS ON PUBLIC TRANSPORT, published by John Wylde, that a proposal to bring four key employees into partnership was frustrated by Miss Normington. Working relationships became strained and unfortunately Miss Normington became ill. By early 1981 Orpington & District was collapsing. Routes faltered and failed, with the final service being withdrawn from the Forestdale route on 27 February 1981.

Tillingbourne Bus Co Ltd
Little Mead, Cranleigh, Surrey

From August 1981 the title for Orpington area operation became:

Tillingbourne (Metropolitan) Ltd
Tillingbourne Valley, whose Surrey operations left the scope of this book when London Transport's Country Bus Department passed to the National Bus Company on 1 January 1970, was purchased from the Trice family by Trevor Brown in September 1970. Absorbing much of the former North Downs Horsham area operations in 1972 Tillingbourne continued to expand steadily. The company's name was changed to Tillingbourne Bus Co Ltd in December 1972 to reflect its wider sphere of operation.

Bus enthusiast Peter Larking, a Local Government Officer, undertook occasional part time driving duties for Tillingbourne. When Orpington & District failed he, together with colleagues Gary Wood and Mark MacWilliams, persuaded Trevor Brown and Barry King, Managing Director of Tillingbourne, that potential for independent bus operation existed in the Orpington area. Tillingbourne agreed to a trial run of a peak hour service on the Forestdale route from March 1981. The results were encouraging and from 21 April 1981 Tillingbourne took up operation of the East Croydon –

Tillingbourne (Metropolitan) Ltd operated 1983-built 53-seat Duple Dominant AEC Reliance reg.no. JTM 109V which originated with 'parent' Tillingbourne Bus Co.Ltd. This Croydon bound bus was photographed in Croydon Road, Hayes Common in February 1982.
G W Morant

Orpington route. In August 1981 Peter Larking and his two colleagues were appointed Directors of Tillingbourne (Metropolitan) Ltd. This new operation proved successful but over the next two years differences in emphasis emerged between the Cranleigh based and Orpington based Directors. In particular Peter Larking and his colleagues were keen to develop private hire and tour work, which activity was something of an anathema to Trevor Brown and Barry King. Negotiations led to a management buy-out with Peter Larking and Gary Wood (Mark MacWilliams having previously left the company) purchasing the shares of Tillingbourne (Metropolitan) Ltd.

Metrobus former West Riding 1972-built Northern Counties bodied Daimler Fleetline reg.no. BHL 624K was photographed pulling away from the Fairfields Hall terminus in Park Lane, Croydon during March 1985.
G W Morant

Metrobus Ltd

The Bus Garage, Oak Farm, Farnborough, Kent

With Peter Larking and Gary Wood as Directors, Metrobus started operations on 24 September 1983 acquiring the routes and vehicles previously operated by Tillingbourne (Metropolitan) Ltd.

C Springham, trading as:

Crystal's Coaches

Bridge Road, Orpington, Kent

Following the collapse of Orpington & District on 29 January 1981 a four month void in service over the Orpington – Biggin Hill route followed until Crystal's Coaches took up operation of the route from 26 May 1981. This view, dating from 15 August 1986, falls slightly outside the time scale covered by this book but has been included because of that date's historical significance. For the next day London Regional Transport introduced its Orpington Roundabout bus network included amongst which was Route R2, which replaced Crystal's Coaches Route 858. Crystal's 1985-built Rootes-bodied Mercedes-Benz LB608D reg.no. C390 CKK was photographed in Sevenoaks Road, Orpington on the very last day of independent operation over the Orpington – Biggin Hill corridor. Just over 23 years after LT had abandoned Route 479 on 16 June 1963, leaving the way clear for independent bus operation between Orpington and Biggin Hill, operation was again restored to London Transport. A G Whitlam

ROUTE PROFILE

Orpington – Biggin Hill – New Addington.

Note:	Restriction on carriage of local passengers between Orpington and High Elms (Shire Lane).
22 June 1963	Introduced by Orpington Rural Transport Association. Operated Orpington – Biggin Hill via Green Street Green and Leaves Green. Saturdays = 5 journeys.
Note:	London Transport Route 479 had operated experimentally on Saturdays over same route from 16 February–16 June 1963.
20 July 1963	Re-routed at Green Street Green to operate via Downe and Berry's Green to Biggin Hill.
7 March 1964	3 journeys introduced on Tuesdays.
1 Sept 1964	Revised to operate: Tuesdays, Wednesdays, Fridays, Saturdays = 3/6 journeys.
5 Oct 1964	Revised to operate: Weekdays = 2/6 journeys.
22 March 1965	Revised to operate: Weekdays = 2 hours.
1 Sept 1965	Revised to operate: Mondays = 5 journeys (peaks), Tuesdays–Saturdays = 1 hour.
28 March 1967	Bifurcated projection introduced beyond Biggin Hill. Revised to operate: either Orpington – Biggin Hill – New Addington or Orpington – Biggin Hill – Tatsfield. Mondays = 3/4 journeys to each terminal. Tuesdays–Fridays = 1 hour to each terminal. Saturdays operated Orpington – Biggin Hill only = 1 hour.
By end May 1967	Operation to Tatsfield suspended due to inadequate condition of road surface in Tatsfield Lane.
11 Sept 1967	Saturday service extended from Biggin Hill to New Addington. Frequency revised to: Mondays (peak only) Orpington – Biggin Hill = 10 journeys, Biggin Hill – New Addington = 5 journeys. Tuesdays–Saturdays Orpington – Biggin Hill = 30 minutes. Biggin Hill – New Addington = 1 hour.
14 Oct 1967	Frequency revised to: Orpington – Biggin Hill – New Addington. Mondays = 7 journeys. Tuesday–Saturdays = 1 hour.
1 Jan 1968	Frequency revised to: Mondays = 6 journeys, Tuesdays–Fridays = 1 hour, Saturdays = 90 minutes.
23 March 1970	Saturday service reduced to operate Orpington – Biggin Hill only = 1 hour.
30 June 1973	Saturday service withdrawn.
Sept 1974	Circular working introduced at Biggin Hill Valley to serve Hillingdale Estate.
28 July 1975	Numbered 858. Now operated by North Downs vehicles on hire to Orpington Rural Transport Association.
12 Dec 1975	Orpington Rural Transport Association disbanded.
15 Dec 1975	Service provided by Orpington & District using Orpington Rual Transport Association licence. Section of route from Biggin Hill – New Addington abandoned. Revised to operate: Orpington – Biggin Hill Valley Mondays–Fridays = 1 hour.
29 Dec 1975	Acquired by Orpington & District. Retained number 858.
22 Nov 1976	Frequency revised to: 70 minutes (60 minutes peaks).
6 Aug 1977	Saturday service re-introduced.
3 Dec 1977	Saturday service withdrawn.
24 Dec 1980	Route temporarily withdrawn due to vehicle maintenance difficulties.
26 Jan 1981	Re-instated.
29 Jan 1981	Route abandoned at midday by Orpington & District.
26 May 1981	Re-introduced by C Springham (t/a Crystals Coaches). Operated Orpington – Biggin Hill Valley Mondays–Fridays = 10/11 journeys. Retained number 858.
12 July 1985	Extant.

Right North Downs last published timetable for Route 853.

North Downs no. 23 (222 CHN) was a 45-seat ECW-bodied Bristol LS5G. Acquired in February 1973 it still retained the livery of its original operator, United Automobile Services, when photographed travelling along Park Hill Road, East Croydon one month later. North Downs purchased full sized saloons which had approximately one year's certificate of fitness period left to run. Lacking adequate workshop facilities themselves to prepare such vehicles for further re-certification, North Downs withdrew them when their CoFs lapsed – a fate which befell no. 23 in February 1974. G W Morant

ROUTE PROFILE

	East Croydon (Altyre Road) – Orpington (War Memorial) via Gravel Hill, Addington, Coney Hall, Keston Mark, Locks Bottom.
Note:	Restriction on carriage of local passengers between Keston Mark and Orpington.
8 April 1969	Introduced by North Downs. Weekdays = 6 journeys.
2 Sept 1969	Numbered 853. Frequency revised to: 1 hour (peaks 30 minutes).
23 Aug 1970	Sunday service introduced. Frequency revised to: Weekdays = 30 minutes (peaks 15 minutes), Sundays = 2 hours.
28 May 1972	Sunday service discontinued. Weekday frequency reduced to 1 hour (peaks 30 minutes).
4 June 1972	Sunday service re-introduced by Orpington & District = 2 hours.
30 July 1972	Sunday service abandoned by Orpington & District.
27 Aug 1972	Sunday service re-introduced by Thamesmead Motor Services. 6 journeys.
15 Oct 1972	Sunday service abandoned by Thamesmead Motor Services.

27 Oct 1973	Frequency revised to: Weekdays = 1 hour (peak and off-peak).
24 Aug1974	Two late evening Saturday journeys introduced jointly with Orpington & District. These journeys diverted at Gravel Hill to double run to Forestdale, these journeys numbered 857.
2 Sept 1974	Frequency increased to weekdays = 30 minutes (peaks 10/12 minutes).
14 Sept 1974	Route 857 journeys withdrawn.
15 Jan 1976	Route 853 abandoned by North Downs.
24 Jan 1976	Re-introduced by Orpington & District. Retained number 853. Weekdays = 60 minutes (peaks 30 minutes). Last two journeys Mondays–Fridays and all Saturday service diverted at Gravel Hill to double run to Forestdale, these journeys numbered 857.
26 July 1980	Saturday 857 journeys withdrawn.
28 July 1980	Revised to operate: Peak hours = 30/45 minutes (Route 853) Off peak = 60 minutes (Route 857)
16 Feb 1981	Reduced to operate Mondays–Fridays peaks only. All journeys followed 857 routeing in Forestdale except four morning peak journeys in East Croydon – Orpington direction which followed 853 routeing.
20 Feb 1981	Routes 853 and 857 abandoned by Orpington & District.
21 April 1981	Re-introduced by Tillingbourne Bus Co Ltd. Re-numbered 353 (direct journeys). 357 (double run via Forestdale). Frequency Mondays–Fridays peaks = 30 minutes (353/7) off-peak = 60 minutes (357), Saturdays = 60 minutes (357).
Aug 1981	Operator became: Tillingbourne (Metropolitan) Ltd.
9 Nov 1981	Monday–Friday off-peak and all-day Saturday service projected beyond Altyre Road to new terminal in Park Lane, Croydon.
24 Sept 1983	Acquired by Metrobus Ltd. Route numbers 353/357 retained.
12 May 1984	1 Monday – Friday and 3 Saturday journeys projected beyond Orpington to Hewitts Farm.
1 Sept 1984	Extension to Hewitts Farm withdrawn at end of fruit picking season, not re-instated in subsequent years.
12 July 1985	Extant.

North Downs no. 21 (OTT 517) was a 1953 ECW-bodied Bristol LS5G originally new to Western National who had subsequently converted it into a mobile trainer unit for use with currency decimalisation in 1971. Sporting North Downs new livery and logo the bus is seen in Kent Gate Way at Gravel Hill heading for East Croydon in March 1973. Behind is an LT DMS bus on Route C1 from New Addington also bound for East Croydon.
Capital Transport

The last full sized saloons bought by North Downs were two Bristol LS6Gs nos. 27/28 (PNN 771/774). Both originated as 39-seat coaches with Mansfield District in 1954. On their sale to Eastern Counties in 1968 both were rebuilt to pay-as-you-enter bus configuration. Sold by Eastern Counties in 1972 PNN 771 went to Edmunds, Rassau whilst PNN 774 joined Gosport & Fareham's fleet. By a singular coincidence both buses met up again in February 1974 when purchased by North Downs. No. 28 is seen loading at Orpington Memorial, Spur Road terminal soon after acquisition during its brief period with North Downs. A policy decision to revert to minibus operation caused the withdrawal of all full size saloons from the fleet by July 1974.
North Downs Collection

Below **Tillingbourne Bus Co.** loaned three AEC Reliances to Metrobus on the latter's formation in September 1983. One was Duple Dominant-bodied reg.no. JTM 109V which had seen previous service in the area with Tillingbourne (Metropolitan). It was photographed in November 1983. This bus subsequently rejoined Tillingbourne's fleet in September 1985.
G W Morant

ROUTE PROFILE

East Croydon (Altyre Road) – Forestdale via Gravel Hill.	
24 Aug 1970	Introduced by North Downs. Numbered 855. Weekdays = 30 minutes (peaks 15 minutes), Sundays = 2 hours.
16 May 1971	Sunday service withdrawn.
19 June 1971	Discontinued by North Downs.
6 Dec 1971	Re-introduced by Orpington & District. Route number 855 retained. Mondays–Fridays = 11 journeys.

Right **The final 18-month period of North Downs operation on Route 853 saw a reversion to the use of three 1969/1970-built Williams Deansgate-bodied 12-seat Ford Transits of similar age and specification to the vehicles with which North Downs had inaugurated the route in 1969. No. 29 (TAY 428H), acquired from Naylor of Kibworth, Leicestershire, seen at Spur Road, Orpington contrasts markedly in both size and style with no. 28 illustrated above.**
North Downs Collection

27 March 1972	Frequency increased to weekdays = 1 hour (Monday–Friday peaks = 20 minutes).
4 June 1972	Sunday service introduced = 2 hours.
11 Feb 1973	Sunday service discontinued.
2 Sept 1974	Frequency revised to = 30/60 minutes.
17 Jan 1976	Saturday service replaced by Route 857.
1 Aug 1977	Frequency revised to: Mondays–Fridays = 15/60 minutes.
28 July 1980	Reduced to operate Monday–Friday peaks only = 7/10 journeys. Off peak service replaced by Route 857.
27 Feb 1981	Abandoned by Orpington & District after morning peak.
2 March 1981	Re-introduced by Tillingbourne Bus Co Ltd. Monday–Friday peaks = 9 journeys.
21 April 1981	Numbered 355.
Aug 1981	Operator became Tillingbourne (Metropolitan) Ltd.
9 Nov 1981	Frequency revised to: Monday–Friday peaks = 6 journeys. One journey commenced from Croydon (Fairfield Halls).
24 Sept 1983	Acquired by Metrobus Ltd. Route number 355 retained.
12 July 1985	Extant.

ROUTE PROFILE

Orpington (Station) – Ramsden Estate (circular).

Note:	London Country Route 493 (Green Street Green – Orpington Station – Ramsden Estate) covered this section of route on weekdays.
23 Aug 1970	Introduced by North Downs. Numbered 854. Sundays only = 2 hours.
28 May 1972	Discontinued by North Downs.
4 June 1972	Re-introduced by Orpington & District. Retained number 854. Sundays only = 2 hours.
6 Aug 1972	Frequency increased to 30 minutes.
11 Feb 1973	Withdrawn.

ROUTE PROFILE

East Croydon (Altyre Road) – Roundshaw (Community Centre).

Note:	London Transport Route 233 (West Croydon Station – Roundshaw) covered this route on weekdays.
23 May 1971	Introduced by North Downs. Numbered 856. Sundays only = 2 hours.
29 May 1972	Discontinued.

ROUTE PROFILE

Biggin Hill – Orpington (Schools).

Sept 1975	Introduced by Orpington Rural Transport Association. Operated by North Downs vehicle on hire. Numbered 859. Routed via Leaves Green and Keston Mark. Schooldays only = 1 journey.
12 Dec 1975	Orpington Rural Transport Association disbanded.
15 Dec 1975	Service provided by Orpington & District using Orpington Rural Transport Association licence.
13 Jan 1976	Re-introduced by Orpington & District. Retained number 859. Revised to operate via Leaves Green and Green Street Green. Schooldays only = 1 journey.
By 13 Feb 1981	Abandoned (exact date uncertain).

ROUTE PROFILE

East Croydon (Altyre Road) – Biggin Hill Valley (Kings Rd)
via Gravel Hill, Addington, Coney Hall, Keston, Leaves Green.

5 Jan 1976	Introduced by Orpington & District. Numbered 860. Mondays–Fridays = 1 hour.
22 Nov 1976	Frequency revised to: 70 minutes (40 minutes peaks) – total 10 journeys.
24 June 1977	Withdrawn.

Above **Commer LB 12-seat minibus reg.no. PNJ 230F is seen at Forestdale on the original bus service provided by that Estate's developers, Wates Built Homes Limited.** Styled 'Forestdale Express' Wates 'free' bus service, introduced on 5 October 1968, linked Forestdale with the London Transport bus stop at the bottom of Gravel Hill offering onward connections to Croydon. Publicity issued at this time stated that Wates will 'continue the service until Forestdale is serviced by London Transport buses in eighteen months time'. In the event such London Transport operation never transpired. Wates subsequently negotiated with John Wylde with the result that, after Wates had agreed to pay a £750 deposit for a new minibus, North Downs introduced an extended Forestdale – East Croydon route from 24 August 1970. J M Aldridge Collection

Above right **North Downs tenure on the Forestdale route was short-lived, John Wylde citing disruption due to traffic congestion and uneven demand as reasons for withdrawal. Ford Transit** no. 8 is seen at Forestdale along with a group of young bus enthusiasts. To the left facing the camera is Peter Larking who showed early support for North Down's activities and later founded Metrobus. In the centre is Barry King who subsequently became Managing Director of Tillingbourne Bus Co Ltd. North Downs Collection

ROUTE PROFILE

	East Croydon (Altyre Road) – Downe via Gravel Hill. Addington, Coney Hall, Keston, Leaves Green, Biggin Hill Valley.
27 Nov 1976	Introduced by Orpington & District. Numbered 861. Saturdays only = 2 hours.
25 June 1977	Withdrawn.

ROUTE PROFILE

	Sanderstead (Church) or Croydon (Fairfields Hall) – Bromley (Churchill Theatre) via Forestdale, New Addington, Hayes.
4 May 1982	Introduced by Tillingbourne (Metropolitan) Ltd. Numbered 354. Operated Sanderstead – Bromley. Mondays–Fridays = 1 journey.
22 Nov 1982	Diverted via Bourne Vale.
24 Sept 1983	Acquired by Metrobus Ltd.
24 Oct 1983	Sanderstead – Forestdale section withdrawn. Revised to operate Croydon – Bromley. Mondays–Fridays = 1 journey.
12 July 1985	Extant.

Orpington & District's 1959-built Weymann low-height bodied Leyland Atlantean PDR1/1 reg no. 44DKT, originally supplied new to Maidstone & District, turns from Addiscombe Road into Park Hill Road, East Croydon in November 1975. G W Morant

Looking distinctly down-at-heel former Thamesdown (originally Swindon Corporation Transport) 1963-built Willowbrook-bodied AEC Reliance reg.no. 132 CMR was caught by the camera at Altyre Road, East Croydon on 14 March 1977 during Orpington & District's near eighteen month operation of Route 860. D M Persson

ROUTE PROFILE

A fleeting scene soon confined to history is encapsulated in this view at Downe High Street on 26 March 1977. Orpington & District's 25-seat Tricentrol-bodied Ford A series reg.no. PKN 581R lays over before departure for East Croydon on Saturdays only Route 861. Both PKN 581R and sister vehicle PKN 580R was sponsored by the GLC in lieu of a grant. Behind London Transport RT4417 (NXP 771) awaits departure time for Bromley on Route 146 – one of the RT class's last strongholds before the 146's conversion to BL class Bristol LH operation on 22 April 1978. D M Persson

	Ramsden Estate – Brighton – Worthing
	via Orpington, Keston Mark, Coney Hall, Addington, Forestdale, Sanderstead, Purley, Coulsdon, thence via A23/M23 to Brighton.
1 May 1982	Introduced by Tillingbourne (Metropolitan) Ltd. Numbered 350. Operated Ramsden Estate – Brighton (Madeira Drive). Saturdays and Sundays only = 1 journey.
26 Sept 1982	Sunday service seasonally withdrawn.
11 Dec 1982	Saturday service seasonally withdrawn.
1 May 1983	Re-introduced. Saturdays and Sundays only, 1 journey. Also operated Tuesdays and Thursdays in August.
24 Sept 1983	Acquired by Metrobus Ltd. Route number 350 retained.
25 Sept 1983	Seasonally withdrawn.
5 May 1984	Re-introduced. Extended to operate Ramsden Estate – Brighton – Worthing (Marine Parade, Dome). Saturdays, Sundays and Bank Holidays = 1 journey. Also operated Tuesdays and Thursdays in August.
30 Sept 1984	Seasonally withdrawn.
5 May 1985	Re-introduced. Sundays and Bank Holidays only = 1 journey. Also operated Tuesdays and Thursdays in August.
12 July 1985	Extant.

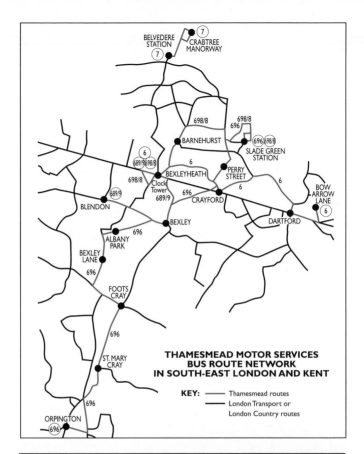

THAMESMEAD MOTOR SERVICES
BUS ROUTE NETWORK
IN SOUTH-EAST LONDON AND KENT

KEY: ——— Thamesmead routes
      ——— London Transport or
           London Country routes

CHAPTER 9

GLC Area Independents 1970–1985

A G Bassom and M Thornton, trading as:
Thamesmead Motor Services
1A Court Lane, Dulwich, London SE21

From March 1971 title became:
Thamesmead Motor Services Ltd
78 Eltham High Street, London SE9

Subsequent changes of office:
By 1975: 7 Alfred Road, Upper Belvedere, Kent
By August 1976: 81 Christchurch Way, Greenwich, London SE8
March 1977: 309A Plumstead High Street, London SE18

Established in 1970 this operator is best remembered for its attempts to plug gaps caused by the withdrawal, or lack, of London Transport (and London Country) Sunday bus services in the Bexleyheath area. Interestingly, two of the early route numbers used, 696 and 698, replicated those formerly used by London Transport on its isolated Bexleyheath area trolleybus system, which had been converted to motor bus operation in the very first stage of London Transport's trolleybus conversion programme, implemented on 4 April 1959. Both such Thamesmead Motor Services routes shared common sections of route with their electrically-powered predecessors – Thamesmead 696 followed a short common routeing with former trolleybus 696 in London Road, Crayford whilst Thamesmead 698 and former trolleybus 698 served a common section of route between Bexleyheath and Northumberland Heath, Colyers Lane. Route number 689 was selected by Thamesmead to fit in with the logic of this 6xx series as well as being a 'complementary' number to London Transport route number 89 over which it replaced the Bexley leg on Sundays. In addition to the Bexleyheath routes in south-east London, Thamesmead had a brief two month tenure, from late 1970, as the operator of celebrated Route 98B between Ruislip Station and Rayners Lane Station in London's north-western suburbs, detailed in Chapter 7.

Thamesmead co-operated with fellow independent operator North Downs by occasional hire of Thamesmead vehicles and crews to North Downs to cover route number 853 (Orpington – East Croydon) as well as, more rarely, to work some of North Downs' Horsham area bus routes. As noted in Chapter 8, Thamesmead took up, in its own right, Sunday operation of Route 853 from 27 August 1972 until 15 October 1972 after both North Downs as well as Orpington and District had given up their attempts to maintain a service on that day of the week.

Below **Thamesmead's first full size bus, fleet no. 2 (DHD 196), was a 1959-built Park Royal-bodied AEC Reliance originally supplied new to Yorkshire Woollen District. Acquired in order to inaugurate the then partnership's first bus service no. 2 was photographed at Slade Green Station (mis-spelt** Slades on the destination blind) shortly after operation started. In November 1971 this bus was sold to J E Maddison's and Miss J M Normington's Orpington & District and was used to inaugurate that operator's Forestdale route on 6 December 1971. A G Whitlam

Above **This view of Thamesmead Motor Services no. 2 at Slade Green Station dates from 23 August 1970 – the inaugural day of Route 698 operation. The conductor standing beside driver Michael Wells is Andrew Bassom, founding co-partner of Thamesmead Motor Services.** A G Bassom

Although timetables were posted at stops, proposals to extend Route 6 from 15 August 1971 with two Sunday afternoon journeys projected beyond Dartford via Greenhithe, Bean and Betsham to Gravesend (as Route 6A) – a road last served on Sundays by London Transport Route 450 on 29 June 1965 – were not implemented. In a similar vein a proposed Monday to Friday peak-hours Route 7 planned for introduction on 9 August 1971 between Belvedere Station and Crabtree Manor Way did not go ahead since London Transport unexpectedly granted the consent to rival operator R D Hall (trading as Belvedere Coaches).

Thamesmead Motor Services aspirations as a bus operator were greater than the network actually operated might suggest. On 5 July 1971 an application was made to London Transport seeking an 'agreement' to operate an hourly-headway 'Limited-Stop' Monday to Friday service between Woolwich Arsenal Station and Thamesmead via Plumstead with the intention that such a route should be extended to Thamesmead Eastern Industrial Estate when road construction was completed. London Transport refused this application on 16 July 1971. A further application to serve Thamesmead was made to London Transport on 17 July 1972. This time a daily route between Thamesmead East Industrial Estate and Woolwich Arsenal Station via Woolwich Industrial Estate and Nathan Way was proposed – to be worked to an hourly headway increasing to 20 minutes during Monday to Friday peak hours. This second application was refused on 17 August 1972. London Transport subsequently extended their Route 177 into Thamesmead from 6 January 1973 along routeing identical to Thamesmead Motor Services' first application whilst new London Transport Route 198, introduced on 17 November 1973, mirrored Thamesmead Motor Services' second application which had been rejected by London Transport fifteen months earlier!

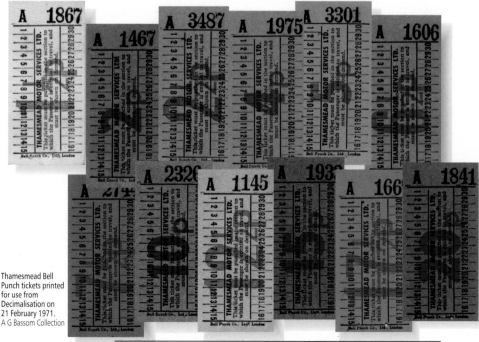

Thamesmead Bell Punch tickets printed for use from Decimalisation on 21 February 1971.
A G Bassom Collection

A third application to London Transport, submitted on 7 January 1972, to operate a local flat-fare Monday to Saturday bus route within the New Addington Estate – prompted by petitioning from the local Resident's Association dissatisfied with the scope of existing London Transport services – was rejected on 20 January 1972. Just over one year later London Transport introduced their own flat-fare Route C5 in New Addington.

It must remain a matter of conjecture as to how the fortunes of Thamesmead Motor Services bus operations might have been altered had these various applications to London Transport for more substantial six or seven day-a-week services been granted. In the event, as may be seen from the Route Profiles, disruption of Thamesmead Motor Services operations occurred in both the winter of 1971/2 and again in the summer of 1972. A final flurry of activity from 17 September 1972 saw Thamesmead Motors Services dramatically increase frequencies on the surviving Bexleyheath routes to Slade Green and Blendon (by then renumbered 8 and 9 respectively). Although it is understood that the bus services were 'breaking-even', a policy decision by the company to concentrate resources upon its coaching activities led to the decision to withdrawn from bus operation, apart from school services, after 11 February 1973.

Thamesmead Motor Services continued in business as a coach operator, re-emerging onto the London bus route scene in a very modest way on 14 July 1975 when acquisition of Belvedere Coaches at long last allowed Thamesmead Motor Services to take up operation of the Belvedere Station – Crabtree Manor Way peak-hour service. Thamesmead Motor Services went on to develop as a leading operator of both British and Continental Tours. Unfortunately, a dramatic slump in that sector coupled with bad debts incurred from contract customers forced the company into receivership in December 1982.

Note: *From 4 July 1971 all Thamesmead bus routes were granted consent to operate on Public Holidays (except Christmas Day and Boxing Day) in addition to their usual Sunday operations.*

ROUTE PROFILE

	Bexleyheath (Clock Tower) – Slade Green Station via Barnehurst, Northumberland Heath.
Note:	i) London Transport routes 122 or 132 covered this route on weekdays. ii) LG Orpwood (t/a C & O Motors) had operated a Sunday service over this route between 6 October 1968 and 11 May 1969 (see Chapter 7). iii) No local passengers could be carried between Bexleyheath and top of Colyers Lane, Northumberland Heath.
23 Aug 1970	Introduced. Numbered 698. Sundays only = 40 minutes (with break in service between 16.30–17.35 hours) – total 16 journeys.
31 Jan 1971	Frequency reduced to 14 journeys.
4 July 1971	Re-numbered 8. Frequency reduced to 8 journeys.
7 Nov 1971	Projected in Bexleyheath from Clock Tower to new terminus in Oaklands Road. Frequency increased to: 1 hour (with break in service between 16.20–17.30 hours) – total 11 journeys.
28 Nov 1971	Suspended.
6 Feb 1972	Re-introduced. Operated Bexleyheath (Clock Tower) – Slade Green Station. Sunday evenings only = 4 journeys.
13 Aug 1972	Suspended.
17 Sept 1972	Re-introduced. Operated Bexleyheath (Clock Tower) – Slade Green Stn. Sundays, daytime = 1 hour, evening = 30 minutes – total 15 journeys.
11 Feb 1973	Withdrawn.

ROUTE PROFILE

	Bexleyheath (Clock Tower) – Blendon (Penhill Road) via Bexley.
Note:	i) London Transport Sunday service over this section of route 89 was withdrawn after 24 January 1971. ii) London Transport maintained a service on Sunday afternoons only on route 124A between Bexley and Blendon. To protect this operation the Thamesmead service was only permitted to operate on Sunday mornings and / or evenings. iii) No local passengers could be carried between Bexleyheath and Bexley Station.
31 Jan 1971	Introduced. Numbered 689. Sundays only = 5 journeys.
4 July 1971	Re-numbered 9. Reduced to operate Sunday evenings only = 2 journeys.
31 Oct 1971	Suspended.
6 Feb 1972	Re-introduced. Sunday evenings only = 3 journeys.
13 Aug 1972	Suspended.
17 Sept 1972	Re-introduced. 2/3 journeys Sunday mornings, 30 minutes Sunday evenings – total = 12 journeys.
11 Feb 1973	Withdrawn.

ROUTE PROFILE

	Slade Green Station – Orpington (War Memorial) via Crayford, Bexley, Albany Park, St Mary Cray.
Note:	This route connected at Orpington (War Memorial) with North Downs Route 853 to East Croydon.
21 Feb 1971	Introduced. Numbered 696. Weekdays, four through journeys plus two short-working Slade Green Station – Albany Park Station. Sundays = 2 through journeys.
27 Feb 1971	Saturday service discontinued.
28 Feb 1971	Sunday service discontinued.
7 April 1971	Withdrawn. This decision was precipitated by the closure of Perry Street, a major traffic artery for the Thamesmead route, for at least four months. A major diversion would have been necessary via Thames Road and Crayford Way to regain the original line of route at Crayford. London Transport would not give Thamesmead permission to stop along this diversion, which was wholly within the GLC Area and the preserve of intensive service by London Country routes 480 and 491.

Thamesmead's 12-seater 1965-built Austin J2 Omnicoach no. 6 (JHK 421C) is seen at Orpington (War Memorial) terminal in Spur Road on Sunday 21 February 1971 waiting time before departure at 14.20hrs on the inaugural return journey of Route 696 to Slade Green station. I E Whitlam

ROUTE PROFILE

Bexleyheath (Clock Tower) – Dartford (Bow Arrow Lane) via Crayford.

Note:	London Country Bus Services withdrew Sunday operation on Route 486 (Upper Belvedere – Dartford (Bow Arrow Lane) after 26 June 1971. Thamesmead's route paralleled the Bexleyheath – Dartford (Bow Arrow Lane) section of this route.
4 July 1971	Introduced. Numbered 6. Sundays only = 5 journeys.
31 Oct 1971	Withdrawn.

Above left **Thamesmead's no. 15 (395 DKK) was a former Maidstone & District Harrington bodied AEC Reliance. This bus was photographed in Colyers** Lane, Erith on 24 September 1972 which was the Sunday following Thamesmead's reintroduction of enhanced frequency services on routes 8 and 9. M Audsley

Above **Thamesmead's no. 2 (DHD 196) is seen at the Bow Arrow Lane, Dartford terminus of Route 6.** M Thornton / A G Bassom Collection

Below **In summer 1972 Thamesmead made the substantial purchase of three former Maidstone & District AEC Reliance saloons, in anticipation of an increase in frequencies of** Bexleyheath routes 8 and 9, needing two vehicles, and the introduction of a Sunday service on Route 853 (Orpington – East Croydon), as detailed in Chapter 8, requiring a further vehicle.

Left to right are: Harrington-bodied 15/14 (395/394 DKK) 1958-built and 16 (293 GKK) a 1960-built Weymann-bodied, in Thamesmead's Blackfen Yard shortly after preparation. A G Bassom

R D Hall, trading as:

Belvedere Coaches

4 Pier Road, Northfleet, Kent

ROUTE PROFILE

	Belvedere Station – Crabtree Manor Way (Circular)
Note:	London Country withdrew peak hour extensions of Route 491 to Crabtree Manor Way after 2 July 1971.
Aug 1971	Previously existing works contract for Beck and Pollitzer Ltd made available for public use. Mondays–Fridays peak hours only = 4 morning, 3 afternoon journeys.
14 July 1975	Operation acquired by Thamesmead Motor Services Ltd. Numbered 7.
16 Feb 1982	Withdrawn.

R Taylor & Son, trading as:

Taylor's Coaches

152 St James Road, London SE1

ROUTE PROFILE

	Brockley (Frendsbury Road) circular
	via New Cross and New Cross Gate.

This short bus service, both in terms of distance covered and survival period, was sponsored by the Telegraph Hill Neighbourhood Council Bus Action Committee. It provided a link over residential roads not served by London Transport to connect with trunk London Transport bus routes, as well as rail facilities, at New Cross and New Cross Gate. Introduced on 1 November 1971, Taylor's Coaches were contracted to operate the weekday service which ran every 30 minutes between 08.30 and 10.30 hours and again between 17.00 and 19.00 hours. In spite of publicity by the Bus Action Committee exhorting residents to support their 'Bus Up The Hill' operation did not last beyond a months trial period, the service running for the last time on 4 December 1971.

Tony Wright recorded the final journey of 'The Iver Bus Service'. Lawrence Coaches 1972-built Williams Deansgate-bodied Mercedes Benz L406 reg.no. TVR 616K is seen with passengers and driver (third from left) about to depart from Richings Park for the last time on 31 August 1977.
T Wright

Locks Coaches Ltd

54B Trundleys Road, London SE8

ROUTE PROFILE

Greenwich – Blackheath.
Unidirectional circular via Grooms Hill, Shooters Hill.

This service, introduced on 5 June 1976, had a daily 20 minute frequency between 10.00 and 18.00 hours. It was aimed at the tourist market but was not a success, being withdrawn at an unascertained date despite being authorised to operate until 31 October 1976.

W J & C J Lawrence, trading as:

Lawrence Coaches

91 Dickens Avenue, Hillingdon, Middlesex

ROUTE PROFILE

	Uxbridge – **Richings Park Estate** via Cowley and Iver.
Note:	London Country Route 459 (Uxbridge – Richings Park Estate via Iver Heath and Iver) was withdrawn after 28 November 1975.
9 Aug 1976	Introduced. Mondays–Fridays = 4 journeys.
4 Dec 1976	Saturday service introduced.
26 March 1977	Saturday service withdrawn.
31 Aug 1977	Withdrawn.

Tandridge Taxis Ltd

26B Chipstead Valley Road, Coulsdon, Surrey

Tandridge Taxis re-instated a service to Clockhouse Farm Estate over the former Banstead Coaches route. Chrysler Dodge minibus reg.no. YKL 351S is seen in Woodmansterne Road approaching Coulsdon on 3 January 1981. D M Persson

ROUTE PROFILE

	Coulsdon – Clockhouse Farm Estate circular.
Note:	Banstead Coaches Ltd operated a weekday service over this route between 8 June 1964 and 31 March 1980. (See Chapter 7)
22 July 1980	Introduced by Tandridge Taxis Ltd. Operated Coulsdon North Station – Clockhouse Farm Estate. Weekdays = 30 minutes.
1 June 1981	Numbered 26B (same number as company's address).

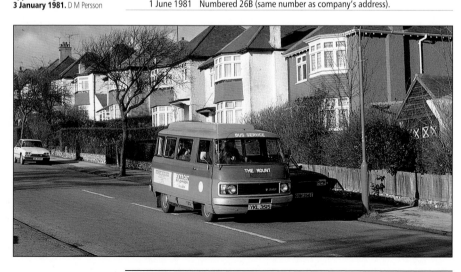

Bristol Street Motors modified 1979-built Ford Transit reg.no. CFX 958T to meet psv regulations for Guards of Caterham. Access for passengers was through the vehicle's rear doors, one of which may be seen opened in this shot taken at Coulsdon terminus.
Photobus / R Marshall

15 June 1981	Extended to operate Coulsdon Woods Estate – Clockhouse Farm Estate via Coulsdon. Mondays–Fridays = 30 minutes, Saturdays = 1 hour.
2 Jan 1982	Frequency became: Weekdays = 1 hour.
27 March 1982	Withdrawn.
15 Nov 1982	Re-introduced by Guards Internationale (Intercity) Ltd (t/a Guards of Caterham) 26 Station Avenue, Caterham, Surrey. Operated Coulsdon (Red Lion) – Clockhouse Farm Estate. Frequency: Weekdays, peaks = 20 minutes, off-peak = 60 minutes. Route number no longer used.
By Aug 1983	Off peak frequency increased to 30 minutes.
30 June 1984	Saturday service withdrawn.
12 July 1985	Extant.

C J Franklin, trading as:

Franklins Coaches

Station Road, Borehamwood, Hertfordshire

Franklin Coaches Monday to Friday peak hour Route HC1 introduced on 3 November 1980 comprised two journeys. The 07.20 departure operated a clockwise circular route from Borehamwood via South Mimms, Potters Bar and Barnet back to Borehamwood. The 17.06 return journey worked the circle anti clockwise. A nimble Derek Persson was hailing former London Country 1971-built MCW bodied AEC Swift reg.no. DPD 488J whilst also photographing the bus ascending Barnet Hill on 7 July 1982. Route HC1 was withdrawn after operation on 31 March 1983.
D M Persson

Lacey's (East Ham) was a substantial coach operator with around 20 vehicles. Coaches were used on the Ripple Road replacement service as evidenced by reg.no. LMU 424P, a 1976 Plaxton-bodied Bedford YMT, seen at Ripple Road (The Harrow) terminus on 7 March 1981. D M Persson

Lacey's (East Ham) Ltd

222 Barking Road, East Ham, London E6

ROUTE PROFILE

Ripple Road – Barking (Town Centre)

While work was undertaken to replace Ripple Road railway level-crossing with a flyover, London Transport Route 87 (Rainham – Harold Hill) was diverted away from Ripple Road to travel via Newham Way. Lacey's route was introduced on 5 January 1981 to give Ripple Road residents living on both sides of the level crossing a bus service to Barking Town Centre. Initially Lacey's route operated every 30 minutes on weekdays, except evenings. Departures from Ripple Road (Post Office) – on the west side of the railway crossing – travelled via St Paul's Road (south side of Barking Town Centre) before cutting south to sprint along Newham Way (A13 East Ham and Barking By-Pass) to gain access to the then bisected eastern section of Ripple Road. Turning at 'The Harrow' the service next completed a double run eastwards along Ripple Road before travelling via Upney Lane and Longbridge Road to reach East Street in Barking Town Centre whence the service continued to Ripple Road (Post Office) terminal. A Sunday service was added from 17 April 1981 followed by the introduction of an evening service from 1 May 1981. The route was completely restructured from 26 May 1981. The routeing along Newham Way was withdrawn and instead journeys travelled via Longbridge Road and Upney Lane in both directions. On the same date departing journeys from Ripple Road (Post Office) were re-routed to give more comprehensive facilities within Barking Town Centre, travelling via Broadway, North Street and London Road. With the construction of the flyover completed, London Transport Route 287 (Rainham–Barking Garage) started to serve Ripple Road from 11.00 hours on 24 November 1982, when Lacey's route was withdrawn.

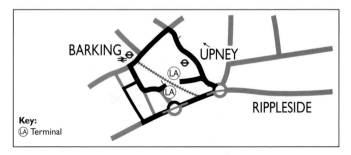

Lacey's bus route between Ripple Road and Barking Town Centre as originally operated in a unidirectional circular form from 5 January to 25 May 1981.

Key:
(LA) Terminal

Lightgray Ltd
11/13 Cricklewood Lane, London NW2

N° 11556

Lightgray Limited
London Airlink

ADULT SINGLE
FROM LONDON

£2

VALID DAY
OF
ISSUE ONLY

ROUTE PROFILE

Gloucester Road (Coach Station) – Heathrow Airport.
Non-stop via Cromwell Road, M4 Motorway.

Advertised as the 'London Airlink' the service was planned to attract Heathrow Airport-bound passengers arriving at Gloucester Road Coach Station – designated 'New West London Air Terminal' on Lightgray's timetable – on the host of London-bound long-distance express coach services which had mushroomed into being following express coach service deregulation on 6 October 1980. The 'London Airlink', introduced on 6 October 1981 with an hourly frequency on Mondays to Fridays reducing to 2-hourly at weekends, was licensed as a stage-carriage service. It competed directly with London Transport's daily 30-minute frequency 'Airbus' Route A1 (Victoria – Heathrow Airport) which had a picking up point at the Penta Hotel in Cromwell Road, near to Gloucester Road Coach Station. On initial application, London Transport had refused to grant a London Bus Agreement to Lightgray Ltd, the applicant only being successful on appeal when Transport Minister Kenneth Clarke overrode his Inspector's earlier decision. Patronage did not prove adequate to maintain the 'London Airlink', resulting in the route's early demise circa April 1982.

A & C Clark, trading as:
Woodside Coaches
188 Portland Road, South Norwood, London SE15

ROUTE PROFILE

	New Addington (Central Parade) – Croydon (George Street).
Notes:	i) Seats had to be pre-booked on a weekly basis. ii) The only intermediate stops were in New Addington at Goldcrest Way, Headley Drive, Lodge Lane, and at Gravel Hill.
13 Sept 1982	Introduced. Monday–Friday peaks only = 15 minutes. Operated New Addington – East Croydon 06.30–08.00 hours, reversed direction 17.00–18.30 hours.
24 Sept 1982	Abandoned.

Woodside Coaches application to London Transport seeking the latter's 'Agreement' to operate a peak hours only 'with the flow' service on the trunk route from New Addington to East Croydon, already served by several London Transport bus routes, not unexpectedly failed to gain London Transport's approval. An appeal by Woodside was rejected by a Ministry Inspector. However the 1980 Transport Act, as well as de-regulating express services, sought to liberalise controls over stage carriage operations. The Minister of Transport, perhaps mindful of the Conservative Government's future aspirations to further de-regulate bus operation, was zealous in promoting the cause of new applicants such as Woodside. As with Lightgray he overruled his Inspector and so Woodside obtained its London Transport 'Agreement'.

Operation was an anti-climax – despite all the effort expended in obtaining the 'Agreement' Woodside's service only survived for two weeks.

Wealden of London Motor Services Ltd

Falcon Estate, Central Way, Feltham, Middlesex

ROUTE PROFILE

Leisure Link	London (Hyde Park Corner) – Windsor (Safari Park) via Gloucester Road Coach Stn, Kew Gardens, Richmond, Twickenham, Hampton Court, Shepperton, Chertsey, Thorpe Park, Staines.
Note:	Last picking up / first setting down point on journeys from/to London was Hampton Wick Station. Restriction on carriage from Hyde Park Corner to Windsor.
20 April 1984	Introduced. Daily = 2 journeys.
By May 1984	Abandoned.

ROUTE PROFILE

The Richmond Heritage Ride	Unidirectional circular from Kew Gardens via Richmond, Twickenham, Hampton Court, Kingston, Richmond Park.
20 April 1984	Introduced. Daily = 1 hour.
12 July 1984	Abandoned.

Victoria Shuttle Service Ltd

16 The Broadway, Stanmore, Middlesex

From April 1985: 34 Grenden Gardens, Wembley Park, Middlesex

ROUTE PROFILE

Victoria Station – Victoria Coach Station.

Introduced on 14 May 1984 this short shuttle service, worked by Dormobile bodied Bedford CFL minibuses, was intended to save inter-changing passengers between rail and road the trek along Buckingham Palace Road. A daily 'continuous' service was provided, for the first week this ran between 12.00 –18.00 hours only but from 21 May 1984 it was revised to operate between 08.00 and 19.00 hours with a break in service between 13.00 and 14.30 hours. The route continued at 12 July 1985.

K S Dhillon, trading as:

New Bharat Coaches

7 Spencer Road, Southall, Middlesex

New Bharat's 1979-built Duple-bodied Volvo B58 reg.no. CAV 621V was photographed at Smith Farm Estate terminus on 9 August 1984. Use of such bold route branding was unusual at this date.
D Stewart

ROUTE PROFILE

Northolt (Smith Farm Estate) – Heathrow Airport (Central Bus Stn)
via Southall, Western Road, and M4 motorway.

This service, introduced on 15 July 1984, was targeted at airport workers at Heathrow, journeys being timed to fit in with shift patterns at the airport Operating daily, initially 8/9 journeys per day were provided although by August 1984 this had been reduced to 4/5 journeys, which frequency was maintained at 12 July 1985.

Willing Bros

ROUTE PROFILE

Richmond (Wakefield Rd) – Roehampton (Queen Mary's Hospital)
via Kew Gardens Stn, Mortlake, Barnes, Putney Hospital.

Introduced on 28 January 1985 this service, sponsored by both the London Borough of Richmond and Richmond Area Health Authority, provided links to hospitals which were not directly accessible on London Transport bus routes. It operated 6 journeys on Mondays to Fridays, which level of service prevailed at 12 July 1985.

Sampson Coaches and Travel Ltd

Essex Road, Hoddesdon, Hertfordshire

ROUTE PROFILE

Waltham Cross Minibus Network.

This operation superseded the long established Breach Barns service detailed in Chapter 2 and also replaced London Transport Route 254 via Parklands, withdrawn after operation on 26 April 1985.

27 April 1985   Introduced:
Route 1:   **Breach Barns – Waltham Cross** via Waltham Abbey. Mon–Sat = 1–5 jnys.
Route 1A: **Breach Barns – Waltham Cross Station** (direct). Mon–Fri = 3 jnys pk hrs.
Route 1B: **Breach Barns – King Harold School.** Schooldays, = 1 journey.
Route 2:   **Roundhills – Waltham Cross** via Parklands, Waltham Abbey.
            Mondays, Wednesdays, Fridays, Saturdays = 2–5 journeys.
Route 3:   **Upshire – Waltham Cross** via Parklands Waltham Abbey, Mon–Sat = 3 jnys.
12 July 1985   Extant.

Beyond the GLC Boundary 1970–1985

On 1 January 1970, when control of London Transport passed to the Greater London Council, 64 daytime Central Area 'red' bus routes crossed over the GLC boundary to reach various terminals in Buckinghamshire, Essex, Hertfordshire, Kent and Surrey. From that same date London Transport's responsibility became that of ensuring the provision of an adequate level of service within the GLC area only. Cross border routes had to be financially self sufficient. For any such routes that were loss making, London Transport had the choices of seeking appropriate subsidies from the relevant local authorities, truncating such routes at the GLC boundary or withdrawing them. As the amount of subsidy needed increased – in 1978 Surrey County Council paid London Transport over £1million to subsidise bus routes – other options were pursued by the councils. This resulted in a number of sections of former London Transport bus routes being replaced by London Country facilities. As an example, in Surrey, new London Country Route 459 (Addlestone – Feltham), introduced on 28 January 1978, replaced both the Chertsey – Shepperton section of London Transport Route 237 as well as the Upper Halliford section of London Transport Route 264.

As detailed in Chapter 5, from the same date, the Walton-on-Thames to Hersham section of London Transport Route 264 was replaced by Ben Stanley Limited whilst Mole Valley replaced facilities previously provided over sections of London Transport routes 201 and 215 from 29 September 1980. At the end of the period reviewed by this book – 12 July 1985 – the number of daytime London Transport bus routes crossing to points beyond the GLC boundary had reduced to 38. Certain of these London Transport bus routes which travelled beyond the GLC boundary led to further fresh 'connections' between London Transport and independent operators.

Essex

London Transport bus routes to both Epping and Ongar, some miles north east of the GLC boundary, were maintained throughout the period reviewed by this book. Most interestingly, against a background trend towards retrenchment from its cross-border operations, London Transport actually stepped up its operations in this area from 4 December 1982. On that date enhancements to bus services, coincident with a downgrading of the Underground's Central Line Epping to Ongar spur from daily service to Monday to Friday peak hours operation only, saw the introduction of new daily London Transport Route 201 (Loughton – Epping – Ongar). This new route also replaced the Epping to Ongar section of London Country Bus Services Route 339 as well as the Loughton to Epping section of London Transport Route 20A.

G F Ward
65 Fairfield Road, Epping, Essex

From July 1973 the title became:

G F Ward Ltd
From August 1979 office at: 30 Bower Hill, Epping, Essex

ROUTE PROFILE

Route 381	Epping Green – Coopersale Common or Toothill via Epping.
9 August 1971	Introduced. Replaced London Country 381, withdrawn 7 August 1971. Mondays–Fridays = 7/8 journeys. Saturdays = 4 journeys.
September 1974	Schoolday jnys projected beyond Epping Green to Broadley Common.
1979	Certain journeys on Mondays, Fridays, Saturdays and schooldays projected beyond Toothill to Moreton Bridge.
13 October 1981	Saturday service withdrawn.
4 May 1982	Acquired by R. and C. Eyres-Scott (t/a Lee-Roy Coaches), Ongar Road, Kelvedon Hatch, Brentwood, Essex. Revised to operate Epping Green – Coopersale Common Mondays–Fridays = 5–8 journeys. Certain journeys on Mondays and Fridays and schooldays projected beyond Epping Green to Broadley Common. These latter journeys further projected on Mondays to Dobbs Weir via Nazeing and on Fridays to Roydon Hamlet.
12 May 1984	Dobbs Weir projections on Mondays altered to run as a circular service via Roydon Hamlet, Bumbles Green and Nazeing Common. Fridays projection to Roydon Hamlet withdrawn.
12 July 1985	Extant.

Crusader Coaches (Harlow) Ltd.

217 Birch Hanger Lane, Bishops Stortford, Hertfordshire

ROUTE PROFILE

	Hastingwood (Bull & Horseshoe) – Epping Church via Tilegate Green.
6 March 1978	Introduced. Mondays only = 1 return journey.
12 July 1985	Extant.

E A and R A Wheeler, trading as:

Anita's Coaches

The Old Bakery, High Wych, Sawbridgeworth, Hertfordshire

ROUTE PROFILE

	Blake Hall Station – Ongar (LT Stn) via Toothill, Stanford Rivers.
6 December 1979	Introduced. Thursdays only = 1 return journey.
4 April 1985	Acquired by C J Blackwell, 1 Wayside, Ongar Rd, Abbess Roding, Essex
12 July 1985	Extant.

Kent

For a short period from 1 April 1978 R S S Fage (trading as Viking Coaches) introduced a route from West Kingsdown to Swanley, at which latter point 'connections' existed with London Transport Route 21A (Swanley – Eltham). As detailed in Chapter 6 West Kingsdown was also the base for Thames Weald's operations.

R S S Fage, trading as:

Viking Coaches

Terra Nova, Viking Way, West Kingsdown, Kent

ROUTE PROFILE

	West Kingsdown – Swanley via Knatts Valley, Eynsford.
1 April 1978	Introduced. Weekdays only = 2 journeys.
Unknown date	Abandoned. No trace of operation by mid-May 1978.

BIBLIOGRAPHY

Birks J A et al, National Bus Company 1968–1989,
Transport Publishing Co 1990.

Burnett G and James L, The Tillingbourne Bus Story,
Middleton Press 1990.

Crawley R J, MacGregor D R, and Simpson F D,
The Years Between – Volume 2 – The Eastern National Story
from 1930, Oxford Publishing Co 1984.

Garbutt P E, London Transport and the Politicians,
Ian Allan Ltd 1985.

Holmes P, British Bus Systems No.3 – Thames Valley,
Transport Publishing Co 1984.

James L, Independent Bus Operators into Horsham,
Rochester Press 1983.

King J T, Bus Operators in the South East – the Private Sector,
The Omnibus Society 1972.

King JT, Persson D M et al, Independent Bus Services in the
London Transport Area 1946–1972, The Omnibus Society 1972.

Lambert A, Hants & Sussex, published by the author 1977.

Osborne A, Transfer of Eastern National Grays Area Services
to London Transport 1933–1951,
The Eastern National Enthusiasts Group 1980.

Osborne E N, Ancestry and History of Green Line Coaches,
The Omnibus Society reprint 1975.

Stewart D, London's Independent Bus Services,
London Omnibus Traction Society 1976, 1978, 1980 editions.

Woodall N, edited by Heaton B, Where's it from? When was it issued?
Car Number Galaxy Publications 1994.

Wylde J, Wylde's Adventures in Busland,

Wylde J, Wylde's Reflections on Public Transport,
both published by the author in 1998 at 4 Osborne Road, Tweedmouth,
Berwick-upon-Tweed, TD15 2HS.

Various editions of Publications

The Little Red Book, Ian Allan Ltd.

Passenger Transport Yearbook, Ian Allan Ltd.

Historical and Current Notes in Connection with Various Tours,
The Omnibus Society.

Current Fleet Lists, Fleet Histories, News Sheets,
The PSV Circle.

Journals and Magazines

Buses Illustrated, Buses, Buses Extra, Ian Allan Publishing Ltd.

The London Bus, London Bus Magazine,
London Omnibus Traction Society.

The Omnibus Magazine, The Omnibus Society.

OPERATORS' INDEX

Aldershot & District Traction Co Ltd:
4, 9, 78, 79, 80, 91, 92, 93, 94, 98, 99, 104, 110.
Alder Valley: 78, 79, 80, 81, 83, 86.
Alexander, W F (t/a Comfy Bus Service): 103, 104.
Anita's Coaches: 173.
Ash, M C (t/a Mole Valley Transport Services): 87, 88, 89, 90, 91, 172.
Ashby Commercial Vehicles Ltd
(t/a Ashline Coaches): 109, 112.
Atkins, L.B. (t/a Beacon Motor Services): 112.
Atlas Coaches: 137, 138.
Association of Public Transport Users: 52.
B & B Services: 64, 65.
Banstead Coaches Ltd: 13, 127, 128, 129, 166.
Barnard J W (t/a B & B Services): 64.
Bassom, A G and Thornton, M (t/a Thamesmead
Motor Services): 2, 17, 138, 142, 159, 160, 161, 162, 163.
Beacon Motor Services (Crowborough) Ltd: 112.
Belvedere Coaches: 161, 162, 165.
Benjamin, E and Brandon, E (t/a Our Bus Service): 32.
Berry, T E (t/a Falcon Coaches): 122.
Birch Bros Ltd: 4, 8, 16, 46, 47, 48, 49, 50, 56, 59.
Bird, R W: 130, 131.
Biss, S G and R P (t/a Biss Bros): 53.
Blackford, D C (t/a Isleworth Coaches): 135.
Blackwell, C J: 173.
Blue Bus Services Ltd: 73, 74.
Blue Line Coaches Ltd: 26, 32.
Bordabus Ltd: 26, 27, 30, 31, 38.
Borough Bus Services: 73, 75, 78.
Brady, A T (t/a Brown Motor Services): 10, 92, 93, 96, 106, 107, 108, 147.
Bream Coach Service: 65, 66, 140.
Browne, P F and Browne, J (t/a Browne's
Transport (Redhill): 101, 102.
Browne's Luxury Coaches (Redhill) Ltd: 101.
Bygrave, J and G: 56,57.
C & O Motors: 142, 162.
Camden Coaches: 126.
Camden, London Borough of: 129.
J W Campbell & Son Ltd: 22.
Campbell Consultants Ltd: 68.
B C Cannon Ltd: 53, 54.
Capital Coaches Ltd: 133, 134.
Carshalton Belle: 133.
Charlwood, A J (t/a Surrey & Sussex Coachways):
99, 100, 106, 108.
Cheek, B J P (t/a Elmtree Transport): 1, 5, 135, 136, 138.
Cheek, H F and Sons (t/a Elm's Coaches): 137, 138.
Chiltern Queens Ltd: 126.
City Coach Co Ltd: 4, 11, 20, 21,35, 37, 39, 40, 41, 42.
City Coach Lines (Upminster) Ltd: 26, 32.
Clark, A and C (t/a Woodside Coaches): 18, 169.
E Clarke & Son (Coaches) Ltd: 131.
Coachmaster Tours: 133.
Cole, A V (t/a Blue Bus Service): 73, 74, 78.
Comfy Bus Service: 103, 104.
Continental Pioneer Ltd: 135, 136.
Continental Pioneer Holidays Ltd (t/a Pioneer
Coaches): 134, 135.
Conway Hunt Ltd: 132, 133.
Cookes Coaches (Stoughton) Ltd: 97.
Coppin's Coaches: 26.
County Coaches: 58.
Crescent Coaches: 76, 77.
Lewis Cronshaw Ltd: 133.
P Crouch & Son Ltd (t/a Blue Bus): 94.
Crusader Coaches (Harlow) Ltd: 173.
Crystal's Coaches: 151, 152.
Cuffley Motor Co Ltd: 57.
Dell, J R G (t/a Rover Bus Services): 14, 64, 66, 67.
Dhillon, K S (t/a New Bharat Coaches): 170, 171.

Digby, G L S (t/a Mildmay Motors): 115, 118.
Dix Luxury Coaches Ltd: 22.
Dorayme Travel: 26, 27, 28, 29.
A Drayton & Son (Barley) Ltd: 54, 55, 56.
Eastern National Omnibus Co Ltd: 4, 5, 9, 10, 11, 14, 21, 22, 23, 24, 32, 35, 36, 37, 38, 39, 40, 41, 42, 43, 47, 59, 60, 62, 70, 114, 119, 123.
Elm Park Coaches Ltd: 22, 23, 24, 32.
Elm's Coaches: 137, 138.
Elmtree Transport: 1, 5, 135, 138.
Esher Urban District Council: 89.
Ewhurst & District Bus Service: 93, 103, 104.
Eyres-Scott, R and C (t/a Lee-Roy Coaches): 173.
Fage, R S S (t/a Viking Coaches): 173.
Falcon Coaches: 122.
Farmer, H E (t/a The Gem): 69.
Finchley Liberal Association: 126.
Finsbury Coaches Ltd: 133.
Fountain Coaches Ltd: 133
Franklin, C J (t/a Franklins Coaches): 167.
French, G L (t/a Pilgrim Coaches): 113.
French, T T (t/a French Car Service): 130.
Frowen & Hill Ltd (t/a Borough Bus Services): 73, 75, 78.
Gem, The: 69.
Godfrey Davis (Home Estates) Ltd: 34.
Godfrey Davis (Parks) Ltd: 34.
Golden Miller Services: 15, 16, 90, 121, 139, 140, 141.
Greens (Breach Barns) Ltd: 33, 34.
E J Green (Breach Barns) Ltd: 34.
Guards Internationale (Intercity) Ltd (t/a Guards
of Caterham): 167.
Hall, R D (t/a Belvedere Coaches): 161, 162, 165.
Hall's Coaches Ltd: 132, 133, 134, 138.
Halls, E C W (t/a The Stag Bus Service): 54.
Hammond, T W and G R (t/a B Hammond & Son):
94.
Hants & Sussex: 9, 13, 93, 103, 104, 107, 110, 111.
Happy Wanderer Coaches: 133.
Harpenden Motor Coaches Ltd: 58.
Hayter, S (t/a Yellow Bus Services): 98.
Hefferman, Dr H N (t/a Thames Weald): 113.
Hicks Bros Ltd: 21, 23, 39.
Horlock, H T & Son: 118.
Imperial: 75, 76, 78.
Isleworth Coaches: 135.
Jackson, R E (t/a Crescent Coaches): 76, 77.
Jeatt, C E (t/a White Bus Service): 77.
KR's Car Hire & Photographic Service Ltd: 130.
W & E F Kershaw Ltd (t/a County Coaches): 58.
Kilner, F H (t/a Sunbeam Bus Service): 103, 104.
F H Kilner (Transport) Ltd. (t/a Hants & Sussex): 9, 13, 93, 103, 104, 107, 110, 111.
Knight, C H (t/a Bream Coach Service): 65, 66, 140.
Knightswood Coaches Ltd: 68, 69.
L and A Coaches: 32.
Lacey's (East Ham) Ltd: 168.
Land & Estates Ltd: 68.
Lawrence, W J and C J (t/a Lawrence Coaches):
165, 166.
Lazzell, A (t/a Ewhurst & District Bus Service): 93, 103, 104.
Lee & District Coach Services: 66, 67.
Lee-Roy Coaches: 173.
Leesway Coaches: 132, 133.
Leighton Coach Co Ltd: 133.
Lempriere, Mrs J M (t/a L and A Coaches): 32.
Lewington Coach Hire Services Ltd: 26, 30, 31.
Lightgray Ltd: 18, 169.
Linkline Coaches: 133.
Livermore, A: 56.
Locks Coaches Ltd: 166.
London Country Bus Services Ltd: 2, 5, 17, 52, 58, 71, 88, 106, 114, 115, 147, 148, 159, 160, 163, 164, 165, 166, 167, 172, 173.

Luton Corporation Transport: 60, 61.
Luton & District Transport: 60, 91.
Maddison, J E and Normington, Miss J M (t/a Orpington & District Omnibuses): 18, 143, 145, 148, 149, 153, 155, 156, 160.
Maidstone & District Motor Services Ltd: 4, 9, 109, 110, 112, 114, 119, 120, 147, 164.
Metrobus Ltd: 18, 19, 136, 151, 154, 155, 156, 157, 158.
Mildmay Motors: 115, 118.
Mitchell, J: 105.
Mitchell, J and M A (t/a J Mitchell): 105, 106, 107.
Modern Travel: 133.
Mole Valley Transport Services: 87, 88, 89, 90, 91, 172.
Monk, H: 10, 53.
A Moore & Sons (Windsor) Ltd (t/a Imperial): 75, 76, 78.
M P H W Sales: 126.
Mullany, J P (t/a Mullany's Coaches): 68.
Nash, A E H (t/a Universal Cars [Hertford]): 58.
New Bharat Coaches: 170, 171.
Normington, Miss J M (t/a Orpington & District Omnibuses): 18, 143, 145, 148, 149, 150, 151, 152, 154, 156, 157, 158.
North Downs Rural Transport Ltd: 106, 107, 108, 146, 150, 160.
North Downs Transport Services Ltd: 146.
North Sussex Rural Transport: 105.
Oborne, W M (t/a Queen's Park Coaches): 62.
Orpington & District Omnibuses: 18, 143, 145, 148, 149, 150, 151, 152, 153, 154, 155, 156, 157, 158, 160.
Orpington Rural Transport Association: 6, 14, 15, 18, 101, 105, 113, 143, 144, 145, 146, 147, 148, 149, 152, 156.
Orpwood, L G (t/a C & O Motors): 142, 162.
Our Bus Service: 32.
Oxford, City of, Motor Services Ltd: 71, 72.
Paynes Coaches (Croydon) Ltd: 126, 133.
People's League for the Defence of Freedom, The: 13, 123, 124, 125.
Perry, J A: 76, 78.
Pilgrim Coaches: 113.
Pioneer Coaches: 134, 135.
Plaskow, A H and Margo, M (t/a Atlas Coaches): 137, 138.
Popular Coaches: 133.
Premier Travel Ltd: 52, 54, 55, 56.
Pulleine Coaches: 131, 132, 133.
Queen's Park Coaches: 62.
R R Coaches (t/a Red Rose): 62.
Rackcliffe, H D: 97.
Reading Transport: 19, 43, 44, 84, 85, 86.
Redbridge & District Motor Services: 29, 35.
Redbridge & District Omnibus Co: 24, 25, 29.
Red Rose: 62.
Red Rover Omnibus Co: 63, 64.
Reid, P W (t/a B & B Services): 64, 65.
Rhees, Mrs H: 97.
Richmond, H V: 56.
Charles Rickard (Tours) Ltd: 133.
Rogers, F: 32.
Rover Bus Services: 14, 64, 66, 67.
St. Pancras, Metropolitan Borough of: 129.
Safeguard Coaches Ltd: 94, 95.
Sampson, P C (t/a Sampson Coaches): 142.
Sampson Coaches & Travel Ltd: 34, 142, 171.
Samuelson New Transport Ltd: 122, 130, 131.
Sargent, Mrs J: 109.
Sargents of East Grinstead Ltd: 109.
Seabrook residents Association: 25.
Seth Coaches Ltd: 131, 133.
Smith, W H: 11, 57.
Smiths (Buntingford) Ltd: 56, 57.
Southdown Motor Services Ltd: 9, 13, 14, 109, 110, 111, 112, 120.
Southend Transport: 4, 43, 44, 45, 84, 86.
Southgate Coaches: 133.
Springham, C (t/a Crystal's Coaches): 151, 152.

Stag Bus Service, The: 54.
Ben Stanley Ltd: 9, 91, 172.
Sterling, A G (t/a Sterling Bus Service): 24, 25, 28.
Stubbington, G F (t/a Bordabus and Bordacoach): 27, 31, 38.
Stubbington, G F (t/a Dorayme Travel): 26, 27, 28, 29.
Sunbeam Bus Service: 103. 104.
Sunnymede Coaches Ltd: 13, 33.
Super Coaches (Upminster) Ltd. (sometime t/a as both Redbridge & District and Upminster & District): 14, 24, 25, 26, 27, 29, 30, 35, 133.
Surman's Coaches Ltd: 69.
Surrey & Sussex Coachways: 99, 100, 106, 108.
Tandridge Taxis Ltd: 129, 166.
Taylor, R & Son (t/a Taylor's Coaches): 165.
Tellings Coaches of Weybridge Ltd: 139.
Thames Valley Traction Co Ltd: 5, 9, 11, 15, 69, 71, 72, 73, 75, 76, 77, 78, 80, 81, 82, 83, 99, 134, 140.
Thames Valley & Aldershot Omnibus Co Ltd (t/a Alder Valley): 78, 79, 80, 81, 83, 86.
Thames Weald Ltd: 113, 114, 115, 116, 117, 118, 133, 173.
Thames Weald Travel Society: 113.
Thamesmead Motor Services Ltd: 17, 153, 159, 160, 161, 162, 163, 164, 165.
Thomas, E: 126.
Thompson, W R (t/a Coppin's Coaches): 26.
Tillingbourne Bus Co Ltd: 150, 154, 155, 156, 157.
Tillingbourne (Metropolitan) Ltd: 18, 150, 151, 154, 155, 156, 157, 158.
Tillingbourne Valley Coaches: 97.
Tillingbourne Valley Services Ltd: 9, 10, 14, 93, 95, 96, 97, 106, 107, 150.
Tourist Coachways, Ltd: 121, 122, 139.
Turner, J C and S M: 33, 34.
Twentieth Century Coaches: 133.
United Counties Omnibus Co Ltd: 14, 37, 47, 48, 49, 59, 60, 61, 62, 70.
Universal Cars [Hertford]: 58.
Upminster & District Omnibus Co: 24, 25, 30.
Valliant Direct Coaches Ltd: 132, 133, 137, 138.
Victoria Shuttle Service Ltd: 170.
Viking Coaches: 173.
Walton Lodge Garage Ltd: 90.
Walton-on-Thames Motor Co Ltd: 9, 78, 90.
Ward, G F: 172.
G F Ward Ltd: 172.
Warren, P G: 113.
Warrens Coaches Ltd: 113.
Warrens Coaches (Kent & Sussex) Ltd: 113.
Wates Built Homes Ltd: 157.
Wealden of London Motor Services Ltd: 170.
Weeden, F E (t/a Weeden's Motor Services): 55.
Wernher, Major General Sir H A Bt: 58.
West London Coachways Ltd: 12, 121, 139.
West's Coaches Ltd: 34.
Westcliff-on-Sea Motor Services Ltd: 4, 11, 21, 37, 39, 40, 41, 42.
Wheeler, E A and R A (t/a Anita's Coaches): 173.
White Bus Service: 77.
Whitefriars Coaches: 126.
F G Wilder & Son Ltd (t/a Golden Miller Services): 15, 16, 90, 121, 139, 140, 141.
Williams, M J (t/a Coppins Coaches): 26.
Williams, M J and Stubbington, G F (t/a Dorayme Travel): 26.
Wimbledon Coaches: 133.
Willing Bros: 171.
Woodside Coaches: 18, 169.
Wordsworth, R W (t/a Upminster & District): 25.
World Wide Coaches Ltd: 138.
Wright Bros: 126.
Wylde, J D, Wylde, Mrs M F and Edwards, R H (t/a North Downs Rural Transport or North Downs): 15, 18, 100, 106, 143, 145, 146, 147, 148, 149, 152, 153, 154, 155, 156, 157, 160, 163.
Yellow Bus Services Ltd: 98.
Young, D (t/a Redbridge & District Motor Services): 29, 35.